Born in 1935, RICHARD J. WHALEN is an author, journalist, and the president of Worldwide Information Resources, Inc., an international consulting firm retained by major American and foreign corporations. A native of New York City and a graduate of Queens College, Whalen has served as a contributing editor for *Time*, an editorial writer on *The Wall Street Journal*, and a member of the Board of Editors of *Fortune*. During 1966-1970, he was a writer-in-residence at Georgetown University's Center for Strategic and International Studies.

Mr. Whalen's biography of Joseph P. Kennedy, *The Founding Father*, was a national best seller for nearly a year and was nominated for a National Book Award. The author is now at work on a history of the Kennedy family since the death of John F. Kennedy.

BY RICHARD J. WHALEN

THE FOUNDING FATHER
  The Story of Joseph P. Kennedy
A CITY DESTROYING ITSELF
  An Angry View of New York
CATCH THE FALLING FLAG
  A Republican's Challenge to His Party
TAKING SIDES
  *A Personal View of America from
  Kennedy to Nixon to Kennedy*

WHALEN, Richard J. Taking sides; a personal view of America from
    Kennedy to Nixon to Kennedy. Houghton Mifflin, 1974.   320p
    74-12076. 8.95.   ISBN 0-395-17271-7.   C.I.P.
Eminently readable but shallow in scholarship, this collection of essays
is the work of a journalist formerly associated with *Time, The Wall
Street Journal,* and *Fortune.* In commenting on our immediate political
past and present problems, the mean between understatement and over-
statement is too often sacrificed for just a little more alliteration and
the neatly turned phrase. In several places complexities are ignored and
the single-cause theory implied: e.g., "In 1968, the Independent Eugene
McCarthy drove President Johnson out of the White House, and the
Independent George Wallace dictated the strategy of Richard Nixon,
including his choice of a vice-presidential running-mate" (p.84). A conservative Republican intellectual who despaired of Richard Nixon in an
earlier book, *Catch a falling flag* (1972), Whalen now sees Nixon as
having been "fascinated by foreign affairs and mostly bored with
domestic problems. Perhaps the greatest of [his failures] was characteristic of the man and his manner: he had withheld the truth from the
American people" (p.276). Of marginal value to the undergraduate.

CHOICE   FEB. '75
Political Science

RICHARD J. WHALEN

Taking Sides

*A Personal View of America
from Kennedy to Nixon
to Kennedy*

WITH AN INTRODUCTION
BY ROBERT D. NOVAK

Houghton Mifflin Company Boston   1974

To My Mother and Father

Veronica R. and George C. Whalen

Portions of this book have appeared in *Fortune* magazine.

FIRST PRINTING V

Library of Congress Cataloging in Publication Data

Whalen, Richard J 1935–   Taking sides.

CONTENTS: Politics without purpose: Nixon:
politics as conspiracy. Kennedy: politics as
illusion. The triumph of media politics. Cultural
politics. [etc.]
   1. United States — Politics and government —
1945–   — Collected works. 2. United States —
Civilization — 1945–   — Collected works. I. Title.
E839.5.W47   320.9'73'092   74-12076
ISBN 0-395-17271-7

Printed in the United States of America

Author's Note
and Acknowledgments

MOST OF the essays in this volume have not previously been published, and those that have been published have been extensively revised and updated. These latter essays have appeared in *Fortune, Harper's, The Saturday Evening Post, The New York Times Magazine, The Nation,* and the Washington *Post,* and are printed here with permission.

Much of the research for the unpublished essays, especially "The Second Cold War," was accomplished while I was Writer-in-Residence at Georgetown University's Center for Strategic and International Studies, and was supported by a grant from the Sarah Mellon Scaife Foundation.

My editor, Grant Ujifusa, provided imaginative assistance in the design and format of this volume, and I am most grateful for his counsel.

Over the past decade, in the writing of four books and scores of articles and essays, my wife, Joan Marie Giuffré Whalen, has been a source of constant inspiration and support as researcher, editor, and, most important of all, friend. Because she is also the house Democrat, her advice is often pointed and always lively. Some of the ideas and much of the work in this volume are hers; it is the latest product of an intellectual collaboration that has enriched our life together.

RICHARD J. WHALEN

Washington, D.C.
June 15, 1974

"Every line of serious work that I have written since 1936 has been written, directly or indirectly, *against* totalitarianism and *for* democratic socialism, as I understand it. It seems to me nonsense, in a period like our own, to think that one can avoid writing of such subjects . . . It is simply a question of which side one takes and what approach one follows. And the more one is conscious of one's political bias, the more chance one has of acting politically without sacrificing one's esthetic and intellectual integrity. What I have most wanted to do throughout the past ten years is to make political writing into an art."

George Orwell, *"Why I Write,"* 1947

Contents

Part Three: What Happened, U.S.A.?

Introduction

by Robert D. Novak

No JOURNALIST writing today has succeeded so well as Richard J. Whalen in correctly forecasting the disasters ahead for our politicians and our people. He was one of the first to perceive the contrived and superficial on the New Frontier. He quickly understood that defects in character would doom John V. Lindsay as savior of the city. Long before most, he recognized the Vietnam War as an unwinnable drain on the nation's will and strength. His most dramatic and most important early warning came in *Catch the Falling Flag: A Republican's Challenge to His Party* (1972). When even liberal journalists were celebrating President Nixon's supposed expertise in governing the nation, Whalen defied the conventional wisdom with his revelation of moral and managerial chaos within the White House soon to be exposed to all by the Watergate disaster.

In sum, he has succeeded remarkably in escaping the superficiality and impermanence that plague our journalistic trade.

A basic reason, I believe, is that Dick Whalen is not truly a Washington correspondent, although he has lived in the capital city for the past eight years. Whereas the archetypal Washington correspondent is consumed by the gossip and inside maneuverings of a one-industry town, Whalen's horizons are broader. His essays transcend the superficial political gossip of Washington and explore what is happening beyond the Potomac that will truly shape our lives and our future: the treacherous cross-currents of international economics, the agonizing problems of American business management, the dangers of the strategic arms competition and negotiation. Whalen's virtuosity and versatility are unique.

What most broadens his scope, however, is his willingness to make large moral judgments and to assign moral deficiencies as the cause for material shortcomings. It is this willingness that leavens Whalen's painfully realistic world view with a thankful strain of hope.

Thus, as an overview of what has happened to America since 1960, *Taking Sides* is at once more bleak and more hopeful than conventional journalism. It is bleaker because Whalen does not stop with Watergate as the source of the nation's malaise but goes on to more profound difficulties, mercilessly deflating the Nixon Administration's widely assumed excellence in foreign policy. The woes of Watergate seem overshadowed by Whalen's grim portrait of a dispirited and disillusioned nation facing the muscular, self-confident, neo-imperialistic Soviet Union of the 1970s. It is hopeful because he eloquently insists that an America rekindled in patriotic self-belief can yet reverse its decline.

Dick Whalen is a conservative but abhors the rigid and crassly material doctrine passed off as conservatism by so many politicians and businessmen. He believes self-styled "conservatives" in the business community have helped spawn "a peculiarly American kind of socialism, cloaked in the rhetoric of enterprise and dedicated to preserving the status and security of the privileged." That amounts to "socialism disguised as conservatism" in Whalen's view.

Worse yet from his standpoint is the conservative approbation of Richard M. Nixon ("the mind of an intellectual and the temperament of a huckster") along with the sloganeering and gimmickry of his Administration. He is harsh on the Republican conservatives in Congress: "Although they knew from personal experience Nixon's limitations and flaws of character, they set no watchdogs on the White House." This, says Whalen, justified "Nixon's contemptuous judgment that he could keep the right wing in line with rhetoric and occasional patronage plums" — a "habit of assent" justifying John Stuart Mill's descriptions of the Tories as the "Stupid Party."

Whalen is distressed by both parties today. "Because they bowed to government by advance men for four barren years, the Republicans in the Congress and the country will be buried under its collapse for a long time to come." Whalen certainly sees no relief from the post-McGovern Democratic Party, which he sees "turning itself into a movement dedicated to purging its past." He sees Watergate as emphasizing a permanent Democratic Party shift far to the left of where most Americans want to go: "Experience teaches that when a party transforms itself into an ideological vehicle and true believers take the wheel, even an election crash produces only a limited corrective reaction."

The demoralization of one great party and ideological derangement of the other assume menacing importance in the face of the perils we face as a nation. The thirteenth essay here should, I believe, be read and pondered by every American, particularly those who have rationalized President Nixon's moral failings as insignificant considering his accomplishments on the world scene. What the President has depicted as peace, Whalen calls "gradual accommodation to emerging Soviet dominance and phased capitulation to Soviet demands." To maintain the appearance of détente as "his most prized and appreciated accomplishment," Whalen accuses Nixon of overlooking Soviet violations of at least the spirit of the SALT I agreement. The warning: "Our children would pay for his deception and our self-deception."

This self-deception he views as rooted in the failure of the American spirit and the refusal of the American people to accept the burden of leadership any longer. He traces that failure to basics — ". . . the family and the church and every other nongovernmental and cultural institution have been steadily drained of legitimacy and moral authority."

But the root cause is the nation's political leadership of the 1960s. "The American people have not failed as citizens — they have *been* failed. They are prepared to make far greater sacrifices than timid leaders realize, provided they are told the truth." Thus does Whalen become the prophet not of despair but of hope and achievable salvation.

To actually achieve that salvation, Whalen envisions a new conservatism based on a concept that rejects the emerging corporate state and is based on questing for *both* human happiness and expanded capital accumulation. To compete internationally, Whalen points to the Japanese "virtues of work, self-discipline and thrift — the same virtues, significantly, that built America's industrial primacy." So, we need not imitate Japanese methods, but "we need to be more ourselves."

As a conservative, a Republican, and an old critic of the Kennedys, Whalen's great surprise in this book is his suggestion that the legacy of John F. Kennedy is the standard to which we should now repair — indeed, a standard to which the Republicans rather than the McGovernized Democrats *can* repair. Whalen recognizes that lost innocence prevents a return to Camelot. He certainly does not want to return to the arrogance and fakery of the New Frontier. Beyond all this, he sees a hard core of value in the Kennedy legacy: "That core is patriotism." He adds:

> Since 1960, America, it seems to me, has come full circle to confront again the kind of questions raised and left unanswered by John Kennedy — questions of our values as individuals, our identity as a people, our purpose as a nation, and our resolve as a civilization under mortal challenge at home and abroad.

Dick Whalen is probably more optimistic than I about the possibility of patriotic leadership renewing the vigor and purpose of the nation. But more than a journalist, he is himself a practicing patriot and, in fact, an activist.

He has been disappointed before. In 1964, he saw some signs of hope, if only tentatively and momentarily, in the conservative movement that nominated Barry Goldwater. A year later, he hoped that John V. Lindsay could manage the regeneration of the American city and was again disappointed. In 1968, he hesitantly and reluctantly served on Richard M. Nixon's campaign staff before the advent of Haldeman and Ehrlichman showed him the grim shape of the future. In these essays, he tentatively suggests that Henry M. Jackson and John B. Connally might have part of the answer, but he is clearly unconvinced and by no means optimistic. The leader to seize that vestigial Kennedy legacy is not at hand.

This is in fact a book of failed leaders. Whalen has been disappointed but not, I believe, discouraged. So, he emerges from this decade of cynicism and despair with a clear unafraid view of his country — a country older, more cynical, more tolerant, but still unique as "a nation created and preserved by ideals."

He asks: "What ails America?" His answer: "Our sickness of the spirit arises from a prolonged absence of just pride in what we have attempted and what we have accomplished. Our cure will come with the restoration of honest, truthful, and effective leadership that demands the best in us . . ." Richard Whalen believes we deserve that kind of leader even after Vietnam and Watergate. And so should the rest of us.

PART ONE

Politics Without Purpose

Nixon: Politics as Conspiracy

I.

BEFORE WATERGATE and related scandals ruined his presidency, Richard Milhous Nixon enjoyed the reputation among sympathizers and enemies alike of being a dark political genius. Condemnation of "Tricky Dick" was typically mixed with grudging respect for his durability and professionalism. Indeed, a British visitor and sometime adviser on Vietnam, Sir Robert Thompson, emerged from the White House to compliment the American people on having sensibly installed their first "professional President." Practically every journalist who caught a glimpse of the man inside the tightly guarded Oval Office reported finding a figure half-Puritan, half-Spartan — calculating, self-disciplined, always "up" for the next challenge. "The major weakness of inexperienced people," said the re-elected President in an early 1973 interview, "is that they take things personally, especially in politics, and that can destroy you . . ." If anyone ever merited Balzac's description of politicians as "monsters of self-possession," it would seem to be Nixon.

Yet the conventional perception of Nixon as a man of iron

self-possession was mistaken, as I came to realize when I worked with him in his 1968 comeback campaign. Several years earlier, in reviewing Nixon's autobiography, *Six Crises*, I had raised an outsider's complaint: "Throughout his career he has tried to synthesize sincerity, when all he had to do was unlock himself and let it out." A year of insidership taught me that behind the locked door lay another and another. The "real" Nixon was the one who seemed so transparently artificial and mechanical, a plastic personality continually trying to derive his selfhood from his circumstances and tactical opportunities. Sometimes as the result of faulty judgment of a situation, he exposed the "wrong" self and lost control completely. Until he became President, his most memorable and damaging mistake was the famous 1962 "last press conference." With the release of the transcripts of the Watergate tapes, which demonstrated the opposite of his claimed innocence, Nixon quite literally destroyed his public self by revealing the private one.

While I served him, I saw evidence of Nixon's skills as a tactician, especially his shrewd sense of when to avoid an issue and retreat into silence, but I saw nothing indicating a larger vision and a strategy for fulfilling it. In spite of his opponents' blunders and misfortunes, he almost managed to snatch defeat from the jaws of victory in 1968, waging a lifeless campaign that cut his plurality over Humphrey to barely one-tenth the margin he expected. Nevertheless, even after Watergate, the myth of Nixon's political mastery persisted. *He couldn't be that dumb*, ran a common reaction. In truth, he could be and was. Watergate, far from being an aberration, was a faithful reflection of Nixon's approach to politics throughout his career: politics as conspiracy.

4

Fiction and films have given the word "conspiracy" misleading overtones. We form a mental image of ruthless, brilliant men scheming for the highest prizes. But stupid men also scheme. Conspirators may be motivated by nothing more than fear of losing what they have. The fictionalized ambition to seize power by a bold stroke becomes in real life the petty desire simply to hang on to the trappings and satisfactions of power — the luxurious jets, the fleet of limousines, the protected villas and retreats, the warm feeling of total security. To most of those who possess it, power is not desired as a means to great ends. It is a perfectly satisfying end in itself. To command that a well-laid fire be set crackling on the hearth in mid-August, even though one's White House office must be simultaneously chilled by air-conditioning — that is to enjoy the psychic security blanket of power. Men who crave power — especially second-raters playing far over their heads and afraid of failing and being found out — may be willing to take irrational, potentially self-destructive risks to preserve it. Because they are dumb, they may take such risks without realizing it.

Lyndon Johnson, whose invective often contained wounding insight, once dismissed Nixon as "a chronic campaigner." In fact, Nixon made no distinction between the politics of campaigning and the politics of governing: they formed a continuum of conflict and struggle. "I believe in the battle, whether it's the battle of a campaign or the battle of this office, which is a continuing battle," President Nixon remarked to Saul Pett of the Associated Press after his 1972 landslide victory. "It's always there wherever you go. I, perhaps, carry it more than others because that's my way." During most of his long career, Nixon, unlike Johnson, the Senate wheeler-dealer, knew scant personal power before entering the presidency. Overshadowed by Eisenhower, condemned for eight years to the purgatory of the vice presidency and then after the bitter 1960 defeat to another eight years of wandering in the wilderness, Nixon reached the White House formed by the scarring experience of frustrated pursuit, confirmed in his combative campaigner's politics and quite remarkably ignorant of power brokerage, accommodation, and compromise — the politics essential to democratic leadership and governing.

Campaign politics, regardless of party and candidate, is inherently conspiratorial. Men band together to achieve their individual and collective ambition for office. Because the only purpose and binding force of the enterprise is victory, almost any means toward that all-important end can be justified after a few moments of rationalization. Everyone not a part of the conspiracy is, by definition, unworthy of trust — an outsider. Because that is where the public, most other politicians, and the press stand, hostility toward them follows automatically. Because the conspirators operate in secrecy, ever conscious of the tactical advantages to be gained from successful duplicity, the moral and practical constraints of governing politics are a hindrance — if they are acknowledged at all.

II.

With a handful of exceptions, the men around Nixon when he came to the presidency were experienced solely in campaign politics. He and they merely continued the ways that had worked well enough to give them what they sought. Most of these men were also strangers to the President and to each

6

other, separated by fear, jealousy, and suspicion, yet joined nonetheless in cynical conspiracy. For the enemy of the "Us" within the White House lay beyond the gates: a vast *Them*. (One of the most pathetic secrets to emerge from the Watergate affair was the White House "enemies list," an unknowing, error-filled, yet frightening document, revealing a sinister combination of naiveté and vindictiveness.) Columnist Nick Thimmesch coined a valuable phrase for the mind-set of the Nixon White House: "the vault mentality." The administration cherished the desire to wall itself off behind a phalanx of guards and escape from untidy, undisciplined reality. During his first term, the President practiced a novel kind of government-by-exclusion. He deliberately estranged himself from the Congress and entire sectors of the executive branch, most dramatically from the distrusted State Department, and constructed a miniature government within the White House. The ignorant, combative view from inside the vault at 1600 Pennsylvania Avenue was expressed by Chief of Staff Haldeman: "I don't think Congress is supposed to work with the White House — it is a different organization, and under the Constitution I don't think we should expect agreement."

Nixon set the tone for his underlings in their dealings with each other and outsiders. He regarded human beings in his service as instruments to be used and discarded when used up, and the broken and forgotten lay strewn along his line of march across the years. Just as he tested himself, he tested and retested others until their loyalty and subservience were total. Only then were they admitted to the inner circle, for they knew better than to attempt to disagree with him or even to advise him candidly. Nixon, the solitary brooder and scribbler on yellow legal pads, was his own final authority on

7

all questions. To be sure, he might feign interest in the opinions of temporarily useful human instruments; he might be genuinely impressed with the talents of a Henry Kissinger; he might find solace in the company of a strong, silent John Mitchell. Ultimately, however, the loner at the center of the conspiracy of strangers believed no one and needed no one beyond himself.

At the outset of the Nixon administration, two men were especially close to the President and seemingly indispensable: Chief of Staff H. R. (Bob) Haldeman and Domestic Adviser John Ehrlichman. They came to Washington as though entering conquered enemy territory. During the transition period in the winter of 1968–1969, a then assistant to President Johnson recalls giving Ehrlichman a tour of the White House. In a basement office he pointed to the ceiling and said impishly: "The trapdoor in front of the President's desk is overhead. The bodies fall down here and we carry them out the back way." Erlichman looked up, all seriousness. Finally the Johnson aide signaled the visitor by laughing at his own joke.

In time, figuratively speaking, Ehrlichman and Haldeman, like many others, would slide through that trapdoor and leave the capital in disgrace, their fall from giddy heights of personal power uncushioned by the President's farewell ("my closest friends on the White House staff and most trusted assistants"). While they stood at Nixon's side, Haldeman and Ehrlichman, especially the former, dominated the White House more completely than any presidential aides in history. Of all the questions raised by the Watergate affair, the most troubling are: How did such men get where they were and why did they stay so long?

8

Haldeman, Ehrlichman, & Company, who came to be known as "the Germans," rose on the side of politics furthest removed from the electorate: the behind-the-scenes realm of the managers, schedulers, advance men, image manipulators, and assorted technicians who package and merchandise a presidential candidate. This was congenial work for Haldeman, the former manager of J. Walter Thompson's Los Angeles office, and he recruited college cronies (such as Ehrlichman) and junior advertising agency types (such as Ronald Ziegler and Dwight Chapin) into the Nixon *apparat*. He gave "the Boss" slavish loyalty and he demanded the same from those below.

The stage managers, working in a closed and secret environment, had a natural antipathy to politicians, including those who were supposedly their collaborators. Through the closing months of the 1968 campaign and afterward in Washington, the Haldeman *apparat* waged jealous cold war against the politicians grouped around Mitchell, Nixon's former law partner and a relative newcomer to the inner group. But the hostile Haldeman and Mitchell factions joined forces ruthlessly to oppose the men inside and outside the Nixon organization, a miscellany of intellectuals and elected politicians, who supposed that "issues" mattered both in campaigning and governing. Shortly after Nixon's nomination in late August 1968, when I resigned from his staff, a purge began that drove all "issues men" either out of his entourage completely or off to the lonely periphery. At the same time, party politicians, regardless of past loyalty and service to Nixon, were fenced off from him.

Early in the fall of 1969, Martin Anderson, a member of the White House staff with whom I'd worked in the campaign the previous year, shot a nervous glance around the busy down-

9

town Washington restaurant and confided the shape of things to come. "Haldeman and Ehrlichman are ready to bring the whole thing under their control," he said. "Pat Moynihan is out, and so is Bryce Harlow. Ehrlichman will run a new Domestic Affairs Council. Haldeman will be the only man between him and the President." Anderson paused for a moment. "You know what's so frustrating? The damned lazy press doesn't have a clue about what's happening."

The campaigners who did much to put Nixon in the White House thus had him almost completely to themselves after he arrived there, and they continued to give him the benefit of their very narrow experience and expertise. This was fine for them but very bad, on the evidence, for him and the presidency.

Long before the abortive burglary of the Democratic party headquarters, the Watergate was a symbol. The chosen nesting-place of the Mitchells and other well-heeled members of the Nixon hierarchy, it symbolized the transience and insularity of men who had taken power almost without bothering to unpack, men basically uninterested in the business of government whose hearts belonged in Westchester and points west, where big money and the good life waited. To be sure, the right of a high official eventually to cash in on his experience and connections in Washington is established by long Democratic precedent. But Democrats who have come to office harboring the ambition to exploit their public service have usually shown patience and a self-protecting prudence. They have known what to expect in Washington, and — far more important — what would be expected of them. They realized, as their unknowing Republican successors did not, that they would be *watched*.

Elected politicians, as a breed, are cautious men because their minds run naturally to the sometimes distant consequences of words and deeds. Intellectuals and "issues men" generally are advocates and want an audience. The former expect scrutiny and the latter crave it. But the *apparatchik,* such as Haldeman, who lacks a constituency or an ideological commitment, does not understand scrutiny — *he* is the watcher and prier into secrets. And the conspiratorial campaign politician, such as Mitchell, who reduces all political problems to deal-making behind closed doors, is contemptuous of it. Sadly for Nixon, he had only these two kinds of men around him — the ignorant and the arrogant.

Haldeman and Ehrlichman and their buttoned-down, scurrying aides had the mission of protecting the President from disorder and enabling him to make the most effective use of his limited time and energy. Haldeman, as manager of Nixon's losing bid for the California governorship in 1962, had seen him come apart under pressure, and he was resolved to prevent it from happening in the White House. What this actually meant was once described by Haldeman in an interview with a friendly reporter:

> We started out trying to keep political coloration as much as possible out of policy and hiring matters. However, we realize that these things make for variety in decision-making, and so within reasonable limits we have tried to keep a spread of opinion on the staff, so that no one is to the left of the President at his most liberal or to the right of the President at his most conservative . . . Ehrlichman, Kissinger, and I do our best to make sure that all points of view are placed before the President. We do act as a screen, because there is a real danger of some advocate of an idea rushing in to the President . . . if that person is allowed to do so,

11

and actually managing to convince [him] in a burst of emotion or argument . . .

Can you imagine Marvin Watson saying something like that about Lyndon Johnson? Or Kenny O'Donnell presuming to enter John Kennedy's mind and judge the "reasonable limits" of what he wanted to hear? By Haldeman's own assertion, his dependency on the President, great as it was, was matched by Nixon's dependence on him to protect him against his own inner weakness and irresolution. These shortcomings are painfully evident in the Watergate transcripts, which reveal the President being treated with open disrespect by his pair of bullying German shepherds.

"Nixon is a great talker," says a close acquaintance of two decades. "He's a salesman and he gets carried away in making his pitch. Sometimes he goes beyond what he intends to say." Nixon indeed has the mind of an intellectual and the temperament of a huckster. Although he knows better, he cannot resist exaggerating and falsifying, bending his plastic personality in what he hopes is a pleasing, impressive shape for the customer's benefit. Haldeman's unique knowledge of the Nixon behind the masks — and the weakness they concealed — was the source of his power.

From entering the President's mind, it was but a short step for his protectors to go even further and *speak* the President's mind. Quite early in the Nixon administration, a shaken Cabinet-level official and old friend of the President's described to me a White House meeting at which Ehrlichman had proposed a new domestic program. The official challenged him, saying that the proposal contradicted what he knew of Nixon's values and philosophy. Ehrlichman coldly informed the of-

12

ficial that the President didn't have any philosophy — he did what was feasible and tactically rewarding.

"Ehrlichman didn't realize what he was saying," the official told me. "I know Nixon has values and a philosophy, but why doesn't Ehrlichman? And why does Nixon rely on a man like that?"

Similarly, the President's dependence for political counsel on Mitchell — called in his heyday "El Supremo" — led him into a succession of avoidable confrontations and disasters. Republican leaders in the Congress, who were ordered to close ranks behind the likes of Supreme Court nominee G. Harrold Carswell, had no voice in the councils leading to such gross misjudgments. Yet the conservative barons of the Senate — Barry Goldwater, John Tower, Strom Thurmond — who had played a decisive role in Nixon's 1968 nomination and election kept their fury bottled up long after they saw both ideology and political common sense betrayed by Mitchell and his client in the White House.

In his turn, of course, Mitchell himself was abandoned. Mitchell knew too much about the "dirty tricks" campaign of which Nixon was determined to remain ignorant and technically innocent. Shortly after the Watergate break-in, Mitchell stepped down as manager of the President's re-election campaign. On first reading, Mitchell's resignation seemed like a happy solution. He would escape the media spotlight while Nixon would continue to have support from his steady, pipe-smoking friend. And Martha would have John home where she thought he belonged. Soon, however, a quite different reading came from sources close to the former Attorney General. It was all over between Nixon and Mitchell.

Two of Haldeman's men — Jeb Magruder and Fred Malek — had earlier moved across Pennsylvania Avenue from the White House and taken over the campaign headquarters behind the front man, former Congressman Clark Mac-Gregor. Mitchell's protégés were swiftly cut down: Harry Flemming, his hand-picked patronage lieutenant; Robert Mardian, who had come over with him from the Justice Department as deputy campaign manager; and Harry Dent, the former White House counsel.

Those who talked to Mitchell after his resignation reported that he spoke of Haldeman with more than his customary antagonism but with an air of fatalism as well, as though he had put the lost battle for the President's ear behind him. Mitchell evidently sensed a sudden coolness toward him on the part of Nixon, and he knew that his old enemies, who spent so many hours each day with the President, would work to freeze the relationship. Their moves against the Mitchell men remaining at campaign headquarters indicated their confidence that they had the upper hand.

The decisive factor, of course, was Nixon's own attitude. The strange, inward man had few political friends who were both old and close. Murray Chotiner was a classic example of the Nixon retainer who was used to being abused. Robert Finch, whom the President once described as being "like a younger brother," went literally months without talking to Nixon and spent much of his time in California, trying to retrieve his once-bright career. So it was not unusual that Mitchell, having climbed over bodies to Nixon's side, should feel the sword of cold indifference biting into his own hide.

"They [meaning Haldeman, Ehrlichman, & Co.] won't be able to run Nixon," Mitchell told a friend. The remark foreshadowed a familiar pattern in Nixon's career, which Mitchell alone had broken in 1968: Nixon's "loner" instinct finding expression in his determination to be his own campaign manager. In 1968, a cautious and worried Nixon, unsure of his inner ability to withstand another defeat, had found strength he needed in Mitchell. A man without conventional political ambition, secure in the kind of big-league legal success Nixon respected and envied, Mitchell could tell Nixon what to do — and more important, what *not* to do. He gave Nixon the psychological crutch that he needed to come back from the land of the lost.

In 1972, Nixon was anything but worried. He saw a big victory ahead — and he saw no need to share the credit with anyone. Nor did he see any need to share with Mitchell and the others the blame for the Watergate break-in and all that lay behind it.

III.

Where, as all this happened, were the professional scrutinizers, the watchmen of the Washington press? They were, for the most part, in a state of culture-shock brought about by the arrival of the first Republican administration they had encountered. And they were without a frame of reference to even begin describing the men who had taken over the White House. Because this was a Republican administration, the prevailing assumption was that it must be "conservative" — whatever that meant. Slogans and gimmickry were accepted at face value. On the eve of the first hundred days, a senior White House staff member boasted to a reporter about the administration's fundamental aimlessness: "There is no

ideology, no central commitment, no fixed body of thought."
He knew that he could dismiss idealism with impunity.

Influenced by the New Frontier to admire tough-minded,
hard-boiled pragmatism, the White House press corps
thought they saw it in Ehrlichman especially, who might have
been a New Frontiersman with his cynical quips that summed
up the Nixon administration's huckstering ("It'll play in
Peoria"). They accepted the facade of neatness, discipline,
and managerial efficiency erected by "the C   nans" without
really trying to look behind it. Haldeman's c.   and brisk
manner were noted, but none of the watchers as   'ind
of man this really was, and what, if anything, he believ
beyond serving "the Boss' and hermetically sealing him o.
from distractions. While the reporters panted after such colorful figures as Kissinger and (while he lasted) Moynihan,
there was almost no critical scrutiny of the extraordinary
White House organization structure and the concentration of
enormous power in the hands of a few men unknown to the
public.

One of my former campaign colleagues, who became a
White House aide, told me: "Haldeman and Ehrlichman
shield the President by monopolizing him. One of them is
present at every meeting — he sees no one alone. He's made
himself their captive. Sometimes 'the Germans' don't carry
out Nixon's orders, or they let papers sit on their desks for a
while, because they're certain he won't find out. How *can* he
find out? All the channels flow back to Haldeman." Nixon,
the willing captive, desired this arrangement so that he would
not know everything Haldeman was doing. From another
member of the White House staff, early in the administration,
came an unwitting prophecy: "The Boss likes things simple

and uncomplicated, and that's the way Haldeman and Ehrlichman serve them up. It will take a catastrophic error to change it."

Reporters covering the administration had daily evidence that they were pressing their noses against a plastic P.R. bubble surrounding and concealing a nongovernment. Yet they did not poke through and expose it. Within the bubble were men who believed in nothing, aspired to nothing, and wanted nothing, except to enjoy incumbency for as long as they could before the mistakes overtook them. A press corps made docile desire for "access" to the powerful played along, pretending the bubble wasn't there and a true government was. In a prescient speech in 1962, the late Lawrence Fanning of the Field newspapers of Chicago had worried about the elitism of the Kennedy administration and the lack of reaction by the press: "It boils down to government by an intellectual elite, and the policies can only be as good as the members of the elite. What happens if the elite is replaced by a venal, arrogant, or power-mad cabal? What happens if it is replaced by an elite of the stupid?"

To save himself after the catastrophic error of Watergate, the President reluctantly forced the resignations of Haldeman and Ehrlichman, who resisted their dismissal because they, too, wanted to keep the protection of high office. But Nixon no longer needed them. Soon after their departure, he found two human instruments to replace them — retired General Alexander Haig as chief of staff and Ziegler as adviser-confidant on domestic policy. Except for sporadic bursts of public exposure to defend himself against Watergate charges, the President resumed his isolated, reclusive ways. The attempt to cover up the Watergate plot continued even as the Presi-

17

dent, his spokesmen, and platoons of lawyers professed to be cooperating with Congress and the courts. If this was transparent, self-defeating sham, it was also too late to expect Nixon to change the habits of a political lifetime.

Long before the legal verdict on the President and his *apparatchiks* had been established, the moral verdict on Watergate was pronounced in the news media. A regime of mediocre men lacking character and intelligence had brought shame on the presidency and the country, and the Watergate transcripts condemned them out of their own mouths. They were the shabbiest group of connivers to occupy the White House in this century — and yet they had very nearly gotten away with everything. Our greatest institutions were more vulnerable than we had supposed.

But this was the least of the truth. The Nixon men had merely exploited the potential for totalitarianism created by the aggrandizement of the presidency during two generations of mostly Democratic rule. The system had been subverted by the combination of concentrated, arbitrary executive power, big campaign money in pursuit of big favors, and secret dealmaking decades before the conspiratorial politicians of the Nixon era had their chance and blew it. Even before Watergate, Americans were thoroughly disillusioned with their political leaders, and no longer expected much moral example from them. But they did expect an essential minimum of skill and competence in the conduct of the nation's affairs. Watergate was shocking mainly because it disclosed gross stupidity in the highest places and thus raised fears of more basic and damaging mistakes yet to come to light. The revealed incompetence of the Nixon regime in managing the hyperinflated economy and the Nixon-Kissinger gambling with national security for the sake of one-sided détente with the Soviet Union were two areas where history might well judge the President's failure far more harshly than his contemporaries judged him for Watergate.

No less disturbing was the thought that Nixon's conspiratorial approach to politics was shared more widely within his party than many Republicans cared to admit; that they were, on the whole, campaigners and oppositionists who had almost literally no idea what to do with governing power on the rare occasions when they won it. The Watergate affair could not have occurred if intelligent, experienced Republican politicians had been in charge of the Nixon government and re-election campaign. But such men did not care deeply enough about the success of specifically Republican policies and programs to wage an all-out fight with the *apparatchiks* and admen for top-level participation in the administration. These foolish partners in the politics of conspiracy, who remained "loyal" even after being completely betrayed, are likely to pay a heavy price for their years of silence. Because they bowed to government by advance men, these Republicans will be buried under its collapse for a long time to come.

Kennedy: Politics as Illusion

RICHARD NIXON would have become President in January 1961 if the nation's votes had been cast (or counted) slightly differently the preceding year. Given the built-in rationale of continuity with the Eisenhower years, Nixon might have concealed more successfully his lack of a sustaining political purpose. As it was, John F. Kennedy, no less a man without a goal beyond personal victory, won by projecting an image of "freshness" and "vigor" in a time of national self-doubt. He practiced a media-oriented politics of illusion, which only a few skeptics challenged.

Among them was the theologian Robert E. Fitch. Writing in *The New Leader* in June 1960, Fitch made an arresting prediction: regardless of which man won, the next President would be a "cool cat," a phrase borrowed from the vocabulary of the Beats. "The essence of the cool cat is that he is controlled rather than committed; that is, he is self-controlled, rather than controlled by ideals to which he has given himself." This could not have been said of the other men who had entered the White House in the twentieth century, the second-rate no less than the great, for there was never any question of the principles to which these men were committed. Kennedy and Nixon seemed to assume and shed commitments casually, as though adapting to changing fashions in opinion as they did in clothing. "It has been fascinating to watch them gradually acquire what are commonly called liberal principles," Fitch wrote, and in the 1960 campaign it would be "still more fascinating to see which one acquires the more liberal principles more expeditiously."

I.

On the morning in July 1960 after his son had won the Democratic nomination for the presidency, Joseph P. Kennedy boarded a jet alone in Los Angeles and flew to New York. From the airport, he telephoned Henry R. Luce, then the editor in chief of Time Inc., and asked "Harry" if he could drop by his office. They made an appointment to meet late that afternoon at the Time-Life Building. An hour or so later, Kennedy called again to say he would be delayed; could the appointment be pushed back? Luce saw no alternative but to extend an invitation to dinner that evening at his apartment, which he suspected Kennedy had been angling for.

The relationship between the pair, extending over thirty years of on-again, off-again friendship, was without pretense. They managed intimacy without affection, for each was conscious both of his own and the other's power, and of the mutual advantages which might flow from being on good terms. Through dinner, they kept their conversation rather deliberately general. Finally, over coffee, Luce decided it was time to come to the point, and he did so with his usual directness.

"Joe, I know why you're here — I'm on your list."

Before Kennedy could reply, Luce continued: "Tell Jack not to worry about the way Time Inc. will treat him. We know he has to go with the liberals on domestic issues, and we'll argue with him politely. On foreign policy, we'll be fair to him — unless he listens to you and turns soft. Then we'll cut his throat."

This thrust, recalling the elder Kennedy's pre–World War II isolationism while U.S. ambassador to Great Britain, was delivered with a smile. Kennedy wore a look of hurt surprise as he replied. "Harry, how the hell could any son of mine be a goddamned liberal? Don't worry about Jack being a weak sister. He'll be tough." *

With that, they rose from the table and went into the next room. Luce turned on the television set.

A crowd of 80,000 had jammed into the Los Angeles Coliseum to hear the candidate make his acceptance speech. As twilight fell over the Pacific, Kennedy performed the obligatory ritual of the nominee, hailing his defeated rivals, calling for party unity, and denouncing the Republicans. Then he moved into the main theme of his address, one which he would develop through the coming campaign. He invoked the classic American myth of the West, recalling the heroism and sacrifice of the pioneers who had toiled across the continent toward the last frontier. "Today some would say that those struggles are all over, that all the horizons have been explored, that all the battles have been won, that there is no longer an American frontier. But . . . the problems are not all solved and the battles are not all won, and we stand today on the edge of a new frontier — the frontier of the 1960s."

* Luce recounted the exchange to me in an interview on October 1, 1962 — ironically the month of the Cuban missile crisis and JFK's greatest testing.

Luce watched and listened intently, much impressed. That night, after his guest left, he drafted a memorandum. The next morning he summoned the writers and editors of *Time*'s National Affairs section for a luncheon conference. Ten of us met in a dining room on one of the upper floors of the old Time & Life Building. Through the skyscraper's windows only clouds were visible.

As we sat down, Luce distributed copies of his memorandum and studied our faces as we read the three pages. When we had finished, he indicated with a gesture that he wanted the confidential document back. We passed the copies to the head of the table. Luce carefully counted them and stacked the pile at his elbow. The most influential publisher in the English-speaking world, a lifelong Republican who had used his influence strenuously on behalf of Dwight Eisenhower, appeared to be seriously considering the idea of supporting a Democrat. He was full of praise for the previous evening's speech and quoted lines that especially pleased him ("Too many Americans have lost their way, their will, and their sense of historic purpose"). The Democratic platform, of course, was too liberal, but he admired its boldness: it offered "a coherent vision of Utopia." *

Luce was a man of headlong, transient enthusiasms, but this was not one of them. For more than a year, the Proprietor, as he was known inside Time Inc., had been caught up in a cause which he pursued with the zeal inherited from his missionary parents. "More than anything else," he wrote in 1959, "the American people are asking for a clear sense of National Pur-

---

* Not surprisingly, this phrase found its way into *Time* (July 25, 1960): ". . . The 1960 Democratic platform . . . is . . . probably the most coherent blueprint for Utopia ever to come out of a convention."

23

pose." *Life* ran a series of essays on this theme by contributors
ranging from the Reverend Billy Graham to Walter Lippmann. A congressional committee launched hearings and President Eisenhower appointed a blue-ribbon Commission on National Goals, headed by Henry Wriston. A semi-editorial in
the guise of a news story was scheduled and rescheduled for
Time's National Affairs section, but each version fell short of
Luce's exhortatory desires. The thankless assignment finally
came to me, the junior writer. With strong guidance from up-
stairs, I wrote a "Nation" lead reporting the supposed debate
astir at the grassroots. All the soul-searching tended to support the assertion of candidate Kennedy: "The harsh facts of
the matter are that we have gone soft — physically, mentally,
spiritually soft."

At lunch, the Proprietor sailed into one of his famous
monologues. As usual his thoughts darted ahead of his words
and he paused frequently to collect them. Sometimes the un-
wary mistook one of his long pauses for a full stop and began
to speak just as Luce took off again. To complicate matters,
he was slightly deaf, a handicap he used to advantage in ignoring disagreeable remarks. Experience taught that Luce
usually signaled the completion of an immediate train of
thought with a slight nod of his head and a barely audible
grunt.

Although Kennedy's performance had prompted Luce's
memorandum, it was the sad state of his own Republican
party that most concerned him. The reverse of every compliment he paid Kennedy and the Democrats was a complaint
against Vice President Richard M. Nixon and the G.O.P.
Where, he demanded to know, was *their* vision of Utopia?

A luncheon with Luce, like a church service, filled up from

24

the rear. So it was that I found myself seated at the Proprietor's right hand. Throughout lunch, he helped himself to my cigarettes but said nothing. Now, as he went around the table polling the group's reaction, I was the last to speak.

It seemed to me, I said, that the cause of the Republican party's plight was plain. Moreover, it was one to which Time Inc. and Mr. Luce himself had contributed. In order to escape the political wilderness, the Republican party had put itself at the disposal of a winning but nonpartisan personality. The party, in effect, had bartered its soul and sacrificed its identity for the presidency. Eisenhower's philosophy, such as it was, could scarcely be defined, much less legislated. All the windy talk of "modernizing" the party came to nothing because the men around Eisenhower had no use for ideas and were convinced that a smart businessman knew all that it was necessary to know about the art of government. (Treasury Secretary George Humphrey, the dominant figure in the Eisenhower Cabinet, often said as much.)

Eisenhower's popularity was nontransferable. The voters trusted Ike for reasons seemingly as obvious as his flashing grin; he was a good man "above party." Nevertheless he was an astute politician adept in the organizational maneuvering learned during his years in the peacetime army. Military budgets then were miniscule, advancement was almost hopelessly slow, and a soldier-politician's career depended on winning the favor of powerful civilian sponsors. Eisenhower's meteoric rise to Supreme Allied Command showed how adroitly he had manipulated his sponsors. His skill in using people did not desert him in the presidency. No matter what went wrong in his administration, blame never fell on his shoulders.

25

Yet the main reason many things had gone wrong was clearly Eisenhower's responsibility: whenever possible, he avoided hard, divisive decisions. By nature he was a conciliator, a patient seeker of consensus, which he fashioned from the materials brought to hand by events. For most of the fifties, the mood of the country and his disposition had seemed perfectly matched. A people anxious to forget war and hardship were content with a Chief Executive who regarded his office as a climactic honor, a burden to be borne, rather than as a center of action. When he drew on the lessons of his Abilene boyhood and offered homespun homilies on thrift, Eisenhower exerted a magnetic appeal. A people uprooted and beset by change felt at home again and were comforted by his affirmations. Eisenhower had administered a regime of immediate satisfactions. He did no evil but deferred and finally omitted doing necessary things that might have been done. And so America had drifted.

Luce heard my countermonologue patiently, nodding once or twice. At the end, as my colleagues shuffled and fidgeted and cleared their throats, Luce fixed me with a stare and said: "So you're a Republican. What's your name?"

By three o'clock, as we rose from lunch and resumed writing the account of Kennedy's nomination, we had received from the editor in chief unmistakable marching orders. There would be a new dispensation of objectivity in *Time*'s treatment of the candidates. If the country needed dynamic leadership, the Republicans would have to prove they could provide it. Luce was not quite ready to endorse Kennedy and his New Frontier (and, in fact, never did), but it troubled him to find his Republicans so *dull*.

II.

A stunning event had thrust the issue of purpose on the American consciousness. On the evening of October 4, 1957, Radio Moscow issued a bulletin to the world. The announcer reported that the Soviet Union had fired the first man-made satellite into orbit 560 miles above the earth. *Sputnik* — the Russian word for "traveling companion" — was racing through the heavens at a speed in excess of 18,000 miles an hour and beaming radio signals back to the planet on which, the voice from Moscow said, socialism would surely triumph.

The feat provoked reactions of alarm and near-hysteria in Western countries, especially the United States. The supposedly "backward" Russians had narrowed, if not closed entirely, America's vaunted lead in science and technology. Only a few weeks earlier, the Soviets had staged the world's first successful firing of an intercontinental ballistic missile, capable, so they claimed, of delivering a hydrogen warhead to any spot on the globe. *Sputnik* thus underscored in spectacular fashion a direct challenge to the United States and its margin of nuclear superiority on which rested the uneasy *Pax Atomica*.

Prominent Democrats quickly took up the challenge, for here, of all unexpected places, the popular general in the White House seemed open to criticism. "We have got to admit frankly and without evasion that the Soviets have beaten us at our own game — daring scientific advances in the atomic age," declared Lyndon Johnson, the Senate majority leader. He announced a special investigation of the lagging U.S. space and missile programs. Other critics broadened the scope of Soviet achievement and American failure, claiming that *Sput-*

27

nik "proved" the superiority of Russian education and scientific training. In their eyes the prestige of the United States was sinking fast. To Adlai Stevenson it seemed that most of the world's population now saw Russia "as more skillful, more powerful, yes, and ironically, more peaceful than we are."

Only a year earlier in the fall of 1956, the "peaceful" Soviets had dealt cruelly with a series of explosions within their Eastern European subject states, culminating in their bloody repression of a nationalist revolution in Hungary. As Soviet tanks rumbled through the streets of Budapest and doomed Hungarian freedom fighters radioed desperate appeals for America to redeem the empty promises of "liberation," Washington did nothing beyond admitting a stream of refugees. The uprisings in Eastern Europe were one of the consequences of "de-Stalinization," a process set in motion by Nikita Khrushchev to consolidate his own power. When crisis came, however, Communism fell back on the methods of the late tyrant. As *Sputnik* soared overhead, America might have remembered this display of Soviet weakness but our memory failed just as our conscience and will had failed earlier.

Robert Murphy, one of America's most experienced diplomats, reflecting on the fear the Soviets inspired through their ruthlessness, wrote afterward: "In retrospect, world acceptance of the Russian aggression in Hungary is still incredible. For sheer perfidy and relentless suppression of a courageous people longing for their liberty, Hungary will always remain a classic symbol. Perhaps history will demonstrate that the free world could have intervened to give the Hungarians the liberty they sought, but none of us in the State Department had the skill or the imagination to devise a way." *

* Robert Murphy, *Diplomat Among Warriors* (New York: Doubleday & Co., 1964), p. 432.

During the three days of intense debate within the Kremlin which preceded their intervention in Hungary, the shaken Soviet leaders recognized the risk of war but they at last faced it and gave Marshal Zhukov authority to use all necessary means to suppress the revolt. The West and especially the United States shrank from even considering the possibility of symbolic, diplomatic intervention in a fluid situation which might have proved a historic turning point. One of Stalin's governing beliefs continued to influence Soviet policy. "Russia and the West both fear war," he once told a Western ambassador, "but we fear it slightly less than you do."

In fact, the possibility of nuclear war was what preserved the truce between East and West. In the early 1950s, when America's nuclear superiority had been overwhelming, the U.S. delivered confident, even belligerent warnings of "massive retaliation" if the Soviets overstepped the line. Secretary of State John Foster Dulles laid down the doctrine of deterrence: "The willingness to wage war, if necessary, is in fact an assurance of peace." The press gave U.S. policy a name Dulles himself never used — "brinkmanship."

The American reaction to *Sputnik* revealed beyond doubt a weakening will to contemplate the risks inherent in the basic U.S. security posture. Now, the Soviet Union seemed strong enough to challenge that posture and call America's nuclear bluff.

A new fear was entering the American consciousness but it could not be admitted openly. Instead, fear lay concealed beneath the clamor against the apparent deficiencies in U.S. defenses, as though an inadequacy in the physical means of destruction were the issue rather than failing courage to even consider using a still enormous U.S. superiority to support diplomatic maneuver. In the months after *Sputnik,* the Democrats warned against an approaching "missile gap." Senator Stuart Symington, one of his party's ranking spokesmen on defense, said that within two years the United States would have only thirty intercontinental missiles to the Soviet Union's one hundred; by 1964, he claimed, the margin against the U.S. would be a terrifying fifteen-to-one. Senator Kennedy warned in a speech that "the deterrent ratio might well shift to the Soviets so heavily . . . as to open to them a new short cut to world domination . . . We cannot expect them to give us the same advantage — by sitting by until our missile power equals their own — that we gave to them during the years of our atomic monopoly." The "gap" would begin to open in 1960, he said, too short a time in which to repair U.S. defenses through "crash" programs. The United States would need a new and more conservative "underdog" strategy, for the nation dared not rely upon "those same policies in effect during the years of our . . . lead." *

In reality, the United States at that time did *not* face a "missile gap." President Eisenhower knew for certain that overall U.S. nuclear strength would be more than sufficient to maintain deterrence through most of the sixties. Secretary Dulles and other advisers urged the President to divulge this information as well as the basis of his certainty, thereby silencing the opposition. But Eisenhower refused. Thus, while Americans reacted anxiously to *Sputnik* and the warnings of imminent inferiority, they remained unaware that U-2 reconnaissance aircraft were flying high above the Soviet Union, their detailed photographs providing, to both the President and Russian leaders, conclusive proof of continued American su-

* John F. Kennedy, *The Strategy of Peace,* ed. Allan Nevins (New York: Harper, 1960), pp. 33–45.

periority. The world would not learn of the U-2 flights until May 1960, when the Soviets finally succeeded in shooting down one of the spy planes just before a scheduled U.S.-Soviet summit conference.

The so-called U-2 incident, which revealed both Soviet inferiority and its long vulnerability to aerial espionage in support of deterrence, gave Soviet Premier Khrushchev a most welcome pretext for calling off the summit and avoiding a situation in which he would bargain from embarassingly apparent weakness. But most of the Western press reacted with keen disappointment to the dashing of inflated hopes for a comprehensive American-Soviet deal, and the real meaning of the U-2 incident was obscured amid Khrushchev's self-protective bluster. Each ascent to the summit, from Geneva in 1955 to Camp David four years later, had produced only momentary euphoria, pressures for American concessions in behalf of "peace," and, inevitably, disappointment at the lack of results. Ill-prepared summit diplomacy changed nothing in the relations of the nuclear powers, except that other nations noted America's rising respect for Soviet strength and adjusted their attitudes accordingly. The Soviets, in spite of their evident weakness and the instability of their system, put on a front of belligerent optimism in sharp contrast to the timid self-doubt of Western spokesmen. A slightly intoxicated Khrushchev, confronting a representative capitalist at a reception in Moscow, affirmed his faith in the eventual victory of Communism. "We will bury you," he roared.

On June 11, 1960, at Colonial Williamsburg, Charles Malik of Lebanon, former president of the United Nations General Assembly, delivered one of the truly great addresses of the time. The press almost completely ignored it. Malik, asking whether the future would redeem the past, spoke with rare insight and courage:

> I am yet to hear one Western leader who, assured to his face that he is doomed and will be "buried," can muster enough courage and conviction, if not to use the vulgar phrase "bury" with respect to Communism itself, at least to use some such civilized expression as that the days of Communism are numbered and that Communism will one day be completely forgotten . . . Whereas international Communism believes and acts on the belief that the days of everything non-Communist are numbered, my deepest fear is that Western leadership believes no such thing with respect to Communism: my fear is that the softening-up process has reached such an advanced state that all now believe Communism is here to stay and that therefore the utmost they can do is to manage somehow to "coexist" with it. The deepest crisis of the West is the crisis of faith in its own values.

America had twice blindly intervened in Europe's wars without understanding that Western civilization was torn by a civil war of the spirit. Each of the "isms" — Marxism-Leninism, Fascism, Nazism — was an armed heresy arising from the decay and disorder of the West, a monstrous offspring sworn to destroy the failing parent. As the chief remaining defenders of Western civilization, the Americans were now faced with an implacable ideological foe and engaged in a conflict for which their national experience left them unprepared. "It has been our fate as a nation," Oliver Wendell Holmes had written, "not to *have* ideologies, but to *be* one."

What were the values the nation lived by and would, if necessary, defend with arms? Was *anything* worth even the smallest risk of war in the nuclear age? Americans could deny the clash of moral ideas and ideals at the heart of the Cold War, but that evasion drained their cause of the beliefs necessary to sustain sacrifice. In an essay written in 1941, as the most terrible of Western civilization's internal conflicts reached full fury, Allen Tate diagnosed "a deep illness of the modern mind . . . our limitation of the whole human problem to the narrow scope of the political problem." Incisively, he wrote: "We are justified in saving democracy if democracy can save something else which will support it."

That "something else" was still lacking a generation later. In the emerging view, the Cold War was a contest of competing materialisms and the stake was physical survival. Democracy, as such, seemed worth neither dying nor living for, an attitude Kennedy sensed and exploited in his heroic rhetoric.

III.

In all terms except its own, America seemed a phenomenal success. Never in history had a society enjoyed such broadly shared well-being. Never had a nation been so powerful militarily and so advanced technologically. Yet every index could be reversed and made to point an opposite judgment: prosperity was crass selfishness, global military commitments overextended the U.S., and technology could turn socially destructive without the discipline of human ends.

The standards by which Kennedy and others judged America's failure were ideal standards, and these commanded an almost religious assent. For a century and a half, the United States had been a proud exception among nations in the continuing attempt to fulfill ideal conceptions and practice the secular faith — "Americanism." Americans committed themselves to act on "self-evident" truths practiced nowhere

33

else in the world. The idea that men were naturally endowed with certain rights and entitled to govern themselves, free to maintain the precarious balance between freedom and responsibility, was as revolutionary and as much open to doubt in 1960 as when the founders proclaimed it. The essence of the American experiment was the choice of the sovereign people. They chose not only their leaders, but also the course which determined what America would become in each generation.

The American had been born through a merging of many ethnic and religious strains, and his character had an unfinished quality. The Europeans, including the Russians behind the imposed facade of Marxism-Leninism, were deep-rooted and tradition-bound in a way the Americans were not. It did not occur to the Russians or the French or the British to ask what kind of people they were becoming. They wore their identities as unreflectively as they drew breath and stood unselfconsciously within centuries-old cultures.

The United States, as the world's oldest republic, could boast a rich political tradition. But as a civilization, America was still unformed and shallow. The "American way of life" extolled from the platform was an appeal to visceral patriotism and a synonym for a middle-class standard of living, not a binding set of shared memories, customs, and associations. The long cultural dependency on Europe had been broken only within the twentieth century. What was distinctive in the American culture was mechanical, technical, and managerial, capable of satisfying human needs and desires, to be sure, yet seemingly incapable of supporting a secure identity. America's finest novelists and storytellers — people who knew who they were — tended to be Southerners and Jews from submerged and untypical subcultures; the Negro, for all his

34

burdens, consoled himself with real music, while the white man listened to Muzak. As a unifying force, culture was much weaker than politics, economics, and technology.

In the fifties, people who had made money during World War II and people forced to defer moneymaking for the duration burst on the marketplace and set in motion the longest sustained prosperity in the nation's history. Second- and third-generation Americans overthrew old class obstacles and pushed their way up in every sector of national life from industry to the professions to politics and the arts. The great metropolitan centers and their suburbs became the special domain of the aggressive new moneyed Americans.

The pre–World War II social structure, weakened by the Depression, did not disappear gradually. It collapsed almost unnoticed, so busy was everyone erecting his part of whatever would replace it. The difficulty was, the old social blueprint was gone too. The replacement lacked a clear, coherent structure by which one might know his rank and the rank of others above and below. Those who stood out in the new scheme of things tended to be either official (politicians), functional (the anonymous corporate elite), frivolous (show business "personalities"), or exaggerated types (oil millionaires). The newly prosperous could identify with none of these groups. The fading of distinctions between "mass" and "class" made the national culture more democratic but also more confused. If upward mobility was open to anyone who could obtain credit, who was anybody?

In such best-selling books of the 1950s as *The Lonely Crowd* and *The Organization Man,* the new middle class read about itself. Among those Americans who worked for large, bureaucratic organizations, and who belonged to them spiritually as

35

well, David Riesman and his collaborators saw the national character changing. The "inner-directed" individual was giving way to the "other-directed" man of the lonely crowd. The "inner-directed" man looked within himself for authority and goals; he forged his own identity. The "other-directed" man looked outside and took direction from his contemporaries, as Riesman wrote, "either those known to him or those with whom he is indirectly acquainted, through friends or the mass media." * His desire to emulate his peers went far beyond externals of dress, consumption, and behavior, extending to "the quality of his inner experience." He sought to *feel* as he imagined others felt, and his frustration led to diffuse anxiety. William H. Whyte's organization man lived comfortably in a protected environment, but his life was shadowed by doubt. He had found nothing satisfying with which to replace the Protestant Ethic and the American Dream of individualism. "The Organization man," Whyte wrote, "seeks a redefinition of his place on earth — a faith that will satisfy him that what he must endure has a deeper meaning than appears on the surface." **

More and more Americans were being drawn into a "class" which could not be adequately defined in economic and social terms. It was characterized by a distinctive state of awareness which tended to make members of the new middle class both actors and self-critical observers of their actions. They took their bearings in a social and cultural environment created by modern communications technology, especially television. Be-

* David Riesman, Nathan Glazer, Reuel Denney, *The Lonely Crowd* (New York: Doubleday Anchor Edition, 1955).
** William H. Whyte, *The Organization Man* (New York: Doubleday Anchor Edition, 1956), p. 6.

36

cause the mass media were organized to serve primarily as a marketplace, where values were manipulated and ideals synthesized to sell products, the American acquired his self-image as a consumer, becoming what he bought. Though warned to be on guard against Madison Avenue's hidden persuaders, the man who defined his place within the new middle class as a consumer could not help studying the social context of ads, seeking in the distorting mirror of the media culture clues to his rank and identity.

Technology had superseded imagination, replacing personal visions with prefabricated illusions. Magazine advertisements and television commercials projected the authentic Americans: handsome, active, and sexually attractive people, families enjoying the good life. The children were most vulnerable as they sat staring at the TV screen. They clamored for the large, fragile plastic toys they saw advertised as tokens of parental love. And yet, once the tokens had been extorted and displayed under the coolly appraising gaze of their peers, the children discarded them.

The upper-bracket man, who hurdled class barriers and enjoyed privileges his parents had only dreamed of, sat beside the swimming pool behind his picture-perfect split-level in the New York suburbs, and remembered the subway rides to Coney Island in the sweltering summers of his childhood. His lunch of sandwiches and fruit stained the brown paper bag he carried, and he frequently patted his pocket, checking the coins tied in a handkerchief. On the way home, the wet, sandy bathing suit chafed his legs. His children took a pool as their birthright. To strive for the next generation's swimming pool was perhaps a goal, but not one to make child or parent feel challenged and fulfilled.

37

The old ways were gone and so was the old morality which laid down rules, prescribed punishments, and determined goals. The old America lay on the far side of the great, uprooting experience of the world war. "So many people are doing things they haven't done before, seeing a part of life which their elders hoped they never would see at all," Margaret Mead wrote in 1945. "So much of life is being lived anonymously, far from home . . ." Through the fifties, Americans searched for the remembered comfort of familiar habits and enduring associations and for the stability of home, trying to preserve the desirable consequences of a code without the code itself. Church membership rose, especially in the suburbs. Clergymen hailed the religious "revival" until they realized many of their new parishioners were less interested in believing than in belonging.

Rising individual dissatisfaction among outwardly successful Americans formed the background of the "issue" of national purpose, which was cultural rather than political. Men and women who felt purpose had seeped out of their lives sought it elsewhere. In this atmosphere of national self-doubt, John Kennedy, more than any other figure, caught the ear and the eye of the new middle class. Though a conventional and traditional politician, he stood within the media culture in which the anxious searched for their self-images. The seeming embodiment of his rhetoric, he offered the reassuring possibility of heroism.

The Triumph of Media Politics

I.

JOHN F. KENNEDY, in his wife's phrase, was "an idealist without illusions." Least of all did he harbor illusions about the profession of politics: the object was victory for its own sake, for the sheer selfish enjoyment of it. "The political world is so much more stimulating," he once told *Time*'s Hugh Sidey. "It is the most interesting thing you can do — it beats following the dollar. It allows the full use of your powers. First there is the great chess game. It's the battle, the competition. There's the strategy and which piece you move and all that. And then in government you can do something about what you think."

If governing seemed almost an afterthought in this perspective, Kennedy was being faithful not to the training he received at Harvard but to the heritage of Irish politics in which he was reared. "In my family," he told another interviewer, understating the obvious, "we were interested not so much in the ideas of politics as in the mechanics of the whole thing."

The "mechanics" were tested and perfected in Massachusetts for more than a decade before he launched his pursuit of the presidency. As a young congressman, he had

among his early tutors a tough-talking Boston pol named Joe
Kane, who had known his grandfather "Honey Fitz." Kane
laid down the basic prescription: "It takes three things to
win — money, money, money." This became the key element
of the proved Kennedy formula: lavish financing of skilled
personnel who were carefully organized and who acted according to a detailed master strategy. His re-election to the
Senate in 1958 by the biggest landslide ever rolled up by an
office seeker in Massachusetts — 800,000 votes — demonstrated the machinery was ready for the drive to the White
House. By then, he and his aide, Ted Sorensen, were already
traveling the country, lining up support among delegates to
the Democratic Convention still two years away. Already laying the organizational groundwork for the presidential primaries were crew-cut, tight-lipped men a generation younger
than Joe Kane but of the same breed, the men whom the press
called "the Irish Mafia."

Yet money and organization were not the only ingredients
of Kennedy's success. Many another wealthy family had converted parochial fame into political power. From 1946, when,
though a resident of Palm Beach and almost a stranger in his
native Boston, he used the family's name (and money) to win a
seat in Congress, through 1952 when he defeated the lordly
Yankee, Senator Henry Cabot Lodge, Kennedy followed a familiar course. (His grandfather, after all, had been beaten by
Lodge's grandfather in a 1916 match between Irishman and
Brahmin.) The Kennedys, campaigning en masse, scored a
spectacular upset by presenting themselves to the Irish Catholics of Massachusetts as aristocrats of their own kind — the
first *Irish* Brahmins. Hundreds of women received socially
correct, handwritten invitations to take tea at receptions hon-

oring the candidate and Ambassador and Mrs. Joseph P. Kennedy. The lines of thrilled and awe-struck women in formal gowns spilled out of the hotels and into the streets. "It was those damned tea parties," said Lodge after his defeat.

Even so, that victory might have marked the summit for the Kennedys. No matter how strong their dynastic impulse or how lavish their spending, the Kennedys, like other locally famous clans, might have been forced to content themselves with ruling their fief. The ethnic and religious characteristics of Massachusetts were unrepresentative of the nation. Jack Kennedy — relatively young and inexperienced, with an unimposing legislative record, scant support among major voting blocs, and the apparent liability of being a Roman Catholic — was scarcely an obvious presidential candidate. A generation earlier, as his father well knew, the presidential candidacy of a man bearing such credentials would have been impossible. By the latter 1950s, however, the great leap could be made from an unpromising base by using the new springboard — the mass communications media.

Kennedy needed a piece of Irish luck. It came at the 1956 Democratic Convention when Adlai Stevenson broke with custom and threw open the choice of his running mate. Kennedy narrowly lost out to Senator Estes Kefauver, who had gained national prominence through the televised hearings of his investigation of organized crime. As Kennedy later realized, he was lucky to lose, for he thus escaped the ticket's subsequent defeat and the inevitable suspicion that his Catholicism had contributed to it. His televised battle with Kefauver gave Kennedy invaluable national exposure as an attractive personality and established him as a future leader of his party.

After 1956, Kennedy brilliantly practiced the new media

41

politics. Every politician, of course, sought every opportunity to publicize himself and his views. But with the rise of television as the decisive medium of political persuasion, the balance between the substance of a man's views and his "style" was permanently tipped. The politician who possessed *charisma* — a Greek word originally meaning a divinely granted gift or talent for eliciting enthusiastic popular support — had the clear edge over an opponent who lacked it.

The gift of being able to stir and manipulate the emotions of the crowd came at a cost, however. The leader easily became the captive of his followers. Kennedy's temperament — dispassionate, detached, and rational — might have disposed him to try to reach men through their reason as well as their emotions, but this was neither the quickest nor the surest way to victory. Although he wrote a book in praise of politicians who had braved unpopularity for their convictions, he was not attracted to their example.

One of Kennedy's friends and early supporters, Mark Dalton, a Boston lawyer who joined him as a volunteer at the outset of his career and who managed his three races for the House, saw a potential for greatness in him. But the candidate and his family refused the risks. During the 1952 campaign against Lodge, Dalton tried once again to convince the candidate to emphasize "issues" in his speeches. He ran head-on into Joe Kennedy, who poked his finger into Dalton's chest and told him: "Jack will have plenty of time to be a statesman after he's elected." After an argument with Robert Kennedy, fresh from the University of Virginia Law School and much impressed with his own authority, Dalton walked out.

"The strength of the Kennedys," Dalton said without visible bitterness years afterward, "lies in their courage, energy, and will to victory. They are all guts, they will work until they drop, and they never doubt for a moment that they will win. But their weakness is a synthetic quality about themselves and their operations. They hire the best brains and attract the ablest people. Jack still thinks he'll find a speech-writer some day who can make him sound like Lincoln. But substance is lacking. The words, the gestures, the campaigns are hollow. There's showmanship and not much else."

In reminiscing on his picaresque career, Joe Kennedy often said that the only business he had ever really enjoyed was show business. In the late 1920s, as he moved from managing and reorganizing Hollywood film companies to personally financing independent productions, he learned the techniques of the buildup for the "star" on whom his investment was riding. It was no amateur's boast, then, when he told his friend Arthur Krock in 1957: "We're going to sell Jack like soap-flakes."

As the undeclared candidate spoke throughout the country, signed his name to magazine articles written by Sorensen and others, accepted all television invitations, and did everything possible to make himself known nationally, he received something more than the publicity a politician craves. He crossed an invisible dividing line and became a glamorous celebrity. Newspaper and magazine stories emphasized the *non*political: Kennedy's youth and good looks, his multimillionaire status, his World War II record (the saga of PT-109 was told and re-told), his colorful and controversial family, and his beautiful wife Jacqueline. He appealed to all audiences and ideologies. He turned up in the women's magazine *McCall's* as both subject and author. The right-wing *American Mercury* found him "the perfect politician." The pro-business *U.S. News & World*

43

Report took respectful note of his fast start in the race for the nomination. As the build-up gained momentum, *Newsweek* and the *New York Times Magazine* published long, favorable profiles, and *Look* ran three articles on the family, as well as part of a book by reporter Joe McCarthy *The Remarkable Kennedys*. By the fall of 1959, promoter Joe Kennedy was boasting: "Jack is the greatest attraction in the country today."

To be sure, not all the publicity was flattering; liberal journals such as *The Progressive* and *The Reporter* were skeptical of the young man in a hurry. The correspondent of *The Economist* made an unsparingly candid appraisal: "Egotism and a fierce will to succeed are Senator Kennedy's ruling characteristics." But at the very least such articles kept Kennedy's name before their readers. A magazine such as *Look* was much more important because of its mass circulation; in its pages, the Kennedys were treated as figures in an American epic, a family risen from an immigrant grandfather's humble station in East Boston to the heights of fame, wealth, and power. Readers who aspired to the middle-class virtue of "togetherness" saw it exemplified in this proud and united fighting clan. No less impressive were the family's links through marriage to the worlds of the English nobility, New York society, and Hollywood. Politics distinctly aside, the Kennedys were presented as an exemplary success story in a society which worshiped success. They were enthroned as aristocrats of the popular culture, a family personifying every value the mass media exploited and the mass audience tried to emulate.

But politics, of course, was uppermost in the minds of the actors on this stage created by the media. The photographers puffing across the lawn at Hyannis Port, capturing the Kennedys as they played touch football, were there for a political purpose. The "intimate" glimpses of the Kennedys' lives were granted to satisfy the voyeurism of the voters. In the intensifying glare of publicity, the Kennedys played the roles their audience expected and applauded. They did not deceive the image-consumers; they merely encouraged mass self-deception concerning the merits of the product.

II.

The influence of the media, working obviously and subtly to Kennedy's advantage, was evident in the preoccupation with the so-called religious issue. Because the electorate was two-thirds Protestant and because Al Smith's 1928 defeat provided the only precedent for a Catholic attempt to break the Protestant monopoly on the presidency, the press could plausibly frame dramatic questions. Would the Democrats defy the religious taboo and nominate Kennedy? Would the nation "prove" its devotion to democratic principle by electing him?

But these were misleading questions. Polls had shown repeatedly that Americans were strongly opposed to religious bias in choosing a President. The prominence of Catholics in public life disproved the existence of any formidable sentiment against their faith. Far from being a liability, Kennedy's religion was one of his solid assets. If he had been a wealthy young Episcopalian bearing the same record and credentials, he would not have received the publicity which made him the front runner entering 1960. And his relevant qualifications for the presidency — or lack of them — would have come under less sympathetic scrutiny.

45

Kennedy and his strategists knew that the media's concern with the supposed issue of bigotry did not accurately reflect the political realities. Prior to the 1956 Democratic Convention, Sorensen drafted a memorandum, later attributed to Connecticut Democratic Chairman John Bailey, asserting the existence of a "Catholic vote" strategically placed in the large industrial states where the party had suffered reverses four years earlier. Although the "Bailey memorandum" mentioned no names, he was known to be a Kennedy backer. His argument came down to a plea for putting his candidate on the ticket to recapture those normally Democratic Catholic voters who had defected to Eisenhower. By 1960, the implicit religious double standard had become a key part of the Kennedy strategy: he righteously pleaded for keeping religion out of politics while appealing to his co-religionists on the basis of their faith. Anyone who opposed Kennedy, on whatever ground, risked being accused of bigotry.

This was the commonplace cynicism of local and state politics transferred to the presidential level. Party ties had weakened. An increasing number of voters called themselves Independents and declared that they voted for the man and not the party label. In fact, of course, as the voters scanned the mostly unfamiliar names on the ballot, they "read" ethnic and religious labels. Kennedy, by making certain his label was clearly displayed, succeeded so well that by early 1960 more than eight out of ten Catholic voters knew he was a Catholic. In trial heats against Nixon, the polls showed him steadily gaining ground among Catholic Republicans as well as Independents.

Throughout the prolonged Kennedy buildup, the men in control of the Democratic party's nominating machinery watched complacently as though their power were unaffected. For the first time in eight years, the Democrats were free of the burden of facing the unbeatable Eisenhower, and their presidential nomination, twice bestowed on Stevenson, was worth having. With a handful of exceptions, such as Chicago's Mayor Richard Daley, the big city bosses stood aloof from Kennedy. The liberals, again with few exceptions, were distrustful of the candidate who had written *Profiles in Courage* but who had not publicly opposed McCarthyism. Labor leaders detected too much enthusiasm in the Kennedy brothers' attacks on corruption in the Teamsters' Union. Negroes and white Southerners alike were unsure of Kennedy's position on civil rights. Party leaders such as former President Truman and Mrs. Eleanor Roosevelt openly expressed their concern about the elder Kennedy's influence.

Each of the factions, blocs, and interest groups making up the loosely knit Democratic coalition seemed to favor another candidate. Stevenson, though he maintained a characteristic posture of indecision, wanted another try at the presidency and had the support of fervent liberal loyalists. Senator Hubert H. Humphrey was more than acceptable to liberals and organized labor. Senator Stuart Symington, an adroit straddler of regional and ideological lines, made known his availability as a dark horse. Senate Majority Leader Lyndon B. Johnson was preparing to stake everything on an eleventh-hour power play uniting the South, the West, and those Northern bosses agreeable to making a deal.

What these ideologues, pragmatists, and deal-makers, professional politicians all, failed to recognize until too late was the mandate building up beneath Kennedy's rising visibility and popularity. A decision directly affecting the lives of 180

47

million Americans and much of the world could no longer be made in a smoke-filled room or even a convention hall. The mass media and opinion polling had transformed the nominating process into a plebiscite, which all but predetermined the outcome of the convention. Indeed, the media — especially television — were replacing the parties as the central aggregating force in American politics. Voters rallied around a candidate's image rather than his party's standard.

The media, though beset by criticism of their "inaccuracy," were, as a rule, quite accurate in disseminating the impressions they were given — which were sometimes false. Thus while the media emphasized the religious issue highlighted by Kennedy's managers and portrayed him as an underdog, his own private polling in the primary states told an entirely different story. In heavily Protestant West Virginia, for example, the Kennedy polls showed that the voters generally were indifferent to sectarian religious questions, but were deeply concerned with the state's depressed economy and high unemployment. Campaigning as a New and Fair Deal liberal, who was incidentally a Catholic, Kennedy presented himself to the voters of the Mountaineer State not as another Al Smith, but as another Franklin D. Roosevelt — and, just to be sure of that identification, he took FDR Jr. campaigning along with him.

The Democratic party bosses, so-called, were themselves manipulated. They too read the newspapers and magazines and watched television. They too saw Kennedy crush Humphrey and the presumed forces of bigotry in West Virginia, roll up an ever-widening lead in the opinion polls, and become, in the judgment of the media, a sure winner in Los Angeles. All the while, the Kennedy delegate hunters kept up their pressure for commitment, and the opposing lines began to buckle.

By the time Kennedy arrived at the convention, the insiders were ready to succumb to the showmanship outside. The nominating machinery waited to ratify the people's choice. Johnson went frantically in search of support, armed with, among other things, an oddly ingenuous and old-fashioned memorandum comparing his substantial legislative record with Kennedy's meager output. He could not comprehend the unimportance to the delegates of this document alongside Lou Harris's polls predicting a Kennedy victory over Nixon. In his frustration, Johnson raged against Joe Kennedy's prewar isolationist views, declaring that he, Johnson, had never been an appeaser and "a Chamberlain umbrella man."

The Stevenson loyalists made a gallant stand. "Do not reject this man," cried Senator Eugene McCarthy in his nominating speech. "Do not leave this prophet without honor in his own party." The galleries erupted in thunderous applause and foot-stamping. During the frenzied demonstration that followed, electric with the excitement generated by true believers and a holy cause, it seemed just barely possible that McCarthy's eloquent plea might be heeded. But Stevenson's rejection had been sealed by two former supporters, Pennsylvania's Governor David Lawrence and Chicago's Mayor Daley. They delivered their decisive votes to Kennedy, whose slogan promised *He Will Win*.

For the Democrats, as for the Republicans eight years earlier, the choice of a charismatic personal leader meant the abandonment of a principled leader — Taft in 1952, Stevenson now — who had maintained the integrity of the party in defeat and insisted on it remaining an instrument of coherent

49

purpose. The parallel between Taft conservatives and Stevenson liberals lay not in their goals but in their underlying agreement that politics served moral ends. Conservatives, finding no sustenance in Eisenhower's modern Republicanism, regrouped on the right, bent on recapturing the G.O.P. for their brand of ideological politics. After a generation in power, however, liberalism had accumulated a body of formalized responses to public questions, a catechism which any politician, especially the pragmatic and agile Kennedy, could adopt and more or less plausibly recite. Far from possessing the all-pervasive influence in the Democratic party attributed to them in right-wing Republican demonology, the anti-Kennedy liberals were an isolated and forlorn minority within a party determined to win in 1960 — and most of them realized it.

As the Democratic party came under the control of a dominant but uncommitted personality, the alternatives facing liberals were plain: they could go into opposition, guarding their principles and hoping for a future return to power; or they could accommodate themselves. Not surprisingly, the course of accommodation prevailed.

The nominee put his special stamp on the first decision of the Kennedy era. Because of his strength in the South, Johnson was offered, and to Kennedy's surprise accepted, the vice-presidential nomination, a choice urged, among others, by Joe Kennedy. While the liberals threatened mutiny and Mrs. Roosevelt flew home to New York still wearing her Stevenson button, the Kennedys relaxed. As a memento of their conquest, the nominee gave his brother Robert a silver cigarette case bearing a light-hearted inscription: *When I'm Through, How About You?*

III.

MEMO TO VEEPEE NIXON: WANT AN AGENCY JOB?

So ran the headline in *Variety* on September 14, 1955, above an account of a speech Vice President Nixon had made before a meeting of the Radio and Television Executives Society in New York. Nixon spoke on "what a candidate should do to use this medium [television] effectively." *Variety* reported that Nixon "advised use of saturation selling of candidates through one- and five-minute 'spots' as he called them because, he said, 'a great number of voters vote only names, not platforms.' " There seemed to be little difference, in the trade paper's judgment, between his counsel on how to handle political candidates and the way advertising men mounted campaigns for their products. An advertising executive, impressed with the presentation, jocularly offered Nixon an agency vice presidency.

If diligent application could make a media politician, Nixon should have been an outstanding success. He closely studied media techniques, fascinated with the small details of how desired effects might be achieved. He was proud of his skill in the mechanics of politics, and especially proud of his skill in using the new image-machine of television. Yet Nixon lacked what diligence could not supply: the sensitive inner prompter which told the successful actor when to perform and when to be at ease. Nixon was never off-stage. Even when he was most in earnest, the manner of contrivance and the whiff of salesmanship clung to him. He gave the appearance of straining to be sincere.

Ironically, the course of Nixon's career had been dramatically altered, propelling him to within an uncertain heartbeat of the presidency, because he once had been true to himself and his convictions. As a young Congressman in the summer of 1948, Nixon had been caught in the confrontation between Whittaker Chambers and Alger Hiss, the former high government official whom Chambers accused of pro-Soviet espionage. "An ex-Communist is one of the loneliest of creatures," Chambers suddenly burst out during a session before Nixon and the other members of the House Committee on Un-American Activities. "Particularly an ex-Communist of my sort, who is in constant apprehension, who is afraid to trust anyone." This struck a chord in Nixon, himself a lonely, shy, and introspective man slow to give trust. He became convinced that the mysterious Chambers, with his bizarre tale of pro-Soviet conspiracy inside the New Deal, could be trusted, and that the handsome, brilliant Hiss, president of the Carnegie Endowment for International Peace and supported by leading figures in the Eastern establishment of law, finance, and politics, was a liar.

Prior to the Hiss case, Nixon had been just another bright newcomer to the House (a fellow freshman in the Class of '46 was Jack Kennedy), another ambitious, small-town lawyer who had scrambled up from the edge of poverty and made his way mainly by grinding persistence. He might have passed uneventfully through Congress, as many like him did, and gone home to California and a solid law practice or a judgeship. As a result of the publicity surrounding the Hiss case, however, Nixon swiftly became an exciting young Republican personality, known across the country. Within four years he vaulted from the House to the Senate and then, in 1952, to the vice presidency, a very junior partner to the great general.

Their distant relationship was painfully revealed during the 1952 campaign. Six weeks before the election, the New York *Post* took revenge on the man who had helped destroy Hiss by running a sensational front-page story: SECRET NIXON FUND! Wealthy California businessmen, the story disclosed, had underwritten Nixon's political expenses, including travel back and forth from Washington and Christmas cards for his constituents. Eisenhower's advisers, who knew Nixon only slightly, panicked. The general proposing to lead a crusade to restore morality in government could not be tainted by the slightest hint of corruption. To save his place on the ticket, Nixon sacrificed his dignity. He gave a tawdry yet effective speech on television in which he laid bare his family's personal lives, their finances, and their possessions, down to his wife Pat's "Republican cloth coat" and his daughters' cocker spaniel, "Checkers," a gift he said he would not return. Afterward, film tycoon Darryl Zanuck telephoned Nixon: "The most tremendous performance I've ever seen." The "Checkers speech" produced a tidal wave of tears and sympathy which swept Nixon into the arms of a forgiving Eisenhower. "You're my boy," he declared as they were reunited. Knowing how close he had come to being abandoned, Nixon turned, buried his face in Senator William Knowland's bulky shoulder, and wept.

The scene was symbolically apt. Knowland, the heir to Taft's mantle, was a natural political friend and ally, but the aloof Eisenhower, and even more the men around and behind him, held the power to fulfill Nixon's ambitions. As Vice President, he sought to ingratiate himself with the Eastern, "modern" Republicans who privately scorned him, and edged away from the Midwestern and Western conservatives who, in time, felt a scorn of their own toward him. Assuming the party burdens Eisenhower shirked, Nixon bore not only the brunt of Democratic attacks, but also occupied a kind of no man's land between the antagonists in his party's unending ideological civil war. In the name of unity, he tried to compromise principles which both sides regarded as far more important than winning elections. ("I have found, over the years," Nixon wrote in his memoirs, "that Republicans have an almost cannibalistic urge to destroy and consume one another whenever they happen to disagree.") The pressures and counter-pressures on Nixon came to a head just before the 1960 Republican Convention. With his nomination assured, the Vice President secretly flew to New York and met through the night with Governor Nelson Rockefeller, revising key planks in the platform to his satisfaction. This gesture of appeasement infuriated conservatives.

It was against this background of suspicion and disunity that Nixon at last broke free of his humiliating subordination to Eisenhower and assumed the authority of the man who might be the next President. He found release for pent-up frustration by taking total, personal command of *his* campaign, down to the most trivial detail. "He did everything," an aide recalled, "but sharpen his own pencils."

In the euphoria of his nomination, Nixon made the decision, and so pledged publicly, to campaign in every state, an obvious waste of time and energy. Even more important was the decision whether or not to face Kennedy in joint television appearances. *"Mister Vice President,"* said Senator Styles Bridges, the astute, behind-the-scenes leader of the conservative forces in the upper chamber, "don't give the *junior* Senator from Massachusetts a platform." Eisenhower and others echoed the advice. But Nixon, in spite of the obvious pitfalls, felt obliged to accept Kennedy's challenge and felt confident of his ability in the proposed format. The candidates agreed to meet in four televised "debates."

Even if he received every Republican vote in the country, Nixon told his campaign planners again and again, he would lose the election by 5 million votes. Victory could be won only by reaching the Independents and wavering Democrats, and the best way was through television. Nixon's aim was to soften what he himself called "the Herblock image" — Nixon as the unrestrained, mud-slinging partisan — and to project instead an image of mature, experienced statesmanship.

His calculations might not have failed so disastrously except for a small mishap. Getting out of an automobile in Greensboro, North Carolina, he hit his knee against the door frame. The knee swelled and became infected. Finally he was forced to spend two weeks in Walter Reed Hospital. This fortnight of convalescence left him hopelessly behind in his fifty-state travel schedule, and his staff pleaded that it be cut back, but Nixon refused and plunged into a hectic round of campaigning. As a result, he approached the first television debate, on the evening of September 26, ten pounds underweight and visibly on the ragged edge of exhaustion. In the hours before air time, Nixon went into seclusion and pored over briefing papers. Kennedy, with a handful of aides, engaged in an informal "cram" session and flipped through index cards containing likely questions and answers. In midafternoon, he moved the meeting to the roof of his hotel and relaxed in the sunshine, restoring the healthy tan that would contrast so strikingly with Nixon's sickly pallor.

The candidates met in the Chicago studio of CBS station

WBBM. A combined radio and television audience estimated at more than 70 million adults, nearly two thirds of the electorate, listened and watched. In publicizing the encounter, the media had likened it to the historic Lincoln-Douglas debates, as though the old methods of persuasion had been transferred intact to the new medium. But the crowds that flocked long ago to the courthouse greens of the middle border saw real men perform; the flow of emotion between speakers and spectators was the essence of the experience. The crowd laughed at Lincoln's anecdotes and applauded Douglas's sallies. Men were amused, moved, and persuaded by the human presence before them. The framework of the event was provided by each spectator's perception of it.

Television imposed its own monolithic frame of reference. The viewer saw only what the camera showed, an edited, enclosed, and intensified "reality," and he reacted in the terms the medium dictated. The viewer passively received an unbroken stream of words and images, issuing from pleasingly made-up faces following scripts timed to the split-second. Lincoln could pause for a moment or two while he gathered his thoughts, but ten seconds of "dead air" made the television viewer uneasy. Lincoln could be physically unattractive yet popular at the same time. The images on the screen were contrived to satisfy the values not of traditional politics but of mass entertainment; and the politicians who entered the realm of the entertainers were judged by their standards.

What drew the enormous audience for the Kennedy-Nixon encounter was not the expectation of reasoned argument, but the novelty of seeing the two most talked-about personalities of the day meet face to face, and the opportunity to measure them side by side. Perhaps the closest historical precedent for the contest was the grisly spectacle of the gladiators in the Roman Coliseum. In the contemporary, symbolic combat, the mob lifted or reversed its thumbs in the subsequent opinion polls.

For Nixon and Kennedy, their encounter had potentially decisive *personal* significance. But it had little meaning for the mass audience because the two men represented nothing coherent or definable outside themselves. Their contest was perfectly in key with the values and critical standards of the new media politics in which the surface was very nearly everything.

IV.

Kennedy and Nixon stood behind lecterns at opposite sides of the gray-walled studio set. The red light on the camera facing Kennedy winked on and his face filled the screen. He spoke rapidly but well, restating in short, emphatic sentences the main themes of his campaign. *I am not satisfied as an American with the progress that we are making . . . This is a great country but I think it could be a greater country.* With the poise and self-assurance of a newscaster, he reeled off statistics — the index cards had served him well — supporting his claim that America was falling short of its potential and slipping in the race with its determined Soviet competitor. *Can freedom be maintained under the most severe attack it has ever known? I think it can be and I think in the final analysis it depends upon what we do here.* He closed with the evocative formula he used in every context: *I think it's time America started moving again.*

In his recollections of the debate, Nixon appraised Ken-

57

nedy's statement as "a very shrewd, carefully calculated appeal, with subtle emotional overtones," one which he believed would "impress unsophisticated voters." He went on to suggest, unconvincingly, that he might have taken "the politically expedient course" of agreeing with Kennedy and then outpromising him, but rejected this approach as "demagogic." Nixon's retrospective analysis was as off-key as his performance. Attacked and hurt more than he realized by Kennedy's opening remarks, Nixon went ahead with his defensive, deliberately muted rebuttal.

Nixon was drawn and hollow-cheeked. A normal-sized shirt collar hung loosely on his neck. Not only did he look weak; his first words sounded weak. *The things that Senator Kennedy has said, many of us can agree with.* Where Kennedy had directed his words at the camera and the audience, Nixon addressed his opponent, as though they were formally debating before a panel of judges. He sprinkled his statement with tributes to Kennedy's sincerity, making it sound as though no major differences separated them. *I subscribe completely to the spirit that Senator Kennedy has expressed tonight . . . I know Senator Kennedy feels as strongly about these problems as I do, but our disagreement is not about the goals for America, but only about the means to reach those goals.*

In a few minutes, Nixon all but threw away the hard-won advantage of his eight years in the vice presidency. The audience watching and comparing the two men could not help but be impressed by Kennedy's confidence and force. Kennedy looked like the stereotype of the television hero, while Nixon more nearly resembled the stereotype of the villain. Kennedy sounded positive and used the word "new" the way television pitchmen did. Nixon sounded like a salesman with a bum

58

product who wasn't too sure of himself. Since the "Checkers" speech, political writers had assumed that Nixon aroused a special empathy among Americans of the heavily mortgaged middle class. But the times and the attitudes of such Americans were changing. Opposite the poised Kennedy, Nixon reminded many viewers of their former selves and of struggles they would rather forget. Faced with the standard Democratic accusation that Republicans were indifferent to the plight of the less fortunate, Nixon, insensitive to the medium's exaggeration of every word and inflection, seemed to lunge for the crowd's sympathy, saying in a tone of self-pity: *I know what it means to be poor.*

A panel of reporters, among them NBC's Sander Vanocur, questioned the candidates. The new media politics, inevitably, bred media men who behaved as partisans, injecting their bias into supposedly "objective" reporting, commentary, and interviewing. Vanocur, a personal friend of Kennedy's, faced Nixon with the manner of a prosecuting attorney, and asked a question of no substance but maliciously damaging implication. A month earlier, just as a press conference closed, Eisenhower had been asked to give an example of a major decision in which Nixon had participated. The President, on his way out of the room, tossed off a facetious reply: "If you give me a week, I might think of one." When the press reported the response deadpan, Eisenhower telephoned Nixon and expressed surprise at being taken seriously, but did not apologize. The following week, the question was not asked again, and Eisenhower did not volunteer an answer. Before scores of millions of viewers, Vanocur now demanded "clarification" from the embarrassed Nixon, who could only explain lamely that Eisenhower did not mean what he seemed to say.

59

Finally the hour ended. Stunned and angry Republicans telephoned Nixon headquarters in Washington demanding to know what was wrong with him. His mother, after watching the debate, called from California to ask his secretary if Richard was "feeling all right." Nixon later assured her he was feeling fine. But his supporters were heartsick. All the old doubts came rushing to the surface. For once, liberals and conservatives glumly agreed: Nixon had blown it.

Kennedy's performance had a tonic effect on the jubilant Democrats. He had demolished Nixon's pedestal of "experience" at a single blow. Overnight, anti-Nixon liberals became pro-Kennedy enthusiasts. Beyond the political effects he achieved, Kennedy had reached the subconscious of the electorate. More than ever he was seen as a glamorous celebrity, combining, as one pleased Democratic Senator put it, "the best qualities of Elvis Presley and Franklin D. Roosevelt." As Kennedy toured northern Ohio after the first debate, drawing large, demonstrative crowds, reporters noticed teen-aged girls on the fringes squealing and jumping. Swiftly, the phenomenon spread to females of all ages and conditions — Theodore H. White, preparing the first of his quadrennial scenarios of democracy, spotted nuns along Kennedy's route demurely bouncing within their habits. America had produced its first presidential candidate with electrifying sex appeal. Caught in the crush of a Kennedy throng ecstatically rocking back and forth, White recorded an unforgettable cameo — a frowsy woman who muttered hoarsely as if to herself: "Oh, Jack, I love yuh, Jack, I love yuh, Jack — Jack, Jack, I love yuh."

Kennedy's command of the newest medium of communication assured his dominance of the oldest — word of mouth. After watching him silently, people felt a need to talk and compare notes on their reactions. In the absence of a major issue between the candidates, it became evident in the closing weeks of the campaign that the election would turn on the voters' emotional response to Kennedy's personality, on how he made them "feel."

Among the poor, the isolated, and the submerged, his presence was less vivid and pro-Kennedy feeling was weak. The people who saw an alien way of life on the television screen, and who heard few words which spoke directly to the conditions they endured, remained indifferent. The greatest number of these Americans were Negroes. If they went to the polls, they would vote overwhelmingly Democratic, following the pattern established in the latter years of the New Deal. But their turnout for elections, in proportion to their numbers, was usually the smallest of any important ethnic group in America. Concentrated in the cities of the large industrial states of the North and Midwest, Negroes, as much as Catholics, held the balance of electoral power, but they had been given no motive, beyond the familiar economic one, to bestir themselves on Kennedy's behalf.

Then, in late October, an event occurred which held only passing interest for most white voters, but which aroused intense concern among Negroes. The candidates, who had made the most coldly deliberate calculations on the factor of race, weighing appeals to black Northerners against white Southerners, received identical advice: do nothing. Nixon, after hesitating, accepted the advice. Kennedy, trusting his instinct, acted.

The event which challenged them was the arrest of the Rev. Dr. Martin Luther King, Jr., along with fifty-two other Negroes, following a sit-in in the Magnolia Room restaurant of

Rich's Department Store in Atlanta. Although his companions were soon released, King was brought before a judge who decided to make an example of him: he found the minister guilty of an unrelated traffic offense and imposed the vengeful sentence of four months at hard labor in the state penitentiary. King's wife, who was pregnant, feared he might be lynched behind the prison walls and frantically began searching for help.

Her apprehension was well-founded. King had become the symbol of everything the intransigent white South feared and hated; crosses were burned outside his home and death threats were received almost daily. At thirty-one, he was older than the collegians who had launched the lunch-counter sit-in movement. As a middle-class preacher, he represented the tradition of submissive Christianity against which many of the impatient young blacks were rebelling. But his symbolic importance propelled him to the fore of the movement. Although the young were discovering their own leaders on campuses throughout the South, none of them could attract the publicity and financial support which King's name guaranteed. He was internationally known as the Gandhi-like leader of the Montgomery bus boycott, in which "nonviolence" had ended Jim Crow seating. That dramatic though limited victory in the heart of the Deep South had captured the attention of the media, and had gained for King unique acceptance and moral authority among conscience-stricken whites. It was their influence and sponsorship, as much as King's passionate eloquence, which raised him above his rivals and established him as the foremost Negro civil rights leader. Therein lay his power and jeopardy. To sympathetic whites, he held out the hope of peaceful and gradual racial accommodation. To his

Negro followers, he promised swift and unswerving progress toward true racial equality. He had staked everything on his desperately uncertain gamble that the hope and the promise could be reconciled, although he had no plan or strategy.

When word of Coretta King's concern reached Kennedy, the near-unanimous judgment of his advisers was that he should avoid a "grandstand" gesture that would cost him heavily in the South. Even before King's arrest, three Southern governors had warned Kennedy headquarters against giving support to the Negro leader's activities. Nevertheless, Kennedy placed a telephone call to Mrs. King in Atlanta. Afterward she told friends, they told the press, and the news of Kennedy's intervention not only flashed in the media but also raced by word of mouth through Negro neighborhoods in cities across the nation. The following day, Bobby Kennedy followed up by telephoning the judge and asking that King be freed on bail. Within a matter of hours, the prisoner was released.

Nixon, meanwhile, was paralyzed between the opposing pulls of principle and expediency. His civil rights record was better than Kennedy's. His running mate, Henry Cabot Lodge, had gone so far as to promise that a Negro would be included in the Nixon Cabinet, a pledge that raised a storm in the South. Attorney General William P. Rogers, who had joined the Nixon campaign, tried unsuccessfully to get White House clearance for a statement saying the Department of Justice would look into the case for possible violation of King's civil rights. Initially, Kennedy had been so unsure of the political impact of his call to Mrs. King that he had made no statement to the press beyond saying simply, "She is a friend of mine, and I was concerned about the situation." Now, as

63

the reaction of strong Negro approval and general white indifference became apparent, and as Bobby Kennedy's call to
the judge was revealed, reporters pressed the Nixon camp for
a statement. Through a spokesman came the deadly response: "No comment."

"They were all for you," the Vice President's Negro chauffeur said of "his people" after the election. "But when Mr.
Robert Kennedy called the judge to get Dr. King out of jail —
well, they just turned to him."

King's father, pastor of the Ebenezer Baptist Church in Atlanta, led the way. Earlier he had come out for Nixon on
religious grounds; now, acknowledging his bigotry without
apology, he said he had discovered he could vote for a Catholic after all. "I've got a suitcase full of votes," he told the
press, "and I'm going to take them to Mr. Kennedy and dump
them in his lap."

Such gratitude was appreciated, but the Democratic National Committee had more ambitious designs. Two million
copies of a pamphlet describing the incident were hurriedly
printed and distributed outside Negro churches on the Sunday before the election. In Illinois, a quarter of a million
Negroes voted for Kennedy, and this enabled him to carry the
state by a bare 9000 votes.

Kennedy won the election by getting the votes he needed
where they counted most. In the populous urban states, his
majorities among Catholics and Negroes ran 70 percent and
higher. The creaking New Deal alliance of the Northeast, the
industrial Middle West, and the Confederacy held together
once again, just barely. The omens of a future collapse were
especially evident in the South: in several areas, Nixon ran
ahead of the Eisenhower record, reflecting the emergence of a
two-party South.

"It was TV more than anything else that turned the tide," said the President-elect. Although the Republicans had spent an estimated $2 million on television in the final ten days of the campaign, it was too late. The election may have been decided in the first joint appearance of the candidates. A nationwide survey for CBS by Dr. Elmo Roper showed that more than half (57 percent) of those who voted believed the debates had influenced their decisions. Fully 6 percent, projected to some 4 million voters from this sample, said their final choice had been made solely on the basis of what they saw on the screen — and these television voters favored Kennedy by three to one.

If Kennedy had indeed won the presidency on television, the statistics of his narrow election were deceptive, for these, adhering to the traditional forms of politics, equated votes alone with power. But Kennedy combined the highest, most visible office in the land with mastery of the instrument of mass persuasion. From that combination came a new form of mastery over the imagination of the people.

Cultural Politics

THE NEWS MEDIA and the liberal intellectuals, whose jurisdictions overlapped in the American communications system, enthroned and mythologized John F. Kennedy and then, quite predictably, became displeased with him for behaving as the cautious politician he had always been. His martyrdom, however, transformed him into a figure of instant legend, and the liberals were again greatly pleased with JFK. For now they could devote themselves to making the Kennedy myth permanent and to protecting their heavy investment in the illusory liberalism recast in his image.

The subsequent left-liberal insurgency against Lyndon Johnson turned the political-cultural elite of the American Establishment into an *anti*-Establishment, shattered the Democratic party as a vehicle of a governing majority, and opened the way for Richard Nixon's election in 1968. While this media-centered, culturally based struggle raged, ordinary people defected from the Democratic party that no longer represented them, their values, and their feelings about the country and its course. Calling themselves "independents," they turned to Alabama's Governor George Wallace who knew and played on the emotions of his constituency with demogogic artistry. Kennedy-style media politics had special appeal to the upwardly mobile upper-middle classes. Wallace-style "gut" politics stirred those who were not going anywhere and who feared being overrun.

In the spring of 1969, at the Woman's National Democratic Club and elsewhere, I gave a series of talks on the new "cultural politics," from which the following essay is adapted.

I.

A few days after the 1968 election, columnist Mary McGrory wrote: "In contemplating the future of the Democratic party, it is important to recognize that there isn't any party." She also wrote (and I will return to this point later): "The Kennedy party is the strongest in the country."

Her diagnosis of the Democratic party may be accurate, but it describes equally well the state of the Republican party, despite its victory and the seeming advantage of occupying the White House. Indeed, at this point in the nation's history, the presidency may almost be a party liability rather than an asset. The public accountability that accompanies the power of that high office may well hamper the Republican party's response to the new political realities of the 1970s. Faced with such urgent national tasks as ending the war in Vietnam, reconciling the races at home, and bringing the runaway economy under control, Republicans may be too harassed to deal with the problem of redefining and reorganizing their own troubled party. As Rogers Morton, the chairman of the Republican National Committee, said in his first postelection speech, the Republicans didn't *win* in 1968 — the Democrats lost. And the obvious question is: *why?*

The Democrats lost, it seems to me, because a majority of the voters blamed them for allowing the country to come apart — politically, economically, socially, and, most important, culturally. America in the 1960s was denied the sense of itself as a "good society" which sustains the morale, confidence, and vitality of our democracy. Insurgents sprang up to condemn America and those foolish enough to believe in it and be willing to make sacrifices for it. The Democratic leadership split in its response, and that spelled defeat for the former majority party. The popular unity forged during two generations of Democratic political ascendancy disintegrated in a few years of cultural insurgency, which had no "politics" worthy of the name.

During the Inaugural events in January 1969, I joined the counter-Inaugural marchers as an observer — in fact, I fell into step with my favorite polemicist, I. F. (Izzy) Stone — and caught the complaints of the angry young on my tape recorder. Facing the police guarding a reception at the Smithsonian Institution, the protestors shouted the usual dreary curses, but a few said more interesting things. One youth shouted: "You know what's wrong with you cops? You're culturally deprived." Pressed for an explanation of why he had come to Washington, another marcher told me: "I came to demonstrate a counter-lifestyle."

That doesn't make a very stirring slogan — "My lifestyle can beat yours!" — but it contains, or so it seems to me, the essence of the central conflict in this country. We have seen the clash of lifestyles most clearly among the rebellious young and the militant blacks, but it is also apparent among the quieter

68

population at large, especially the millions who voted for George Wallace in 1968 and the additional millions who wanted to.

Looking at the future of the Democratic party and of liberalism as well, Arthur Schlesinger, Jr., has written: ". . . The issues of the '60s do not square with the battle lines of the '30s. To an increasing degree, politics in the '60s — and this will probably be even more true of the '70s — has begun to divide according to the level, not of income, but of education."

A steadily rising average level of income and education, contrary to the expectations of the New and Fair Deal Democrats, has *not* brought social harmony within a great, all-embracing American middle class. Quite the contrary: it has sharpened awareness of the remaining class and status differences — the cultural differences — among us. Increasing equality, ironically, has intensified social envy, resentment, and hatred.

For most of the past generation, most Americans had a pretty clear idea who they were and where they stood politically, economically, socially. Union members were workers and down-the-line Democrats. Well-paid white-collar people were loyal Republicans. This is no longer true. The strongest party in the country today, in terms of its rate of growth, is neither the Democrat nor the Republican, but the Independent. Certainly those who say they "vote for the man and not the party" are the voters most avidly courted by the politicians. They are the voters who swing close elections, and they are attuned to a new politics.

What is this new politics? Let me offer an illustration — literally an illustration: a photograph that filled almost a full page in the society section of the Washington *Post* in late Feb-

69

ruary 1969. It showed Mrs. Edward Kennedy being greeted at a White House reception by President and Mrs. Nixon. The President was wearing his usual mirthless smile. Mrs. Nixon was trying to smile, but her gaze was fixed on Mrs. Kennedy's minidress, which ended five inches above her knee — a "maxi-mini." It was the only such dress on display at the White House on that very formal evening.

Mrs. Kennedy's dress made a statement: "See, my husband and I are *with it.*" And Mrs. Nixon's stare said everything a "square" could say in reply. The photograph captured a wordless dialogue in the new politics.

While America is deeply divided, our divisions are no longer primarily political, at least not in the accustomed sense. Rather, they are *cultural,* in the broadest sense of that word, which the poet Allan Tate once defined with exquisite simplicity as "the way we live." Certainly it has always been true that Americans lived in different ways, and displayed different tastes and styles, depending on how much of the good life they could afford. But as recently as the 1950s there seemed to be general agreement on what the "good life" was, and on what "good taste" was. There was fairly broad agreement on the beliefs and attitudes implied when we heard the phrase "the American way of life."

There is no longer an "American way of life." There are now several ways of life, several cultures, several moral codes, all of which are at odds with each other. This struggle, which has no obvious political resolution, nonetheless lies at the heart of our new politics.

America's culture traditionally has been both a way of life and a way of looking at life. It has been rooted in our values as a people. Our new divisions spring from the uprooting of

70

belief in these values. Another poet, Peter Viereck, describes values as "those loving identifications with persons, families, places, institutions, traditions or rituals that unite the individual and the group, the present and the past, the expressible and the inexpressible. Values make up most of our selfhood, our true personal life, as opposed to the surface life of conscious formulas and abstractions."

As recently as John F. Kennedy's Inaugural Address in January 1961, an American cultural consensus seemed to remain intact and serve as a secure political foundation. He could urge his "fellow Americans" to ask what they could do for *their* country — and almost everyone knew what country he meant and felt himself a part of it. Those who heard his words could identify with the values behind them, could feel — and be proud of — a wave of loving identification with their country and a desire to serve and, if necessary, make sacrifices for it.

John Kennedy appeared to embody those attitudes and qualities — those values — that Americans generally held in high esteem. He was living proof of the success of the system and the society. He lived as most of us wanted to live. Abroad, this youthful and vigorous President was regarded as a symbol of America's maturity as a culture and a civilization. We need only recall the extraordinary worldwide mourning of his death, from the streets of Moscow to the villages of Africa, to realize that John Kennedy was a new kind of leader.

As a practicing politician, Kennedy was conventional in approach and method — and, it must be said, not very successful in getting his bills through Congress. As the central, unifying "image" of the society, addressing the people over the heads of other politicians, he was brilliantly successful. He trans-

71

formed the presidency, as we realized only after his death. The highest seat of democratic political authority also became, during his tenure, the symbol of America's cultural fulfillment and legitimacy. It was this new, extra dimension of the presidency — the role of cultural exemplar — that his successors could not fill, in part because our society's moral arbiters rejected and opposed them.

I recall a conversation with an alarmed left-wing Democrat in the spring of 1968. "Johnson is a classic tyrant," he declared. A couple of weeks later, the supposed tyrant voluntarily stepped down, in one of the most unselfish gestures seen in our recent political history. President Johnson realized that he had personally become the chief issue in our bitterly divided society, that he faced a discontented majority, and so he removed himself from the scene.

His successor cannot afford to harbor any illusions about the extent of his popularity. Nixon was elected in 1968 by barely one tenth of the plurality he expected and predicted. He is the first President in more than a century to be elected without gaining control of at least one chamber of Congress. Nixon is clearly a President on trial, representing the enthusiastic choice of only a minority of the discontented majority.

President Nixon's strategy, signaled in his Inaugural admonition to "lower our voices," is to reduce the visibility of his office as a symbol, to appear before the public only under controlled circumstances, and to project an image of prudence in pursuit of what the discontented majority wants — the restoration of order. This will require, I believe, the simultaneous attempt to restore our shattered cultural consensus. There are legitimate causes of disorder in our society, and these must be dealt with forthrightly and courageously. Certain reforms must be urged and undertaken because they are right, as well

72

as urgently necessary. In short, our values must be redefined and their moral authority revived before we can be confident of a return to civilized order — and this is the task the President cannot escape.

It is too early to make any firm judgments on the new administration, but we can already see some potentially crippling weaknesses. The Nixon administration lacks a clear identity and a central, guiding vision. In fact, it gives the impression — and reports from within confirm it — of being several mini-administrations, unconnected and vaguely suspicious of each other, all searching for something greater to belong to.

II.

John Kennedy's successors must somehow cope with the central fact of the new cultural politics: public *awareness* on a mass scale never before experienced in human society. The television screen is a picture window on other worlds, giving us access to distant strangers on more intimate terms than we have with our neighbors next door. Indeed, the dramatic "reality" enclosed on the screen has more immediacy than the mundane reality around us.

Television reaches us through our senses and penetrates to that part of our beings which is at once beneath and beyond reason. It penetrates to that subconscious region of the human spirit where our personal values are rooted — or uprooted by the thrust of sweeping social change. Television radically changes our way of looking at the world, and therefore our sense of ourselves and our lives.

We may see with our own eyes and believe what is simply not objectively true. Consider, for example, the unemployed coal miner in West Virginia, whose shack is falling down and whose children live precariously on government-provided food. When the pollster came to seek this man's opinions on the leading issues in the 1968 presidential campaign, you might have expected that he would put a job and a decent chance for his children at the head of the list. But no, in this remote county where no blacks live, the miner emphatically declared that rioting in the cities, which he watched on television, was the overriding issue.

You do not have to venture into the hills of West Virginia to find this anomaly. In suburbs where the only Negro faces are those of domestic workers, pollsters uncover anxiety about crime and racial disturbances bordering on hysteria. In the suburbs of Washington, in tranquil Montgomery County, would-be vigilantes took over public hearings and shouted down a proposed gun-control law, in a reaction to what happened in downtown Washington — and what television showed them.

In 1968, the McCarthy "kids" also were marching along with the militant blacks. The "New Politics" — the supposed wave of the future — became identified with the campus and the ghetto and therefore students and blacks became the main actors in the nightly televised news drama.

Then, suddenly, the news media discovered Governor George Wallace and began to take him seriously. Newsmen began asking who the Wallace people were. And some of them began to correct the media's fundamental error in perceiving and reporting the 1968 campaign. About a year after the election, Richard Harwood and Lawrence Stern of the Washington *Post* sounded a self-critical note: "Political journalism did not celebrate its finest year in the 1968 presidential election campaign. Rarely, in fact, have the experts wandered so far off base in their analyses and assumptions in what was taking place in that huge and unfathomable ocean, the protoplasm called the body politic."

Harwood and Stern had discovered, long after it was of any use to the reader or viewer in making a rational democratic choice, that things were not the way they appeared to the media in New Hampshire early in 1968, or as they were presented by the media's coverage of the Wallace movement. "It was a universally accepted truism that Senator McCarthy's New Hampshire primary vote was a manifestation of spreading public dissatisfaction with the war in Vietnam, the desire for peace," wrote the *Post* reporters. Belatedly, as the result of scholarly research by Warren Miller and his colleagues at the University of Michigan Opinion Research Center, the neglected side of New Hampshire came into view. "Among McCarthy's supporters in the primary," the Michigan study found, "those who were unhappy with the Johnson Administration for *not* pursuing a harder line against Hanoi outnumbered those advocating a withdrawal from Vietnam by nearly a three to two margin." Harwood and Stern wrote: "Many of those who covered the 1968 primaries formed a mental picture" — mark those words well — "of the McCarthy constituency that was based on the glowing young men and women who came to serve his cause in New Hampshire and Wisconsin. They were intellectual, earnest, and ranging in ideologies from liberal to radical. Sam Brown, the divinity school dropout who organized McCarthy's children's army, seemed the very embodiment of it all."

The McCarthy movement, as the media perceived it, seemed to be embodied in Sam Brown. But Brown was not an image. He was a human being and therefore complicated in his motivations. Even so, print journalism, trying to catch the reader who runs or who throws down the paper and turns on the tube, seized upon this personality and said: *This is what it is all about.* Reality was personalized — and falsified. The Michigan survey presented evidence utterly contrary to the mental picture formed by the gentlemen of the news media. The survey showed that a slight plurality of those Democrats who supported *McCarthy* before the convention expressed a subsequent preference for *Wallace,* whom they chose over eight other Republican and Democratic presidential aspirants.

The Michigan researchers told us a year after the election that the Wallace phenomenon was far more important and more complicated than the McCarthy movement. What they discovered was a deep and potentially disastrous alienation spreading among the American lower-middle class. The Michigan survey concluded that the Wallace candidacy had greater impact on this relatively stable social and economic group than anything in the preceding forty-odd years, since our last significant three-party race. What the survey found — again, counter to the media perception and the transmission of that perception — was that a surprisingly large number of Wallace supporters were well under the age of thirty. Wallace strongly appealed to the middle-aged and elderly but he also attracted an enormous following among the young. These young people didn't look like Sam Brown. They were less visible, less articulate, lower in their expectations of financial rewards and social position than the tiny academic vanguard of middle-class radicals and revolutionaries. But the pro-Wallace young formed one of the most important new influences in American politics.

The Wallace followers turned out to be far more numerous,

and far more formidable as a political force, than the students and the blacks combined. At the peak of his strength in the late summer of 1968, Wallace was the preferred candidate of one voter out of five. At his peak, Wallace would have received 20 million votes — only 11 million less than Nixon. His base was impressively broad. He had the support of close to one third of the young workers (those aged twenty-one to twenty-nine), who far outnumbered the campus population. These workers represented a quite different wave of the future — an enduring "New Politics" based on real grievances and interests.

A good description of the Wallace voters was provided in October 1968 by Senator Edward Kennedy:

> Most Wallace people are not motivated by racial hostility or prejudice. They are decent, respectable citizens who feel that their needs and their problems have been passed over by the tide of recent events. They bear the burden of the unfair system of Selective Service. They lose out because higher education costs so much. They are the ones who feel most threatened, in the security of their jobs, the safety of their families, the value of their property and the burden of their taxes. They feel that the established system has not been sympathetic to them and their problems of everyday life — *and in large measure they are right* . . . We cannot expect our citizens to pay taxes to solve other people's problems in our country — as they will have to — when their own problems are not being met. *Government programs must no longer be directed to one race or one class,* but to all Americans.

Television and opinion polling now combine to dominate our politics. The combination is novel and potentially dangerous to our form of democratic government. An estimated two thirds of the adult population receives most of its news through television. During the late 1960s, the nightly diet of angry blacks and violent leftists on television fed the prejudices of the ordinary white middle-class citizen. It reached into his subconscious — and when the pollster arrived, the citizen sounded off. His opinion was gathered, coded, cross-indexed, analyzed, and presented to the candidates in thick bound volumes. The advisers then counseled: *This is what the people are saying. Repeat it back to them.* And so we had, in the campaign of 1968, a pseudo-debate on a pseudo-issue: law-and-order.

Ignorance and prejudice on the part of the citizenry are now regularly transmitted into public debate and public policy. We have seen only the beginning of the dangerous movement from indirect to direct electronic democracy. Why, some may ask, is such democracy dangerous? Ours was intended to be a *representative* democracy. In theory and practice, our system provides for settling differences rather slowly and at a distance from passionate conflicts, in the halls of government where cooler and wiser heads are supposed to prevail. But our system clashes with our impatience. When the questions thrust before us with electronic urgency — questions of *values* — do not lend themselves to compromise, we confront each other directly. We have seen in recent years not only the ugly reality of direct democracy — that is, mob action — but also the brutality of no-compromise politics, summed up by students and black militants in the command: "Up against the wall . . ."

Rebellious students and blacks have neither the numbers nor the power to make their arrogant commands stick. They are minorities who reject majority rule, which is the basis of their protection so long as the majority is restrained by the Constitution and the laws. They are violent romantics who imagine that they can overthrow the system and impose a dictatorship upon the disorganized majority. This is a suicidal fantasy, for the system under assault will defend itself and change in the process.

Let us recall the reaction to the disorders at the Democratic Convention in Chicago in August 1968. The demonstrators outside the Hilton were right when they shouted: "The whole world is watching!" But what the viewer saw on his television screen depended entirely on his values and attitudes. Television commentators, network and magazine executives, the editors of the *New York Times* — perhaps most of the educated liberal audience — saw brutality on the part of the police sworn to preserve civilized order. But others not so well educated, not so affluent and tolerant, saw on *their* television screens a kind of order they wholly approved. They saw spoiled children throw a tantrum and get the spanking they deserved from the police.

Two weeks after the Democratic Convention, the pollster Oliver Quayle sampled fifty households in Warren, Michigan, a suburb with homes in the $15,000 – $25,000 class. Many of those who live there are members of the United Auto Workers, traditionally the most politically "progressive" American union. (Incidently, the UAW estimates that it has more than 150,000 members who earn more than $15,000 a year.) In the 1968 election, the district including Warren voted heavily for Humphrey.

Quayle asked this question: How do you feel about the way the police handled the demonstrators in Chicago? Only two of those who responded thought the police were "too tough." Twenty-six said "about right." Twenty-two said the police were "not tough enough." *No one checked the box "don't know"* — which was perhaps the most significant response of all.

The events in Chicago clearly *involved* people, but *not* along party lines: these fifty suburbanites in Michigan were in favor of the police and against the demonstrators regardless of the presidential candidate they preferred when they were polled, and regardless of the support most of them later gave Hubert Humphrey. Lou Harris offers this explanation of the change occurring in our politics: "The privileged whites have become the progenitors of change, while the under-privileged whites have become the steadfast defenders of the status quo." And not only the whites.

The black middle-class citizen may feel equally threatened and betrayed if his values and beliefs are trampled on by demonstrators while politicians do nothing. Consider this judgment on Chicago: "When hard-line organized forces announce publicly they'll run amok in your downtown district, break windows, invade hotels, paralyze vital services, what does a city government do? It can, of course, sit by and let the provocateurs take over, as Lindsay did at Columbia. Or it can do as the loathed and brutish Daley did. It can stoutly defend the peace of the city, the rights of its citizens, and the safety of its guests . . ."

Who said that? The Chicago *Tribune?* No. It was written by an honest man named Roy Wilkins, who was struggling for liberal causes before the Chicago demonstrators were born.

III.

The closed, police-ridden society of the Soviet Union seems the very opposite of our open and tolerant society — until we see a police state in-the-making in the streets of our cities. It is useful to compare Soviet society and our own to remind ourselves of the sources of our freedom.

80

In Soviet society, public dissent, even on a very limited scale, is a recent phenomenon. In our society, it is a right and a tradition protected by our founding documents and enshrined in our institutions. In Soviet society, a rigid bureaucratic elite holds a monopoly of political power and legitimacy. The party establishment exercises total ideological authority. Any retreat from this position, however small, is seen as dangerous to the entire system. In our society, power is widely diffused among a great many elites, most of which are not directly political. Similarly, there are many sources and symbols of legitimacy, reflecting the diversity of our population and culture. Far from holding a monopoly of authority, the national government derives its authority from the consent of the governed. This depends upon the competition of shifting minorities which, through the democratic process, are formed into an effective political majority for the pursuit of limited objectives.

Today we speak in the United States of a "silent majority," composed of Americans described as "forgotten." This is a way of saying that we are not sure an effective political majority exists.

Is there something on the American scene worthy of the name "establishment"? There is, if we are to take the word of the dissenting and increasingly violent minorities, all of which aim their attacks against something called the Establishment. By this, they usually mean those who wield power. But political power is not synonymous with moral authority. Coerced obedience is not the same thing as freely given consent.

In spite of the sharp contrasts between Soviet society and our society, in spite of the fundamental differences between our systems, we can detect an interesting point of identity. In both societies, the issue raised by dissenters is legitimacy. And when we are compelled to rely on the police power of the state to repress violent dissent and preserve civil order, we are aware of a disturbing parallel between such tactics and the more ruthless and comprehensive exercise of police power by the Soviet authorities.

Clearly, when we must resort to violence to suppress violence, something has gone basically wrong within our society and system. I do not need to dwell upon the succession of shocks and upheavals we have experienced since the assassination of John F. Kennedy. From the Berkeley student uprising in 1964 to the Watts explosion in 1966 to the March on the Pentagon in 1967 to the nationwide racial outbursts in 1968, we have seen militant protest spread from assaults on particular institutions to general warfare against the system as a whole. I use the word "warfare" advisedly, for those who have taken to the streets and those who watch the turmoil on their television screens are alike convinced that a state of war — revolutionary conflict — exists. We are witnessing a cultural civil war — and the first casualty has been the Establishment, not as a political entity, but as a widely diffused cultural entity, representing the society's established values and norms.

In this sense, every conscientious parent is a member of the American Establishment. For it is the family unit which is responsible, in our society and under our system, for instilling the values, goals, and self-discipline the child requires for full citizenship. But the family and the churches and every other nongovernmental institution have been steadily drained of cultural legitimacy and moral authority. To a greater or lesser degree, they have defaulted on their crucial responsibilities. This cumulative default of responsibility — like a line of dominoes — has fallen with literally crushing impact on our nation's schools and colleges, which are unable — even if they were willing — to discharge it. We ask, pathetically, for educators to make citizens of children whose formative years have been spent in barbaric ignorance of the connection between freedom and order, responsibility and civilization.

Between the polar opposites of total authority and total anarchy stands the mediating force of an Establishment in the sense that I have defined it — one confident of its values and capable of asserting the nonpolitical forms of governance. It is an act of such governance for a parent to rear and discipline a child. If the parent abdicates, then the authority of the state and its police power eventually come into play.

Doubtless this has an old-fashioned ring, but ours is a society resting on very old-fashioned ideas and moral ideals. We constructed our society on these lines to escape, if we could, the dreary fate of other societies from antiquity down to this day, namely, the total dominance of the state over the life of the individual, the reduction of man to a narrowly political abstraction. But we can preserve limits on the power of the state and balance political authority with other forms of authority only by accepting and discharging our individual responsibilities.

In spite of the fashion of pessimism and despair, and the abundant evidence to support it, I am hopeful that we soon will see the re-emergence of a true Establishment, based on restored belief in the integrity and worth of the individual. Many of the young people are making this act of belief if we will but hear them. And some rising leaders of American business and labor are taking up social, cultural, and moral responsibility as individuals and citizens. They are acting, con-

83

fidently and creatively, as exemplars of those values which cannot be imposed, but must be embraced freely if our society and system are to survive.

We are the mirror image of the Soviet Union, but the image of our free society urgently needs to be sharpened to contrast more clearly in every citizen's mind with its police-state opposite. Whatever danger we face from the Soviet state, the greater danger is the rise of an all-powerful state here at home if our democracy fails.

IV.

In 1968, the Independent Eugene McCarthy drove President Johnson out of the White House, and the Independent George Wallace dictated the strategy of Richard Nixon, including his choice of a vice-presidential running-mate. The interesting thing about McCarthy and Wallace, wholly dissimilar men, is that neither created his following. Their followers found them, in their search for spokesmen who would express the values they cherished. Both men campaigned against the liberal establishment.

The two major parties are organized, to the extent they are organized at all, along traditional lines of economic, group, and sectional interest, which are becoming less and less relevant. There is something quaintly old-fashioned about Arthur Schlesinger's act of faith in the future of the Democratic party — that it will continue to be "the chosen instrument of social justic and social progress" in the United States. We may reasonably ask: *who* will choose, and *whose* idea of "justice" will prevail? The old coalition of the New and Fair Deals has

84

come apart. During the Johnson administration, the last major items on the liberal agenda were enacted. The liberals, who always were a minority within the Democratic party, are themselves divided and no longer can rely on a Democratic majority in the country. Irving Kristol has expressed the dilemma of American liberalism: "It cannot come up with legislative programs that appeal to the majority, and it has not been able to create viable programs for the various minorities that need help."

There is no dependable working majority in the country — and there hasn't been for more than a decade. Lyndon Johnson's landslide victory in 1964 was the result of Republican defections from Goldwater. Nixon's very narrow victory in 1968 was the result of those Republicans coming home and the Democrats being split.

Traditional politicians of both parties, whose attitudes were shaped during the New Deal, believe there is a majority out there in the bushes, if only they can put together the right appeals. I am inclined to doubt this theory, unless we see a major recession that would recreate the kind of economic and social pressures responsible for creating the broad New Deal majorities. Assuming (as the voters universally do) continued prosperity and full employment, I think we will see continued government by minorities, organized either as parties or as cultural-interest groups. The Republican administration must rely on the Southern Democratic subparty in Congress to get legislation passed or to sustain presidential vetoes. Should this subparty ever break its formal ties to the national Democratic party — and this is a real possibility — the Republican party would acquire additional Strom Thurmonds, for whatever they are worth.

The shape of the "New Politics" cannot be clearly discerned. The most active and vocal cultural-interest groups, the radical students and the militant blacks, are playing at revolution rather than practicing politics. Old-line Democratic leaders are not about to share power with kids, mainly because their power is slipping away. They can't deliver their followers. The Democrat who moves to the suburbs becomes an Independent, and votes for the man who best reflects his outlook and way of life.

In this situation, the Republicans have the advantage of being a comparatively homogeneous cultural minority, united around a fairly clear-cut set of values and a suburban-oriented way of life. However, the Republican party has a long-standing "people" problem. It is an unrepresentative minority, and its leaders are not really dissatisfied to have it that way. The party of the risen and the prosperous can talk *about* "forgotten Americans," but it has very little to say directly *to* them. The unrepresentative nature of the Republican party does not stem from the evident scarcity of Republican blacks and young people. It stems from the relative weakness of the party among the American majority, made up of middle- and working-class whites whose allegiance to the Democrats has weakened to the point where they might be attracted by a campaign aggressively aimed at them.

The marketing men of Nixon Inc. have tried to harness the anger and frustration of the white lower-middle class without extending genuine compassion, making reasoned arguments, or offering specific solutions to real problems. In this, as in so many other respects, the Nixon men have borrowed, belatedly and not too wisely, from the Democrats. Another problem is that the predominant Republican lifestyle doesn't have much appeal even to the quiet and nonradical members of the rising generation. These potential recruits to the ranks of the affluent and educated, the class which has tended to be most heavily Republican, aren't attracted to the party of Spiro T. Agnew. Right after the 1969 Inauguration, at a banquet thrown by his friends in Annapolis, Agnew positioned himself on the new cultural battleground by declaring: "We're all middlebrows here." Regardless of their inherited party loyalty and their principles, which are often fairly conservative, the college-educated young have taken to heart one crucial element of John Kennedy's legacy: the passion for, and the pursuit of, excellence. A generation of strivers and achievers will be neither satisfied with nor drawn to a reign of mediocrity.

This brings me to Mary McGrory's judgment that "the Kennedy party is the strongest in the country." Just as the Republicans cannot succeed by replaying the political themes of the 1950s, so the Democrats cannot unite themselves, or the country, by trying to recapture the 1960s. The 1970s will not be mastered by a return to "normalcy" or the New Frontier. We have lost the innocence that made possible the illusions of those years — the Republican illusion of escape and the Democratic illusion of a fresh start.

The chief strength of Senator Edward Kennedy is the tragic legend of his family, which now lies at the center of our popular culture. That same legend, paradoxically, is his chief weakness. He inherits trust and suspicion, love and hatred, a following and an opposition. Because the "New Politics" turns on the personality of the leader, rather than on the party, because it appeals to the senses and emotions — to "awareness" rather than to reasoned understanding — the all-pervasive image of Senator Kennedy gives him obvious advantages. But he faces an equally obvious challenge — to exemplify values appealing not only to the insurgents and the dissenting liberals but also to the broad restless middle of decent and respectable citizens.

Who will represent the center of the American electorate? There is no unifying figure in sight.

We will see a continued search for personal, charismatic figures to represent us, leaders who are less political than cultural. We are also likely to see growing alienation within the lower and middle classes, the result of frustration below and cynicism above. Finally, as the Michigan study of the 1968 election anticipates, we may expect a struggle within the younger generation in the next decade or two: a class and cultural struggle between a privileged minority and those in the less-privileged majority. The minority will expect deference and hope for power. The majority will demand greater equality — and it will have the power to enforce that demand by one means or another.

We journalists and academicians who report and analyze events are more sympathetic to the minority than the majority. We who make and respond to intellectual appeals have a fellow-feeling toward those like ourselves. We are out of spirits and out of touch with the great body of the people, those whom we label "Middle Americans." And they are "fed up to here" with intellectuals who want to interfere in their daily lives on behalf of abstract good intentions. The people are right and they will prevail.

The stake in the new cultural politics is our civilization. The values of the free and responsible society — the values of humanity, tolerance, and order with justice — the values of liberalism — are what we have to conserve.

88

PART TWO

Alternatives

Barry Goldwater and the
New American Conservatism

A DECADE after the 1964 election, we can see clearly that the one-sided contest between President Lyndon Johnson and Senator Barry Goldwater was anticlimactic. The result was preordained by the popular emotional reaction to the trauma of John Kennedy's assassination. Goldwater, as his apologists argued, was forced to run against History. (With equal accuracy, his detractors noted that he also ran against himself, his habit of putting his foot in his mouth, and his abysmally inept campaign organization.)

The true significance of the Goldwater candidacy was twofold: it marked a shift in the balance of power within the Republican party, and it reintroduced ideology to interparty debate after the bland Eisenhower era. Two new issues, prophetic of rising controversy, emerged from the Republican side in 1964: attacks on partisan bias in the news media and complaints against "crime in the streets." By 1968, the latter would become the central domestic issue.

Behind Goldwater, the Republican conservatives succeeded in recapturing the G.O.P. — their main objective in 1964. Four years later they remained solidly in control and were responsible for bestowing on the loyalist Nixon — who stayed with Goldwater while Nelson Rockefeller did not — his second chance at the presidency, a favor many of them have regretted ever since. Today, the conservatives are still in command and are therefore obliged to play the leading role in rebuilding the party after the debacle of Nixonism. They are more experienced and disillusioned than they were a decade ago, but they persist in many of the attitudes that sent them crusading behind Goldwater. Therefore, it is worth retracing the origins of contemporary conservative thought and political activism.

I.

Arizona's Senator Barry Goldwater had long been the favorite son of a state of mind. Until the spring of 1963, that was about all that he seemed to be. Then, with astonishing swiftness and without an announcement of his candidacy, the lean-jawed, jet-flying, outspokenly conservative senator soared into the lead for the 1964 Republican presidential nomination. Nothing in prior U.S. political history quite compared with this stunning change of fortune. But within the Goldwater phenomenon lay a deeper stirring — the resurgence of aggressive, self-confident conservatism.

At the core of Goldwater's political following was an ideological following — the conservative movement. These Americans knew where they stood before they read Goldwater's *Conscience of a Conservative* or heard the Arizonan lash out at overgrown government and runaway spending. Though they were delighted with his presidential prospects, they did not have the professional politicians' absorbing concern with winning. Nor were they dazzled by Goldwater's personal attractiveness. Their ferocious dedication ("I'd give Barry my blood and the marrow from my bones," one admirer remarked) was inspired by his affirmation of their convictions. Goldwater was a mirror reflecting certain truths which they held to be self-evident.

The individual conservative, of course, saw in this mirror largely what he wished to see. In advancing opinions about the "cause," conservatives almost without exception noted that they could speak only for themselves. There was no systematic ideology of conservatism. Rather, conservatism was a *way* of thinking, and Goldwater expressed it. Around his person, the conservatives achieved a degree of unity beyond anything they could hope to achieve by attempting collectively to define their philosophy.

In April 1962, the Young Americans for Freedom (YAF) packed Madison Square Garden for an evening of speeches and awards, the latter going to such widely different talents as the renowned economist Ludwig von Mises and the YAF's P.R. man Marvin Liebman. The climax of the rally was an address by Senator Goldwater. His speech was greeted with earsplitting cheers and a barrage of gaily colored balloons, but it was remarkable mostly for its insensitivity to the occasion. More than 16,000 souls had waited past midnight to hear Goldwater's message, which proved to be that the Republicans, having come close in a recent by-election in New York's Queens County, would yet prevail with a little bit of luck and a lot of hard work. It was a speech that would have been just passable on the G.O.P. rubber-chicken circuit; it was hardly the stuff to set conservative hearts pounding and eager legions marching; it was, in short, a disappointment, made all the more poignant by the fact that it was not unexpected.

93

The disproportion between the senator's lackluster performance and his reception illustrated that the conservative resurgence was a phenomenon independent of personality or organization. The crowd in the Garden that April evening came, not to receive a message from anyone, but publicly to affirm a commitment, of which Goldwater was the chance symbol. "Well, we filled the Garden," said one sleepy right-winger to another as they trudged away.

The conservative activists were proudly conscious of their opposition to another group of activists who wore the label "liberal." The conservatives' most conspicuous characteristic was an intense resistance to the expansion of the powers of the federal government. Against this expansion they defended the rights of individuals, of localities, and of the states. They condemned "fiscal irresponsibility" in the form of chronically unbalanced federal budgets and ever increasing spending. They distrusted any "thaw" in the Cold War and proclaimed victory as the only realistic goal in the world contest with Communism. Many Americans felt vaguely the same way about one or another of these questions. What distinguished the conservatives was the comprehensiveness of their opposition to the dominant political tendencies of the preceding thirty years. They felt a distrust of the power of the federal government that went beyond opposition to this measure or that program. Were Congress never to pass another law, the conservatives would not be content; they would seek to roll back much of the coercive authority already at the command of Washington.

The conservatives expressed much more clearly what they were against than what kind of government they would give the country if they were in power. This lack of "program" was partly a result of deliberate conservative emphasis on "principle," and partly the inevitable characteristic of a movement that developed as an opposition.

The conservative movement resembled a parade. Actually it was a merger of several tendencies, each a response to different circumstances over the past generation. Those who had been on the march longest tended to regard themselves as veterans of a Thirty Years' War that began with the New Deal, a struggle — as they saw it — against the spread of alien collectivist ideologies into every area of American life. Those in the middle ranks, whose political consciousness began with the postwar reaction against Soviet aggression and subversion, tended to regard their anti-Communism as the touchstone of their political convictions. The members of the youthful vanguard, who had come of age since World War II, tended to be libertarians of the great Whig tradition.

The conservative movement brought together strong-willed, contentious individualists. The arguments of conservative theoreticians on doctrinal questions would tax the dialectical agility of a thirty-third-degree Trotskyite. Nevertheless, the intellectual discord within the movement was not evidence of incoherence, but rather of vitality.

Resistance to unnecessary change was the classic conservative posture. The new conservatism gained strength from spontaneous resistance to change — change which was occurring in the form of increasing government authority over the individual citizen. Sometimes the transgression on individual freedom seemed trivial. Congressmen were surprised by the avalanche of mail from their constituents opposing the introduction of taxpayer identification numbers on savings accounts. This was one number too many in their lives. A

95

Midwestern businessman, groping for an explanation of Goldwater's explosive popularity, detected a new national appetite. "Perhaps there is a hunger in people's hearts for someone who doesn't promise to give them something for nothing."

True enough, Goldwater believed the majority of the American people weren't looking for promises. He observed: "In Washington, we legislate most of the time for about five percent of the population; the other ninety-five percent are the forgotten Americans. They pay taxes, play, pray, send their kids to school, and raise them as well as they know how. And they don't complain; but they are beginning to complain."

The conservative resurgence was sometimes attributed to the evident fact of America's affluence. People, the argument went, were merely protecting what they had. But it was too glib to assert that possession of split-levels, sports cars, cabin cruisers, and color televisions inspired a widespread conversion to conservatism. As a people, the Americans were not the grasping materialists they often accused themselves of being. On the contrary, they were remarkably susceptible to ideals, crusades, and unselfish commitments. In the absence of these, prosperity was insufficient to appease the inner emptiness and the starvation of the spirit which so many observers detected within America.

Conservatism, in Senator Goldwater's view, was "a very moral movement, which starts from a religious position and argues for acceptance of those principles that are equally good today and tomorrow." The conservative usually came to his position intuitively; his allegiance was more sensed than reasoned. He made an act of faith in the moral vitality of principles that others more cynical regarded as outworn platform phrases — for instance, "fiscal integrity." The conservative did not view the bloated federal debt as a stupendous and remote abstraction, but as a personal obligation irresponsibly foisted on future generations. The conservative held men, individually and collectively, morally accountable for what they did — and for what they failed to do. Although there was no "typical" conservative, he was likely to be the "inner-directed" man of David Riesman's sociology. (The chances were good that he hadn't read Riesman, and therefore did not realize that he was a vanishing American.)

The conservative proclaimed the need to restore an older America of virtuous public servants and upright citizens. No matter that this America never actually existed, that it was a romantic myth. Myth was an integral part of the conservative ideology, inspiring commitment, action, and self-sacrifice. What conservatives were saying, in a number of ways, was that America was surfeited with realism (and cynicism) and woefully short of idealism. While they rejected the notion of man's perfectibility, they also disputed the modern heresy that he was incapable of living his own life, making his own decisions, and taking the consequences as they came.

Real people earnestly wanted to live in the America that never existed; they believed, simply, that it *could* exist. In the Dallas suburb of Richardson, a bedroom community for employees of Texas Instruments, Ling-Temco-Vought, and other electronics and aerospace firms, a petition bearing 5000 signatures compelled the school board to give up the federal subsidy for school lunches. Parents preferred to pay seven cents for their child's half pint of milk rather than three cents; the difference, as they saw it, was principle. One young man went so far as to cancel his "socialistic" GI life insurance. Goldwater, needless to say, was Richardson's candidate. A

97

young housewife described him this way: "He stands for the original spirit of this country — do everything for yourself that you possibly can and help others to help themselves." Said another Dallas Goldwaterite: "The American people are seeking. It might be the salvation of this country if people got back to what is right and what is wrong and then stand on their own two feet."

The conservatives had an uncommonly clear idea of the difference between right and wrong, and they were troubled by the desire of their society's liberal arbiters to beg the question. The conservatives and their liberal critics seemed to live in different countries and speak different languages. When, for example, the urbane James Reston, the resident moralizer of the *New York Times,* chided Goldwater and his followers for being "anti the whole complex spirit of modern American life," he spoke the tribal dialect of the Eastern seaboard intelligentsia, which was all but unintelligible in Middle America, the region west of the Appalachians.

II.

An Eastern visitor to the middle of America in the summer of 1963 was taken aback by the strong feelings he encountered there on issues that seemed to have drifted out of view in New York and Washington — for example, coexistence with Communist Cuba. Even more than the Soviet leader Khrushchev, Fidel Castro was hated by conservatives in the heartland, for he impudently defied their vision of American power and purpose. Conservatives saw their country tolerating what had long been branded intolerable and forbidden under the Monroe Doctrine — a Communist base on our doorstep.

An American newsman who happened to be languishing in a Havana prison at the time of the 1960 Republican Convention was surprised to learn on his return to the U.S. that Goldwater's name had been put forward for the vice presidency. On the basis of several trips around the country afterward, he evolved a theory. "The man responsible for the conservative resurgence isn't really Goldwater, it's Castro. He's the last straw for an awful lot of people. Foreign policy isn't something remote any more. There are the Communists right on top of us. The darkness has moved across the ocean."

In the Middle American region where isolationism had flourished before World War II, to the consternation of Eastern internationalists who then sought a more venturesome foreign policy, the conservative resurgence of the early 1960s brought a reversal of roles. Now accusations of retreat and default flew from west to east. And the target often chosen was the *New York Times*.

The *Times* stood as a symbol of the concentration of the communications industry in a metropolis with the unique ability to spread and enforce its unrepresentative views over the country as a whole. Conservatives accused the mass media of habitually giving only "one side" of the story. They talked of New York City as though it were the headquarters town of a monolithic liberal Establishment. (This, of course, was untrue, as any member in good standing of the Establishment would testify.) New York was the nation's intellectual center, and the ideas and opinions it transmitted reflected the predominantly liberal consensus in intellectual circles. Like everyone else, opinion-molders proceeded on the basis of what

99

reasonable men — that is, their colleagues — assumed to be true. Conformity, rather than conspiracy, produced one-sidedness in the communications media.

Conservatives outside the East had long shown a deep-seated inferiority complex growing out of a generation of frustration within the Republican party. The goal of conservatives was to present a "clear choice" between the parties. They asserted that many voters went fishing on Election Day rather than choose between two liberals. They pointed to John Kennedy's narrow victory in 1960 and said the result might have been reversed if Nixon had projected a stronger conservative image — that is, if he had reflected what conservatives believed to be the consensus of both the G.O.P. and the country as a whole. "There was hope for Nixon," a Cook County (Chicago) Republican leader remarked in the summer of 1963, "until he made his famous trip to see Rockefeller."

To Easterners, Nixon's visit to the Rockefeller mansion on the eve of the 1960 convention seemed routine fence-mending and was quickly forgotten. Not so in the Midwest and Southwest, where it was a vivid, bitter memory years later. Professional politicians tended to fault Nixon on tactical grounds: they said he should have made a similar gesture toward Goldwater. Rank and file resentment went much deeper. The visit had an infuriating symbolism: once again, someone in New York City had the last word.

Money was the taproot of hostility toward New York. Well-to-do conservatives in the Midwest and Southwest had nothing in common with the Populists of yesteryear, except a feeling akin to the old agrarian dread of the money power of the metropolis. Mention of "the Chase bank" in conservative circles brought instant recognition; it was the command post of the liberal plutocracy. Goldwater's remark that the country would suffer little loss if the Eastern seaboard were sawed off and set adrift belonged in this context. He had first made the quip as a Phoenix department store executive who could not get Eastern banks to accept his commercial paper.

A veteran Eastern political writer set the conflict between the regions in the political-financial perspective: "People fail to realize that there's a difference in kinds of money. There's *old* money and there's *new* money. New money buys things, but old money calls notes. Old money has political power, but new money has only purchasing power."

At the 1960 convention Goldwater had promised the right-wing underdogs that they would soon have their day, and they labored to fulfill that promise. As early as the spring of 1963 an experienced Republican professional and former party chairman, Kentucky's Senator Thruston Morton, believed that the intraparty balance had tipped. He predicted that the next convention would reveal a shift in the center of gravity of the G.O.P. from the East to the Midwest. "It's out there beyond the Appalachians," said Morton, "and its heart belongs to Barry."

III.

Before the coming of the New Deal, there was no conservative movement for the simple reason that none was necessary. Harding, Coolidge, and Hoover suited the temper of the twenties, and both parties went to the country pledged to uphold free enterprise and individualism. Not even the stock market collapse in 1929 and the grim onset of the Depression seemed to affect this popular consensus. With the smell of victory in the air, the Democratic party platform writers, toiling in Chicago in the summer of 1932, confidently promised more rigorous application of traditional principles to restore prosperity. Among other things, the Democratic platform called for "an immediate and drastic reduction of government expenditures . . . to accomplish a saving of not less than 25 percent in the cost of Federal Government."

After his election, Franklin D. Roosevelt ignored his party's platform and acted as though he had been given a mandate for radical change. As he expanded government intervention to stimulate the paralyzed economy, conservative Democrats saw betrayal in his pragmatism and opportunism. Prophecies were gravely spoken. "The present pseudo-planned economy," declared Lewis Douglas, a disenchanted conservative Democrat, "leads relentlessly into the complete autocracy and tyranny of the Collective State."

The conservative counterattack within the Democratic party, launched through such organizations as the Liberty League, founded in 1934, was determinedly ideological. At a banquet in Washington's Mayflower Hotel in early 1936, two thousand Leaguers and sympathizers, including a dozen du Ponts and many leaders of business and finance, heard Al Smith assail the Roosevelt revolution. "Let me give this solemn warning. There can be only one capital, Washington or Moscow. There can be only one atmosphere of government, the clean, pure fresh air of free America, or the foul breath of communistic Russia." Among those who applauded this oration was an anti–New Dealer named Dean Acheson, who as Secretary of State would one day ironically be called to answer for the New Deal's alleged laxity with respect to communistic Russia.

The conservative opposition to Roosevelt took positions that made it extremely vulnerable. The stark prophecies did not come to pass, at least not so recognizably that the man in the street could see the point. The indictments had an abstract quality, unappealing to an electorate urgently concerned with concrete and immediate problems. And the tone of the opposition revealed a self-righteous assumption that the business community was without responsibility for the economic crisis. Conservatives were frozen in a resolute No, entrapped in their emotions and rhetoric. They wore the frightened look of reactionaries, and Roosevelt showed them no mercy.

In the savagely fought election campaign of 1936, the President succeeded in running against the forces of "organized money." In a moment of egotism, he cried out that these forces had met "their master" in his administration. Conservatives seized upon the phrase and assembled evidence of radical New Deal tendencies, but the voters were no longer listening. After Roosevelt's landslide victory, conservatives were out in the cold, warmed only by their hatred of "That Man" and by their waning hope that the American people would finally "wake up."

All that remained of conservatism during the rest of the thirties was a scattered rearguard. Short-lived coalitions of men with generally dissimilar interests formed to offer ad hoc resistance to the administration. In Congress, Republicans and Southern Democrats joined hands across the aisle in a sporadically effective coalition to block such measures as Roosevelt's "court-packing" scheme. Organizations sprang up to defend the republic, and most died on their feet. Denunciations of the Roosevelt tyranny came from the American Bar Association, the U.S. Chamber of Commerce, and the National Association of Manufacturers — from precisely those quarters where FDR had led the voters to expect and discount harsh words. Anti–New Deal arguments gradually became mechanical, guaranteed to drive away all but the true believers. During these bitter years, conservatives became confirmed in the habit of talking mainly to one another, of plucking up their forlorn hopes with impassioned variations on drearily familiar themes.

With the threat of American involvement in war, a broad coalition formed to oppose U.S. entanglement in Europe's troubles. The Chicago *Tribune* and the Hearst press exulted: here was the issue on which conservatives could stage a comeback. But the politics of the leading antiwar organization, the American First Committee, despite its denunciations of Roosevelt, began at the water's edge. When war came, the unnatural front of conservative factions, united by a single issue that had now been decided, crumbled and dispersed.

In 1940 the Republican party turned East for its presidential candidate, "a barefoot boy from Wall Street." The utilities lawyer Wendell Willkie was soundly beaten and promptly went to work for the third-term President, admitting that his criticism of Roosevelt had been just so much campaign talk. He too was a liberal. In the conservative heartland, this admission smacked of treason. The conviction grew that the enemy was now within the camp. At Republican national conventions over the next dozen years, thwarted isolationism found an outlet in truculent sectionalism.

In the mid-1940s, Republican conservatives in the Congress formed ranks behind the commanding figure of Ohio's Senator Robert A. Taft. Almost singlehanded, he rescued conservatism from the backwater of reaction and restored it to the political mainstream. He did not attempt to edge toward the ruling Democrats, and he looked with suspicion on those Easterners in the Republican party who did. But neither did he oppose for the sake of opposing, ignoring real problems unless they fitted the abstract answer in hand. Taft was willing to dirty his hands on grubby problems of everyday life. Sometimes he came up with a solution that displeased doctrinaire conservatives, as when he supported public housing because a desperate housing shortage awaited the GIs who had won for all Americans, themselves included, the right to pursue happiness and own their own homes.

Spare and balding, with a high-pitched voice and a painful shyness which he masked with a brusque manner, Taft nonetheless had the special quality that enables a politician to attract a devoted following. He wanted badly to follow in his father's footsteps to the White House, but it was his fate to lead the minority party in Congress through lean days, upholding an unpopular cause with great integrity. The time was out of joint for Taft. The political movement he led could make only limited, tactical gains in a hostile atmosphere.

The frigid climate of opinion had little to do, actually, with the conservative political performance during the thirties and the war years. The most cogent conservative arguments imaginable would have fallen on deaf ears among the influential intellectuals who were determined to defend the accomplishments of the New Deal against "reactionaries." During a decade in power, liberalism hardened into an ideology, intolerant of unorthodox opinions.

Artists, intellectuals, and journalists who defected from the camp of liberalism found themselves outcasts and wanderers. Novelist John Dos Passos, a radical firebrand who had gone to jail for his agitation on behalf of Sacco and Vanzetti, went to Spain to see the civil war for himself and returned to condemn the Communists for murdering nonconforming leftists on their side of the barricades. Later, during the palmy days of U.S.-Soviet friendship based on antifascism, Dos Passos spoke out against the neglected totalitarian enemy of democracy on the left. That was the blind side of liberalism, and liberal critics reacted in fury. Dos Passos remained America's leading novelist but his name became anathema.

How could a Dos Passos, the scourge of the House of Morgan, comfortably align himself with conservatives who were almost exclusively businessmen and political defenders of business? There was nothing recognizable on the other side toward which a disenchanted intellectual could move, unless he wanted to join the public relations department of the National Association of Manufacturers. Wealth was abundant among the conservatives, but brains and funds to mobilize brain power were lacking. The only intellectual journal hospitable to thoughtful conservative writers was *The Freeman*, founded in the twenties and long edited by the essayist Albert Jay Nock. But this small-circulation periodical struggled along without the support, moral or financial, of the conservative business community. The businessman sought comfort in the *Reader's Digest* and a good Republican newspaper. His convictions, he believed, were shared by the majority of Americans, and needed only to be defended with more vigor in Washington, not argued in obscure little magazines. Still, it disturbed him that so many young people espoused radical ideas, whose source puzzled him.

Until the late 1940s conservatives not only lacked an intellectual journal; they were also without a sympathetic publisher. In 1945 a young Chicagoan named Henry Regnery, Jr., was so impressed by the V-J Day speech of his good friend, the University of Chicago's President Robert M. Hutchins, that he brought it out in a pamphlet. Regnery, whose family was in the textile business, gradually took up publishing as a sideline, but the well-known liberal Hutchins was the first author of what became the nation's leading conservative publishing house. From the presses of Henry Regnery Co. came books offering controversial views that otherwise would not have seen the light of day. Until well into the 1950s, almost the entire output of books by conservatives was published by Regnery, Devin-Adair (a small New York firm), and the Caxton Press, out in the wilds of Caldwell, Idaho.

With the coming of the Cold War, conservatives, having few illusions about Communism and the Soviet Union to shed, found themselves suddenly out in front of shifting public opinion. Liberalism was thrown on the defensive, particularly after the sensational confrontation of Whittaker Chambers and Alger Hiss, leading to the latter's trial and imprisonment. Many liberals refused to accept the verdict against Hiss, for he was too patently the symbol of a generation of "progressives" and his guilt implied their complicity. The drama of the Hiss case was played against the backdrop of Communist advances in Eastern Europe. With the outbreak of the Korean War, a climate was created in which the question of domestic Communist subversion could not be ignored.

What followed, tragically, was a collision of the obstinate and the vengeful, of those liberals who refused to accept the abundant evidence of Communist infiltration and those opponents of the liberals determined to exploit to the hilt that refusal. A plausible case can be made that the flesh-and-blood Senator Joseph R. McCarthy was never actually seen by his friends and enemies; that those who hailed him as a hero and martyr, and those who condemned him as an awesomely powerful figure of evil, were glaring through him at each other.

McCarthy aroused intense popular interest in Communism, but his own credentials as a student of the subject were meager. Although his sympathizers publicly defended him — indeed, loved him — for the enemies he made, privately they expressed horror at his recklessness. One evening in the early 1950s, the journalist Forrest Davis showed McCarthy the manuscript of an article he had written for *The Freeman,* a critical analysis of U.S. foreign policy in the Far East. After scanning it, McCarthy asked if he might use it as the basis of a speech, thereby gaining a wider audience for its thesis. Davis agreed. Whereupon McCarthy imposed his own judgments on what was a responsible piece of journalism, converting the article into his "twenty years of treason" attack on the Democrats and former Secretary of State George C. Marshall. Heartsick at what McCarthy had done, Davis loyally kept silent.

McCarthy was a supreme opportunist. Organizations such as "For America," which sprang up to cheer him, lingered on in a limbo of fading echoes for lack of a larger purpose. He drew a host of vocal recruits, but his "conservatism" consisted of little more than visceral anti-Communism, as his voting record in the Senate showed. He was a conservative by association, who founded no movement and left no doctrinal legacy. History had created the necessity for a free society to make the crucial distinction between heresy and conspiracy; but when that necessity brought no adequate response from abler men it became McCarthy's opportunity. He led conservatives on a reckless, cathartic fling, leaving them compromised and weaker.

If McCarthy found many Republican conservatives eager for a crusade, one reason was obvious. Their champion, Taft, had been outmaneuvered at the 1952 Republican Convention amid accusations of vote-stealing. It was an incredible charge to level at "Mr. Integrity." But then, conservatives found the nomination of General Eisenhower — a man of no discernible partisan conviction — no less incredible. Above all, they hated the Easterners who engineered Ike's victory with the argument that he was a sure winner.

But many others were willing to be led out of the wilderness by Eisenhower. In Arizona, the man who liked Ike best of all was Barry Goldwater, who rode his coattails to a seat in the Senate. Eisenhower was assumed to be a conservative at heart. Yet the purpose that seemed so apparent in Eisenhower's sincere words and manner became blurred in practice.

Conservatives were baffled and infuriated by Eisenhower's undefinable "Modern Republicanism." An Indiana businessman and Republican fund-raiser said in the spring of 1963: "Eisenhower remains a complete enigma to me. I'll never understand the contradiction between what he said and what he did." Throughout Eisenhower's second term the conservatives grew increasingly restive. They were disillusioned by the lack of U.S. response to the 1956 anti-Communist uprisings in Poland and Hungary. They were incensed by the $12.4-billion budget deficit in fiscal 1959, which seemed clear evidence of government gone out of control. Ideological opposition to liberal Republicanism carried some conservatives into a "hard" commitment. Evidence of this was the blind enthusiasm for state "right-to-work" laws, which contributed to election disasters for Republicans in Ohio and California in 1958.

A much broader manifestation of the yearning for straightforward conservative doctrine was the popularity of a little book published in early 1960. In the foreword the author said he had "crossed the length and breadth of this great land hundreds of times and talked with tens of thousands of people." He found that "America is fundamentally a conservative nation." In *Conscience of a Conservative,* which sold some 600,000 copies within a year, Senator Barry Goldwater said what many within and outside the Republican party urgently felt.

At the 1960 Republican Convention, although Nixon was certain to be the nominee, or perhaps *because* of that fact, the emotional favorite of many delegates was Goldwater. He had denounced the Nixon-Rockefeller compact as the "Munich of the Republican party." The conservatives insisted on placing their hero's name before the convention. When he appeared on the rostrum, a throng of young people staged a frenzied demonstration. In his speech, Goldwater asked that his name be withdrawn and admonished his followers to close ranks behind Nixon. "Let's grow up, conservatives," he said. "If we want to take this party back, and I think we can someday, let's get to work."

Overnight Goldwater leaped into national prominence. Significantly, in contrast to his right-wing supporters, the politician Goldwater saw the intraparty differences of the Eisenhower years as more semantic than substantial. Congressman (and later Senator) Robert A. Taft, Jr., looking back, diagnosed an important source of discontent. "Modern Republicanism was born of the frustration of people who were trying to make the party appear anything but conservative. They had no real quarrel with the idea of conservatism, only with the name. The Republican party is conservative on fiscal matters, but fiscal conservatism was frustrated by the Eisenhower administration. The momentum of the government machine was never slowed down."

IV.

Conservatism during the fifties steadily gained strength at a level where it had been weak. A number of writers appeared who challenged the liberal near-monopoly on the intellectual front. In attempting to define their political principles, they drew mainly from two streams of thought, very different from each other yet capable of feeding the same movement in practical politics.

The first stream was traditionalism. Perhaps the major conservative intellectual achievement of the fifties was the publication of *The Conservative Mind,* by Russell Kirk. This scholarly and eloquent book, the work of a young (then thirty-four) and vigorous advocate, appeared in 1953 and announced to a startled audience that society's deepest questions had been reopened for discussion. Kirk took his stand within a universal moral order, appraised man as an imperfect creature led astray by his fallible reason, defended the necessity of class distinctions, and denounced the folly of government attempts to reconstruct society. While the book has come to be regarded as a landmark in the conservative advance, he wrote on the edge of despair. His publisher, Henry Regnery, recalled that Kirk came to him after the manuscript had been rejected by a large New York firm. "He wanted to call his book *The Conservative Rout*," Regnery smiled, "but we talked him out of it."

Although the book went on to become a best seller, Kirk's original choice of a title was not without merit. The conservatism he expounded was under relentless attack, not merely from radicalism, but from the vast forces of industrialism and urban civilization. He recognized the great law of change, yet could not accept the forms of change he encountered on every hand. He sang the praises of heroes from Burke to Santayana who stood by tradition and old establishments, who clung to honorable prejudice and abided by ancient prescription. His was a melancholy and nostalgic song, all but drowned out by the din of a Detroit that had no place in his doctrine.

The second intellectual current rising during the fifties went by a number of names — libertarianism, laissez-faire capitalism, or classical liberalism. A leading figure in this movement was F. A. Hayek, who came to the U.S. from England, where he wrote his classic *Road to Serfdom* as a warning against what he had seen happen under the overgrown state in Germany. Working within the Old World framework of anti-statist liberalism, Hayek specifically disavowed the label of "conservative." In *The Constitution of Liberty* he called himself an Old Whig. His argument for freedom rested, not on tradition and prescription, but on reason and the rule of law. The most important source of the libertarian revival was the University of Chicago, to which Hayek came in 1950. But before that, there had been a Chicago "school," which included the economist and social philosopher Frank H. Knight, the free-market economist Henry C. Simons (who died in 1946), his disciple,

Milton Friedman, and such independent-minded but kindred spirits as the economist Aaron Director, the man of letters Richard Weaver, and the moral and political philosopher Leo Strauss. These men and others, such as the dean of the classical economists, Ludwig von Mises of New York University, produced a continuing critique of statism *in operation,* and proclaimed the necessity of restoring individual freedom. They preached, in fact, acceptance of a more rapid and more fundamental change than any left-wing radical. The traditionalist and the libertarian, despite the huge differences between them, could suspend their arguments and join forces against the overweening state.

In an article published in 1949 entitled "The Intellectuals and Socialism," Hayek outlined the undertaking that subsequently occupied a growing community of thinkers and writers:

> We must make the building of a free society once more an intellectual adventure, a deed of courage. What we lack is a liberal Utopia, a program that seems neither a mere defense of things as they are nor a diluted kind of socialism, but truly liberal radicalism which . . . is not too severely practical and which does not confine itself to what appears today as politically possible . . . The main lesson which the true liberal must learn from the success of the socialists is that it was their courage to be Utopian which gained them the support of the intellectuals and therefore an influence on public opinion which is daily making possible what only recently seemed utterly remote. Those who have concerned themselves exclusively with what seemed practicable in the existing state of opinion have constantly found that even this has rapidly become politically impossible as the result of changes in public opinion which they have done nothing to guide.

At New York University, Professor von Mises noticed a number of surprisingly young men attending his lectures.

They turned out to be students at the Bronx High School of Science, a school for the academically gifted, who formed a study group that met on evenings and weekends. To them and others like them, the old libertarian ideas were excitingly new.

Utopia is the special province of the young. Frank Chodorov, editor of *The Freeman,* understood this. The journalist and libertarian recalled the founding in 1905 of the Intercollegiate Socialist Society, which had novelist Jack London as its first president. The ISS had influenced a generation of talented young men and women who shaped their society as teachers, writers, labor leaders, politicians, and government officials. A distinguished ISS alumnus, Walter Lippmann, once gave this summary of his group's objectives at Harvard: "In a general way our object was to make reactionaries stand-patters; standpatters, conservative liberals; conservatives, liberals and liberals, radicals; and radicals, Socialists. In other words, we tried to move everyone up a peg . . . We preferred to have the whole mass move a little, to having a few move altogether out of sight."

With the same objective in mind, but in reverse, Chodorov in 1952 — he was then in his sixties — founded the Intercollegiate Society of Individualists (ISI). "We are not born with ideas," he wrote,

> we learn them. If socialism has come to America it was because it was implanted in the minds of past generations. There is no reason for assuming that the contrary idea cannot be taught to a new generation. What the socialists have done can be undone, if there is a will for it. But the undoing will not be accomplished by trying to destroy established socialist institutions. It can be accomplished only by attacking minds, and not the minds of those

114

already hardened by socialist fixations. Individualism can be revived by implanting the idea in the minds of the coming generations.

A businessman who read Chodorov's article sent a contribution of $1000 and ISI was launched. Beginning with a list of 600 students' names, ISI mailed paperback copies of such publications as Frederic Bastiat's *The Law,* Henry Hazlitt's *Economics in One Lesson,* and Hayek's *Road to Serfdom.* There was no "attack" on unwilling minds: with each mailing went a postcard asking the student to indicate whether he wished to continue receiving such material. Through the process of self-selection, students entered the stream of libertarian and conservative thought. Within ten years, ISI's mailings had gone to more than 58,000 students, and from its ranks came scores of able scholars and writers.

In 1951 William F. Buckley, Jr., announced his arrival on the intellectual scene by hurling a brickbat of a book at his alma mater, *God and Man at Yale.* Buckley, then only twenty-six, inquired into the "superstitions" of academic freedom and asked by what right a university took money from conservative, God-fearing men to turn their sons into radicals and agnostics. Buckley wrote for *The American Mercury,* which had sunk into disrepute following Mencken's death, until, as one reader noted, remembering what it had been and seeing what it had become caused a shock akin to finding one's sister in a whorehouse. Buckley decided the conservative cause deserved better, and he spent a year raising $275,000 to launch a journal of opinion. *National Review* made its appearance in the winter of 1955. Among the editors and contributors were L. Brent Bozell (Buckley's brother-in-law), James Burnham (former Trotskyite and author of *The Managerial Revolution*),

Russell Kirk, John Chamberlain, Frank S. Meyer, Richard Weaver, and Henry Hazlitt. The magazine introduced and developed an exceptional number of young writers; one issue in the late 1950s consisted entirely of contributions by writers under thirty — a feat no liberal journal could match. From the beginning, conservatives embraced *National Review* uncritically, for it was evidence of intellectual respectability and arrival. (A snobbish but discerning liberal critic noted that the letters from readers in early issues used "the language of people not accustomed to expressing themselves on paper.")

But Bill Buckley, unlike the editors who shaped the liberal weeklies in their early years, found literary chores confining. He swiftly became second only to Goldwater as the idol of young conservatives and launched subcareers as a columnist, a television personality, and above all, an entertainer. He was apparently cast for life in the role of dashing captain of the Yale debating team.

The bright, youthful appearance of the new conservatism surprised and delighted Republican leaders. "When I first began speaking on college campuses in the early fifties," said Goldwater a decade later, "I was lucky if I had an audience of twenty-five people. If I were going to make a speech in New York or Cincinnati, I would bet that I could name the people in the first five rows — all with gray hair or no hair, all fat-catty looking. Now they're all young strangers."

The emergence of the young strangers encouraged some older conservatives to imagine a "wave of the future" building up on the campuses. The truth was that conservatives remained a minority within the tiny minority of collegians who cared about ideological questions. The quality of the heralded "revolt on the campus" was open to question, too.

Much of what passed for conservatism was in fact only youthful rebellion; and when the relative leisure and security of undergraduate life passed, the high spirits would evaporate. It was clear by the early 1960s that conservatism had gained at best only a tenuous beachhead in the realm of ideas, and that the advance or retreat in the next generation would depend on whether gifted young men and women would choose intellectual pursuits over careers in business and industry.

The businessman did not arouse much admiration in young conservatives. An editorial in the *Liberator* ("Published irregularly, not for profit, by students and alumni of several colleges in Louisiana") raised this typical complaint:

> As proponents of private enterprise, it would be reasonable for us to expect help from the practitioners of private enterprise. With some laudable exceptions, however, the logic fails. The persons to whom we in most cases must turn are, unfortunately, *businessmen.* The term means more than just persons engaged in commerce; a businessman must be above all else a "realist." As a realist he must give all his time to making money today, rather than concern himself with preserving freedom for his grandchildren . . . The "realistic" businessman will tell us frankly, "Son, I'm in business, and I can't take sides; I must be everyone's friend; you understand, don't you?"

The young conservatives didn't understand. Nor did the former businessman Goldwater, who said bluntly: "Businessmen in my generation are more for the dollar than for preserving the system."

Businessmen as a rule avoided not only the conservative movement, but also active political involvement of any sort. An exception, John V. Burkhard, president of the College Life Insurance Co. in Indianapolis, traced this noninvolvement to "the guilt complex" businessmen acquired during the thirties. "They were battered financially and then by government investigations. They completely lost confidence and the people lost confidence in them."

Fear of retribution from Washington was not the only reason businessmen refrained from aligning themselves with conservative activists. A perfectly valid reason was that much of the activity accomplished little — and not for lack of money. Following the 1960 Republican Convention, about 100 of Goldwater's youthful supporters met over a weekend at William Buckley's family estate at Sharon, Connecticut, and formed an organization called Young Americans for Freedom (YAF). Hopeful adults hovered attentively, and raised some $70,000 to get YAF rolling. The organization rented glossy offices in midtown Manhattan, hired a public relations man who specialized in right-wing causes, cranked up the mimeograph machine, and went into high gear. There was enough enthusiasm for such an organization to send membership climbing rapidly toward a claimed 18,000.

The Young Americans for Freedom were furiously busy: they picketed in support of the House Un-American Activities Committee; they took a boat ride up the Hudson River to present a plaque to Newburgh's city manager when he gained a quick (and doubtful) reputation for cracking down on welfare-chiseling; they descended on the 1961 National Student Association convention in Madison, Wisconsin, equipped with ample funds and walkie-talkies, and raised hell among the liberals. Then in 1962, as mentioned earlier, YAF filled Madison Square Garden — a rally that grossed some $80,000. Dazzled by affluence and attention, YAF leaders boasted halfseriously of filling Yankee Stadium. But it was not to be. In

118

the organization's early exploits, Buckley approvingly noted "an appetite for power." Soon the appetite turned cannibalistic, and YAF's officers fell into unseemly brawling: when one faction tried to gain access to the books, the other threatened to call the police. Within a couple of years, the leaders went their separate ways, some to new careers as professional young conservatives, and YAF became just another right-wing organization.

It might almost be said that conservatism gained ground in the 1950s and early 1960s in spite of efforts to organize. The movement of organized "conservative" groups was long on self-appointed leaders who were egotists, dogmatists, hucksters, and eccentrics, all engaged in a childish sandbox politics and being very noisy about it. Often referred to by liberals as "the radical Right," such organizations were more accurately described as the irrelevant Right. An unusually forthright liberal, historian John P. Roche, the former president of Americans for Democratic Action, put the right-wing "menace" in perspective when he ranked it twenty-third on his scale of priorities — "between fear of being eaten by piranha and fear of college presidents."

One right-wing group, the incredibly (and maliciously) overpublicized John Birch Society, became an American household word as Democrats gleefully beat the Republicans with the Birch stick. The organization should have been called the Robert Welch Society, in recognition of the guru who founded and dominated the cult. In 1958, he assembled eleven patriots in Indianapolis and proceeded to talk for two days, at the end of which he proposed the creation of the Society. Incessant criticism helped rather than hindered the Society, for its whole appeal lay in the thrilling exclusiveness of the ideology contained in Welch's *Blue Book,* the text of his two-day monologue, and in the slick monthly magazine, *American Opinion.* Welch held out the promise of unique insight into the Communist threat and how it arose. In a flier offering a series of reprinted books ("One Dozen Candles"), he told uninitiated outsiders: "Long before you have finished reading these . . . you probably will be jumping up and down in amazement and alarm, exactly like the rest of us."

Whatever might be said of Welch, the California State Senate Subcommittee on Un-American Activities, headed by the majority leader of the Democratic-controlled Legislature, concluded at the end of a two-year detailed study of the Society that "most of its members are not 'mentally unstable, crackpots or hysterical about the threats of Communism.'" Nor was the Society "'secret, Fascist, subversive, un-American nor anti-Semitic.'" Epithets aside, the word to describe the Society — and similar right-wing organizations — was juvenile. Birchism was a symptom of arrested political development.

John Stuart Mill, the nineteenth-century liberal, scornfully called the conservatives "the Stupid Party." Conservatives merely sat and thought; mostly, they sat. In ordinary times, conservatives were required to do nothing more. But these were extraordinary times, and when conservatives stirred from their natural state, they often became extraordinarily concerned. Commonly, they experienced a semireligious "awakening." The stimulus might be a dramatic event, a provocative book or article, a lecture — almost anything. In the case of one conservative, a man in his early forties employed in the middle management of a large corporation in an Eastern city, the stimulus to activity was a film he saw in 1960. It was *Operation Abolition,* made up of newsreel shots of the student riots against the House Un-American Activities Committee in San Francisco. Among those identified as leaders were several Bay area Communists. After the film was shown at a men's club, two speakers, a conservative and a liberal, debated its authenticity.

In an interview in the spring of 1963, this man described to me what amounted to a "pilgrim's progress" of a newly awakened conservative:

Before I saw that film, I went merrily along, not liking the things I saw in government and politics, but never getting very concerned about it. I used to read headlines and that was about all. The film and the debate really kicked me off. I thought: how could this be? How could a good solid American stand up and say this is an absolute fraud? I got conservative books and liberal books. I read everything I could get my hands on . . . I didn't know what to believe. After nine or ten months of reading, I came to a conclusion: "My golly, we're in trouble in this country!" . . . I wrote to my friends and tried to get chain letters to our congressmen started . . . I took the political action course at the Chamber of Commerce . . . I heard about the Birch Society and bought *The Blue Book* — not that I swallowed every bit of it; but the more I read, the more concerned I got.

About this time, I joined the Conservative Association. It was to be a party or a group to express our ideas. I was an early member, but not formally active. I didn't think the company would like it . . . I know a lot of people; I thought I could influence them. But they were indifferent, a little sympathetic, but indifferent. I thought of leaving the country but there's no place to hide . . . I decided to show the movie *Operation Abolition* to my college alumni group. Afterward I said: "We can either go home and forget what we've seen or we can go home and do something." My wife and I had brought literature to pass out, but several of my friends wouldn't take it. I thought some of them would call me later. Not a single one did . . . I came to the conclusion that you don't win anyone by being emotional — they just say, "Oh, so-and-so is hipped on it." Only in the last six months have I realized something else — that you don't get anything done by organizing conservative organizations. Since then I've become active in the Republican party — done everything they've asked and volunteered, too.

This conservative did not feel that he compromised his convictions by forsaking an avowedly conservative organization for the Republican party. On the contrary, he believed he had become more effective. He found an outlet for his concern in specific tasks, pursued under the supervision of experienced, practical leaders. Instead of trying to save the country in one swoop, he was learning to advance toward concrete goals one step at a time. Much was heard about the alleged danger of right-wing extremists taking over the G.O.P. No such danger existed. But, as this personal case history illustrated, the Republican party was recruiting and reorienting newly awakened conservatives whose dedication needed only discipline to make them useful workers. They, of course, had every reason to expect effective leadership in return.

V.

In September 1973, Barry Goldwater, wearing the mantle of elder statesman among conservative Republicans, pronounced judgment on the Watergate affair in a series of articles on the Op-Ed Page of the *New York Times*. His indictment of the Nixon administration was severe, but without realizing it, Goldwater also indicted himself and the other elected political leaders of the conservative movement.

"The Nixon Administration would not find itself in the situation it does today if it had been manned at the top by staff people strongly committed to the principles of conservatism," Goldwater wrote. "It was not the existence of conservative ideology in the White House or in the Committee to Re-elect the President which brought on the stupidities and the irregularities of the Watergate. Rather — and let me emphasize and underline this assertion — it was the lack of ideology and the lack of experience and the lack of a deeply rooted philosophy of life which brought on the unfortunate and unforgivable activity that has been uncovered in the Watergate investigation."

The blame for the absence of conservatives in the administration hierarchy belonged, not to Nixon and the Haldeman-Ehrlichman clique, but to Goldwater and like-minded politicians in the Senate and the House who failed to use their considerable leverage on the President they had nominated and helped elect. Although they knew from personal experience Nixon's limitations and flaws of character, they set no watchdogs on his White House. Although they were painfully aware of the arrogance and ignorance of the men around the President, who systematically humiliated them, they made no protest. They did not even demand the bare minimum due them as the administration's loyal legislative shock troops — continuing private access to the President. They took their orders from underlings and confined their grumbling to the Republican cloakroom, fully justifying Nixon's contemptuous judgment that he could keep the right wing in line with rhetoric and occasional patronage plums.

In the fall of 1971, a group of conservative intellectuals finally "suspended" their support of the administration, but they were given no support — on the contrary, they were scolded — by Goldwater and other right-wing stalwarts. On the whole, the pre-Watergate performance of the conservative political leadership was hopelessly weak. But quite apart from the shortcomings of individuals, the failure of conservatives to offer timely opposition to the Nixon regime revealed basic weaknesses in their cause and movement.

The conservatives have not yet evolved anything resembling a coherent, systematic program for implementing their avowed principles. These hang suspended in midair, unsupported by concrete analysis and a plan of action. The dominant conservative impulse is to react — negatively to liberal proposals, positively to those bearing the Republican label, almost without reference to their specific contents. This habit of assent — knee-jerk conservatism — is symptomatic of a weak-mindedness apparently peculiar to Republicans. It naturally combines with a short-run perspective and a not very demanding opportunism — if the society's leftward trend is slowed temporarily by the defeat of a particular measure, conservatives light bonfires, uncork jugs, and celebrate victory, forgetting that the enemy will be back the next day with the same measure repackaged, eager for another round of battle.

A contemporary conservative program, it seems to me, must begin with a rigorous, clear-eyed analysis of the American economy, the role of government in it, and the mechanisms for achieving socially desirable ends, such as expanded private ownership of assets producing not only human happiness but also the capital essential to the next generation's freedom, progress, and well-being. Such an analysis must come to grips with the realities of power and political finance symbolized by John Connally. He won ready acceptance by the managerial business elite, who enjoy a reputation for conservatism while practicing state capitalism under expanding government protection. Watergate, among other things, disclosed the cash nexus (to the tune of more than $60 million in Nixon campaign contributions) between big business and big government. On the Democratic side, of course, the same connection exists between big government and big labor. Conservatives are obliged to give up the ritual denunciation of liberals long enough to decide what they think of the reality of the emerging Corporate State.

If they cannot put aside the stale "free enterprise" rhetoric that spares them the pain and difficulty of serious thought, if they cannot grasp the root of the matter — money aspiring to become power and multiply itself under government auspices — then they are foredoomed romantics, for whom the time will always be out of joint. But if they can survive their complicity by default in Watergate and hurdle the Goldwater generation of nonleaders, offering the nation new spokesmen of talent, energy, and unsparing realism, they have the opportunity to capture the imagination of those Americans now caught between big government, big business, and big labor who have gone too long unrepresented. Therein lies the challenge to the new American conservatism.

Crossing the Line I: John Lindsay
and Charisma at City Hall

In 1965, John V. Lindsay, the handsome young congressman representing Manhattan's silk-stocking district, was one of the brighter stars in a Republican sky darkened by the Goldwater debacle. He had the same charisma and enjoyed the same easy success with the news media as the Kennedys. Bored in the House, he decided to make a bid for national prominence, which was understandable. But he chose one of the toughest jobs in American politics, a graveyard of ambitions and reputations. He declared his candidacy to become the "reform" mayor of New York City, the rotting Big Apple wasted by dreary Democratic hacks, indifferent business and financial interests, and avaricious municipal labor unions.

Attracted by Lindsay's foolhardy optimism, I campaigned for him and wrote a book about the man-made misfortunes of my native New York — *A City Destroying Itself*. When he won, I was delighted. But within the first hundred days of the Lindsay administration, which began with the avoidable disaster of a citywide subway strike, I began to have doubts about the practical effectiveness of the new mayor's "image politics," which I reported in *Fortune*.

I.

No other mayor of New York City in modern history has gone about his job the way John Vliet Lindsay has. As only the fourth non-Democratic mayor elected in this century, and the first since the colorful Fiorello H. La Guardia more than a generation ago, the Republican-Liberal Lindsay is something of a novelty no matter what he does. But what truly sets him apart is his daring, even reckless, embrace of a pair of debatable propositions: namely, that huge, dreadfully run-down New York *can* be basically reformed; and that the best way to go about it is in hurry-up, uncompromising fashion.

To appreciate the risks inherent in that approach, it should be noted at once that Lindsay heads a divided government. While he was being elected, his running mates for comptroller and City Council president were losing to their Democratic opponents; and large Democratic majorities were being returned to the council and the powerful Board of Estimate. Though he had been elected to Congress four times as a Republican, Lindsay acknowledged the political realities of New York — where Democrats outnumber Republicans better than three to one — by running for mayor as a "fusion" candidate, alongside a renegade Democrat and a Liberal. Thus Lindsay, a formally nonpartisan mayor, is practicing his politics from a very shaky power base, an unstable coalition of the disgruntled.

Some experienced observers doubt that such unconventional politics will succeed. From the Democratic side of City Hall comes this assessment: "The Lindsay people have behaved as though he were Franklin Roosevelt and this were 1933, but that isn't the political situation at all. Lindsay is just

127

a lonely oak in a forest of scrub pines, and he had better learn to bend." Another critic, this one very much on Lindsay's side, wishes the mayor were "a more skillful operator" who would attempt to "cultivate a community consensus."

Such criticisms concentrate on Lindsay's not very surprising weaknesses, which grow out of his inexperience at the level of municipal power politics. But there is another level of politics on which Lindsay is stronger and more successful. During his first months in office he has shown a considerable flair for getting across an image of himself as the hard-driving champion of the public interest, opposed and sometimes thwarted by narrow defenders of the status quo. It's true that he must learn to put combinations together in order to get results, but it is no less true that he must meanwhile sustain his popularity, without which fundamental reform is impossible. In taking up by far the greatest challenge in urban America, Lindsay detected possibilities in what had been branded an impossible job. How well he does at it will depend on how well he unites the politics of power and the politics of image.

Though in office less than six months, the handsome forty-four-year-old Mayor is engaged in running battles large and small along a spectacularly wide front — and he is fighting practically alone. Responding to the pressure of civil-rights groups, he moved early to shake up the self-satisfied hierarchy of the police department, and to install as commissioner a stranger from Philadelphia who had shown he could live with a citizens' complaint board run by civilians. When Lindsay finally unveiled his civilian review board, New York's uniformed cops, through their Benevolent Association, swore to fight it to the last ditch. In another battle, he took on the despotic septuagenarian Robert Moses and his network of influ-

CROSSING THE LINE I: JOHN LINDSAY

ential friends in politics and finance by proposing that the city's transportation policy-making be brought under the control of Lindsay's newly appointed transportation administrator. Able to give that fight only divided attention, the mayor has been forced steadily to give ground, surrendering most of his original proposal.

Simultaneously, Lindsay was waging his most important contest. He urged an end to the city's increasingly costly borrowing to meet current expenses and proposed a half-billion-dollar tax program, including a hotly controversial new income tax on city dwellers and suburban commuters alike. His package contained new business taxes that fell particularly hard on banking and insurance; and Lindsay's old friends in the better clubs were shocked when he publicly chided business for failing to pay its way. The New York Stock Exchange threatened to leave town if a higher stock-transfer levy were imposed, but nobody seemed to be listening. Through it all, relations between Lindsay and the business and financial establishment had become so distant that a group of businessmen led by Chase Manhattan Bank's David Rockefeller had to wait a month for a meeting with the mayor. As each day brought new skirmishing somewhere, Lindsay, with an embattled air, told visitors: "It's just like La Guardia — I haven't got anybody with me except the people."

Lindsay isn't the sort of politician who expresses such sentiments ironically. He is wholly in earnest. A rather tense, tightly wound activist, he frequently cracks jokes, but his humor is studied and merely underlines the intensity of his determination. He is moved by a moral impulse, which is at once a source of his appeal and a potential weakness. "This Lindsay," as New Yorkers from Harlem to Eastern Parkway to

Flushing came to call him during last fall's exciting campaign, retains his grip on the public imagination as the bold newcomer who means to challenge and uproot the old order. During the grim siege of the twelve-day transit strike in January 1966, which began when his administration was only five hours old, Lindsay launched his most memorable attack, declaring: "The government of this city will not capitulate before the lawless demands of a single power group. It will not allow the power brokers in our city, or any special interests, to dictate to this city the terms under which it will exist in New York." No recent mayor had ever talked like *that*.

Reporters pursued Lindsay to learn just who these mysterious "power brokers" were. The only answer finally given was, "*They* know." That vague, unsatisfying response, along with much rhetoric in a similar vein, has earned Lindsay a reputation for moralizing and some unflattering nicknames ("Mr. Clean" and "Captain Marvel" are favorites among the Room 9 press corps at City Hall). Some sophisticated New Yorkers began to wonder whether the mayor wasn't a square. However, such doubts do not yet trouble the ordinary New Yorker, in whom naiveté and cynicism are peculiarly blended. He knew — or thought he knew — who "They" were, and he approved the mayor who nourished the citizen's inbred sense of being the victim of unseen malevolent forces.

Quite early, then, the tone and style of the Lindsay administration became established. It is much too soon for definitive judgments, but Lindsay's performance so far suggests that his militant campaign ideology may be getting in the way of the achievement of his very ambitious proclaimed objectives. He remains in a highly combative posture, continuing from inside City Hall the outsider's attack on various "establishments."

His administration is still basically a campaign organization, and most of the bright young men suddenly elevated to power incline naturally to the tactics of frontal assault. Whether they will settle down to learning the subtle art of government depends on how they interpret their painful rebuffs. A sympathetic observer, who has himself served in city government, laments "the frightful air of amateurism about it all," and wishes the learning process would go faster, while there is still time.

A less sympathetic but equally knowing onlooker, who was an adviser to former Mayor Robert F. Wagner, believes serious damage has already been done. "The lines of battle have been drawn, and now everything Lindsay proposes becomes part of the battle," he says. That comment echoes the complaint of one of Lindsay's young men, who says bitterly that "any change that comes, no matter how small, will be a battle."

II.

The battle is less about forcing change than it is about catching up with the consequences of change. New York, like most large U.S. cities, is badly organized and poorly financed to cope with the massive problems being thrust upon it. The present crisis of the cities is similar to the organizational crisis that faced the federal government in the late 1930s under the impact of the Depression and the proliferation of new agencies and responsibilities in the New Deal. At that time the presidential Committee on Administrative Management was created, and it inspired a thoroughgoing reorganization which consolidated federal agencies and set up the Office of the President with a strong professional administrative staff.

Lindsay's avowed intention is to go beyond the city's charter revision of a few years ago, and to bring about a sweeping overhaul of the sprawling and ill-coordinated municipal government and a budget second in size only to the federal budget. Yet this fantastic spending scarcely enables the city to hold its own.

For a decade, the crisis of organization and finances was "met" by deferring it — by paying the minimum price of immediate needs through the least painful expedients, and worrying about the long run when it arrived. By the time Lindsay came on the scene, the future had been used up. Hence he proposed during the campaign, and later commissioned a task force to draw up, a plan of reorganization that would consolidate about fifty city agencies, departments, and offices into a dozen major agencies. Related programs scattered through various departments would be pulled together under the appropriate administration, eliminating overlapping functions and clearly defining responsibilities. Along with that structural reorganization would come program planning, budgeting, and management, through which the mayor would be enabled to match resources with objectives, fix timetables, and evaluate performance.

Although it has reason and necessity to commend it, reorganization faces an extremely uncertain future. If it does not survive or emerges badly mauled, the mayor must bear at least part of the responsibility. For little of the necessary groundwork has been done among those who must concur in an enormous change. Lindsay seems more interested in taking ground by storm. It is his aggressive conviction that "the more you go on more fronts, the more you will get action, and the better chance you have that people will bend to your will."

The Democrats obviously may need to be pressed by the mayor. Yet they are also bound to respect his popularity and authority. Beyond that, they cannot very well ignore the urgent needs of the city without bringing down criticism on themselves. So, if Lindsay had been moved to emulate Wagner's cautious technique of lining up partners in advance of major proposals, a measure of Democratic collaboration could not have been denied him. Instead, Lindsay has declined to accord the Democrats a full share of responsibility for meeting a crisis aggravated by their long neglect. He has disdained anything that smacks of "deal-making," which he identifies as an evil practice of the old regime.

Lindsay's strategy of going it alone is in the best tradition of crusading reform, and some admirers are unembarrassed to speak of his "gallantry." Certainly his courage cannot be faulted, nor his willingness to champion the broad public interest. Moreover, he is entitled to that compassion which is the due of any mortal elected mayor of New York. (As President Lyndon Johnson once told the nation's mayors, "When the burdens of the presidency seem unusually heavy, I always remind myself that it could be worse — I could be a mayor.") All that said, however, it must be added that, while Lindsay has shaken up New York, he has thus far barely nudged it in the direction of concrete, significant reform.

Like every politician, the mayor is burdened with unworkable specific hopes and promises. Some are already being cast off. But these are the commonplace equivocations of politics. Lindsay's real peril arises from the fact that he is the captive of extravagant expectations, most of which he aroused himself.

133

His campaign was shrewdly directed not so much against his pallid opponent, former Comptroller Abraham D. Beame, as it was against the general malaise of the city itself. Everything wrong with New York — and the catalogue of shortcomings is almost endless — could be transformed into a vote for Lindsay under the alchemy of his call for change. But, in seeking and getting a mandate to make good on that open-ended promise, Lindsay overlooked the impersonal source of his victory: it was the city and its seemingly intractable ills that had actually defeated the Democrats.

From November to January 1965, the mayor-elect, working in makeshift office space in a midtown hotel, conscientiously prepared himself for office. Drawing on the personnel and resources of the local nonprofit Institute of Public Administration, as well as experts recruited from the city and outside, he began assembling more than a dozen task forces to recommend action on city problems. Nothing altered his conviction that drastic measures were in order because the city's situation, in many respects, was truly desperate. A Democrat, long a fixture in City Hall, agrees, but adds a crucial qualification. "Of course the situation is desperate, and it was desperate under Wagner, too. The situation in New York is *always* desperate."

However that verdict may sound, it expresses quite the opposite of defeatism, and it reveals a truth about governing New York. It is the genius of the city's 7.5 million inhabitants, who lead lives of notably unquiet desperation, never to yield to their circumstances, not even under the added stress of blackouts, riots, subway strikes, or other disasters. Though the city works badly, by some kind of continuing miracle it does work. It works because there is acceptance of the neces-

134

sity of accommodation, as there must be when people of so many different races, creeds, ethnic strains, and persuasions must somehow live and work and compete at close quarters. The necessity of accommodation does not rule out the possibility of change, even change of a radical nature; but it does set limits on the pace of change and defines the method by which change is most likely to come about. As the prime mover, the mayor must do more than upset the existing balance of interests; simultaneously, he must strike a new one on a basis that has been prepared well in advance.

III.

Lindsay entered City Hall in an hour when the city's sense of desperation was especially acute. He came buoyed by his mandate and armed with documentary evidence that New York was close to the brink. And then, just before dawn on New Year's Day, 1966, the city was given one of the rudest shoves in its history.

The bus and subway strike, one of those rare misfortunes immense enough to affect the entire metropolis, turned out to be a stroke of personal good fortune for Lindsay. In their affliction, New Yorkers turned to the new mayor and discovered a rallying figure. Lindsay kept the city's spirits up through frequent televised reports, and set an example of fortitude by walking four miles to work. He won sympathy, respect, and popularity while escaping blame. He was especially fortunate in having an adversary such as the blustering transit workers' boss, the late Michael J. Quill, who played his self-described role of "elder statesman among public monsters."

Only after the strike had been settled, on rather high terms, did doubts arise about Lindsay's handling of the situation. Even granting that he was a newcomer to the complex politics and economics of New York transit, some doubts would seem to be in order.

By coincidence, Wagner's term and the transit union's contract both expired on New Year's Eve. Weeks before that deadline, it was clear that Wagner did not intend to negotiate a contract on his successor's behalf. For his part, Lindsay was determined to stand aloof from the bargaining until he took office. This left the Transit Authority to deal with the union, but as a practical matter it could not. The authority could not make an offer that might upset the fifteen-cent fare, which politicians of both parties, led by Lindsay, were sworn to maintain. So everyone marked time for several weeks.

Everyone, that is, except Quill. For once, there was substance to his biennial strike threat, provided by the mounting discontent he faced within his union. His customary strategy of noisily making extreme demands and quietly accepting modest settlements could no longer satisfy the rank and file. Skilled workers particularly were complaining, with some justification, that contract maneuvering in the past had left them well behind other public employees performing comparable work. Under pressure from below to catch up, Quill needed an above-average settlement this time around. The election of Lindsay, a Republican to whom the union owed nothing, removed the chief obstacle to a strike and created an opportunity to demand a very high price indeed.

Though he stayed away from the bargaining table, Lindsay took a gingerly step toward Quill in mid-December, meeting secretly with him at a private club. Naively enough, the mayor-elect tried to impress the union leader with the seriousness of the city's financial plight. But Quill, of course, wanted to know only what Lindsay had to offer. Their meetings failed to produce any real communication between the pair. They addressed each other chiefly through the press, radio, and television, Quill heaping abuse on the man he called "Lindsley" and Lindsay preserving an air of calm dignity. This clash of opposites was good theater, but it further separated the main actors as the strike deadline neared; and that was hardly good for the city.

An observer close to the unfolding crisis offers this appraisal: "It was obviously difficult to deal with a man like Quill. Lindsay was unfamiliar with bargaining, which you can't blame him for. The fault on his side was an unwillingness to assume responsibility. He stood off from everyone; he wouldn't get together with the Transit Authority and agree on a strategy. And he didn't talk the language of negotiation. The trouble was that he *wasn't* a power broker, at a time when there was no substitute for the key people sitting down and talking."

The strike probably became inevitable during the final week of December. A three-man panel of mediators had been summoned, but there had been little to talk about. Lindsay did not discuss strategy with the Transit Authority and the mediators until almost literally the eleventh hour. A decision was reached to make an offer of $25 million. In a showdown, it was further agreed, the Transit Authority would go as high as $40 million. "And that," Lindsay was heard to remark, "would make me sick."

Considering the late hour, the move was bound to be ineffectual. The $25-million offer, which fell far short of the

137

$38.6-million transit settlement two years earlier, was unrealistic. When the offer was made, the union negotiators hooted. The $40-million figure then was tentatively advanced — "it floated around," recalls one who sat at the bargaining table — but by then it was too late.

After being sworn in on New Year's Eve, Lindsay set the tone of the drama, declaring, "Ours is a proud city." For almost the next fortnight New Yorkers, having no real choice, bore their ordeal bravely and continued as best they could the business of living. But the practical consequences of the strike — frayed tempers, sore feet, business losses, missed paychecks — were obscured by an overlay of theatrical rhetoric and gestures, tending to depict the calamity as a great contest whose outcome would "prove" something. Against a background of editorial thunder and public applause, Quill and his lieutenants were marched off to jail for defying a court order. A group of outraged citizens took newspaper ads demanding an end to the strike, and suggesting as a last resort that the National Guard be called out. In a dramatic climax, the mayor then lashed out at the "power brokers."

In the end, the strike settlement "proved" nothing. While the walkout had plainly violated a state law forbidding strikes by public employees, the law's harsh penalties were not imposed; the union was, in fact, specifically exempted from punishment by the legislature. (The alternative to this shabby expedient was another strike.) Even the symbolic jailing of Quill, who immediately collapsed and was removed to a hospital, had no practical effect beyond making negotiations more difficult. The strike ended after twelve days because a bargain was made, at a cost to the city estimated at around $60 million a year.

The bargain came only after Lindsay turned, very reluctantly, from image-making to deal-making. Recalls Douglas MacMahon, who had become the union's chief negotiator: "I got the impression for days — and each day was like a year — that Lindsay was not serious. He seemed to be up on Cloud Nine about what it would take to settle this."

Lindsay entrusted the first groping movement toward the realities to Robert Price, his long-time campaign manager and closest aide. The thirty-three-year-old Price, a brusque and aggressive product of the Bronx, is prematurely balding, and has a Nixon-like beard that gives his jowls a permanently bluish cast. He looks every inch the mayor's personal "power broker," but he is more than that. Quick-minded, decisive, and highly organized, he is Lindsay's most intimate political associate and the most powerful man in the administration after the mayor. After he had managed the campaign, Price tried to return to his law practice, but Lindsay prevailed on him to accept the title of deputy mayor and to take up the role that no one else could fill. "If Price hadn't come back," remarks one of the mayor's assistants, "this thing would have been a total disaster."

Just before the strike began, Price advanced the $40-million offer. A few days later he secretly visited Quill's bedside, bearing a $50-million offer. MacMahon, unable to communicate directly with Quill, received the same offer skeptically, and asked for a breakdown into "cents per hour." Price declined to untie the package. The main object of MacMahon's concern was the key rate in the dispute — the $3.46 hourly pay of skilled transit workers, which in the case of mechanics was $1.10 below the hourly pay of comparable city employees. "Lindsay just didn't think in terms of $3.46 and

$4.56," says MacMahon. "He didn't seem to realize that I couldn't go back to my boys without half of it." Ultimately, the mediators proposed terms that would appease MacMahon and his "boys," and the mayor accepted them. Although the strike settlement amounted to a victory for the union, won in defiance of the law and public opinion, Lindsay emerged with his image untarnished.

IV.

After the strike, the mayor took up the interrupted task of organizing his administration. He has experienced continuing difficulty in staffing the upper levels of the city government. Lindsay requires topflight people whose professional abilities match up with the city's enormous needs. So far he has not had notable success in recruiting them. Such men are in short supply nationally and most are wary of risking their reputations in a city that has hurt many a promising career. In some cases, Lindsay has been able to lure experts to New York only by creating consultative assignments outside the government, and by leaving his recruits free to study the city's problems and propose solutions before deciding whether to join him. He has brought in Edward Logue, the prime mover of Boston's urban-renewal program, and Mitchell Sviridoff, head of New Haven's antipoverty program, to act as consultants and to draw up blueprints for two of the new city administrations. Their studies, administered by the Institute of Public Administration, have been financed by Ford Foundation grants amounting to almost $300,000.

It took some resourceful arranging to create these posts for

Logue and Sviridoff. At first the foundation was lukewarm to the mayor's proposal, and Lindsay, in the midst of the transit crisis, was forced to slip away for lunch with John J. McCloy, chairman of the foundation's board. Within two weeks the projects were approved. Sviridoff thoughtfully outlined his impressions of the city and the mayor's task. "You can't deal with New York as though it were a city. It's five major cities, it's a country," he said. In Sviridoff's view, "The city is governed by semiautonomous concentrations of power," which won't be changed all at once. "There is just so much change that this system can digest, just so much opposition that the Mayor can handle."

The validity of this judgment is illustrated by the reverses Lindsay has suffered in his first major attempt at government reorganization, in the field of transportation policy. A dominant figure in this confused scene is Robert Moses, New York's master builder and most influential nonelected official. In recent years Moses has gradually relinquished most of his titles, but he remains chairman of the Triborough Bridge and Tunnel Authority and coordinator of highways within the city constructed primarily with state and federal funds. It was from this formidable base of semiautonomous power that he counterattacked against Lindsay's proposals to unify transportation policy-making.

In January 1966, Lindsay, by executive order, created a new city Transportation Administration, embracing in whole or in part such departments as highways, traffic, and public works. Moses's opening criticism of the Lindsay scheme — "fantastic" — was scarcely disinterested, but he did have a point. For Lindsay proposed to overthrow and rebuild, at a single stroke, much of the complex structure of existing legal, financial, and political relationships in the field of transportation. Reform that went this far approached revolution, and many who were sympathetic to the mayor's objectives balked at granting him so much power. Within two months after they were announced, Lindsay's proposals had been compromised to the point where some legislators considered what remained meaningless.

The lessons of this adventure are there for the Lindsay administration to learn, assuming it wants to. If the episode does nothing else it should make it very clear that entrenched, resourceful defenders of the status quo, of whom Moses is the prime symbol, cannot be dislodged without the most deliberately planned and carefully concerted campaigns.

So far the Lindsay administration has done little more than stage dashing light-cavalry attacks against heavily fortified objectives. With a headlong rush, major proposals are advanced almost on a take-it-or-leave-it basis, as though they were the *only* answers. Often the answers are sound enough in principle, but they are presented in such a way as practically to guarantee stiff opposition and court eventual defeat. A close and rather cynical Democratic observer believes that Lindsay, in pursuing the politics of image, has settled on a "strategy of failure," explaining, "Lindsay asks for big reforms with a flourish. He gets turned down. And then he asks the people for more support so that he can slay the dragons who are thwarting the people's will."

The metaphor of the unsuccessful dragon slayer is somewhat unfair to Lindsay. Still, it is hard to discern a strategy bent on concrete success in the way he is waging his most crucial battles. What Lindsay stands to lose are some of his most important stated objectives. All that he may preserve intact is his shining image as a crusader.

V.

When Lindsay left City Hall after eight years on December 31, 1973, the *New York Times* hailed him as "a Mayor of vision, who dared to raise the sights of his fellow citizens." Whatever Lindsay did to his fellow citizens, they were undeniably different after his tenure, as the *Times* reported a few weeks later. A poll conducted for the paper by the Yankelovich organization revealed that, in spite of New York's reputation as the most liberal city in the country, most New Yorkers regarded themselves as conservatives (33 percent) and moderates (31 percent) rather than liberals or radicals (27 percent) — a stunning turnaround from similar polls in earlier years.

Lindsay, too, was different. He was middle-aged, graying, and lined where it showed and scarred where it didn't. He was no longer a Republican, having switched to the Democratic side in 1971 in an abortive attempt to "go national" from his crumbling city base. And his political future, once so bright, seemed behind him. A statewide race for the governorship or the Senate would buck an even stronger conservative trend than the *Times* found in the city. What had happened to Lindsay?

Charisma turned out to be as perishable as lox left un-iced, as unfilling as a Nathan's Famous Hot Dog, as irrelevant as yesterday's *Morning Telegraph*. Lindsay's head-on, polarizing brand of politics upset the city's precarious ethnic and racial power balance, and threw him into conflict with the white lower-middle class and the less well-off Jews, especially in the outlying boroughs. To be sure, Lindsay built solid support among the blacks and Puerto Ricans, and turned it into victory in his three-way contest for re-election. Perhaps his most notable success, at once a tribute to his bravery and energy, was to walk the city's racially tense neighborhoods in the summer of 1968 and keep New York relatively cool while a hundred other cities burned. But he paid a heavy price for becoming too closely identified with those at the lower and upper ends of the social scale at the expense of the mass of New Yorkers in between.

Lindsay and his image-managers hoped to take the 1972 Democratic presidential nomination by media blitz, but he bombed out, partly because the practical consequences of his liberalism — especially the clashes between Jews and Negroes over schools and housing — frightened too many New York liberals, who spread the word that Lindsay spelled trouble. Many of his reforms were useful (government reorganization, introduction of modern management techniques) but of doubtful permanence. He could not keep such men as Logue and Sviridoff at their key jobs when greener and calmer pastures beckoned. Above all, Lindsay had failed to restore the ordinary citizen's confidence in the future of "Fun City," which struck the subway-riding, tax-paying New Yorker as still a jungle run for the benefit of the savages. The responses to questions concerning social issues in the Yankelovich poll revealed personal fear as a main source of the city's newfound conservatism. No fewer than 68 percent favored the death penalty for certain crimes. Two-thirds approved life sentences without parole for drug pushers. And a 59 percent majority believed the city had become "a welfare dumping ground" for the rest of the nation.

The irony of ironies was Lindsay's successor, the man whom he had beaten in his original campaign. After eight years of image politics, New Yorkers turned to Abe Beame, a squat, totally uncharismatic Brooklyn Democrat and veteran city bureaucrat. "Abe the bookkeeper" offered nothing but reasonably competent power brokerage and the prospect of conflict-management through ethnic-bloc accommodation — in short, the pre-Lindsay politics, which now seems blessed "reform."

Crossing the Line II: John Connally
and the Emerging Corporate State

IN THE LATE WINTER of 1970, following the disappointing mid-term elections, President Nixon made a move that stunned his allies and opponents alike. He appointed John Bowden Connally, three-time Democratic governor of Texas, to the key Cabinet post of Secretary of the Treasury. Speculation on the kind of deal the two had made quickly arrived at a consensus: Connally would receive the vice-presidential nomination on the 1972 ticket in return for delivering the electoral votes of Texas to Nixon. On the basis of interviews with sources in Washington, New York, and Texas, however, I concluded that Nixon and Connally, whose shared first principle was flexibility, had not made any kind of binding deal. Instead, they were joined in a pragmatic "arrangement" based on short-term personal and political advantages. This judgment was subsequently confirmed in private talks with Connally and reported in *Harper's*.

Quite apart from Connally's role in presidential politics in 1972 and beyond, his arrival in Nixon's Washington fascinated me for another reason. He personified a new, little-understood "conservatism" widely shared among the business and financial leaders of the emerging Corporate State. Traditional

146

American capitalism, with its emphasis on ownership, enterprise, and the free market, was being replaced by a managerial state capitalism centered on Washington. The mainspring of the system was no longer the market mechanism; it was political bargaining and manipulation. In return for political submissiveness, large private interests were protected against the hazards of competition and the consequences of their own mistakes. The collaboration of organized labor, subsidized agriculture, regulated business, and other politicized elements of the Corporate State produced a peculiarly American kind of socialism, cloaked in the rhetoric of enterprise and dedicated to preserving the status and security of the privileged.

This socialism disguised as conservatism had its roots in the Southern wing of the Democratic party. Since the New Deal, the South and Southwest had enjoyed a disproportionate share of federal favors and money. The agriculture and industries (oil, aerospace, textiles) of these regions were especially dependent on government subsidies, contracts, and protection. But as the politics of these parts of the country became increasingly Republican at the presidential level, the influence of men such as Connally within the national Democratic party waned, and they saw persuasive reasons of self-interest to make other arrangements.

As he soon demonstrated, Connally represented another important new force — an aggressive economic nationalism which was determined to end outmoded and one-sided trading and monetary relationships with such prosperous competitors as the West Europeans and the Japanese. Accustomed to an official American internationalism, these complacent allies were shocked and frightened by Connally's table-pounding demands for a more equitable sharing of burdens and markets. He presided over a dollar devaluation and a unilateral retreat from convertibility with such a flair that this humiliation was made to appear a triumph. (The Japanese, who have their own unique form of business-government cooperation, as we shall see, were especially impressed with Connally's tactics, and made concessions which were unimaginable before he came on the scene.)

Thus, Connally's tenure at the Treasury, though scarcely a year and a half, shed light not only on his personality and political skills, but also on the system of power underlying the new American corporatism and the hard, demanding face it turned to the world.

I.

By nightfall, the news of Connally's appointment had heads shaking from Wall Street to Zurich to Tokyo. The President-watchers in Washington, who supposed they had Nixon figured for a methodical percentage player, were paralyzed with amazement. Known to the world beyond Texas chiefly as the survivor of Dallas, Connally had none of the credentials expected of a Secretary of the Treasury in a professedly sound-money Republican government. To be sure, he was a senior partner in a prestigious Houston law firm, a director of a couple of banks, and a self-made millionaire — his fortune derived mostly from his work in the fifties as lawyer, business manager, and, ultimately, coexecutor for Fort Worth oilman Sid W. Richardson. (His fee for helping settle the $105-

million Richardson estate amounted to $750,000.) But the sniffish Eastern reaction to Connally ("Can he add?") grew out of the undeniable fact that, millionaire or not, he wasn't a businessman or banker. His profession was politics.

During the week after Connally's appointment was announced, the top assistants at the Treasury heard nothing from him, but received calls from friends outside the government reporting that the new Secretary-designate was checking on them. This interlude allowed some tempers to cool and resignations to be reconsidered. When Connally finally showed up, he overwhelmed the staff with his charm, intelligence, and obviously diligent homework. He continued his education through prolonged question-and-answer sessions at the daily 8:45 A.M. staff meetings. "He's very emphatic and direct, and he doesn't waste any time getting to the point of what he wants to know," said one exposed to his interrogation. "If he doesn't like what he hears, he can really blow his cork."

Connally established two rules: he expected loyalty first and last, and he expected to be kept informed of everything his people were doing. The senior staff, a group of unusually able professionals, found they liked the discipline. "The Treasury is a vital force again," said a pleased assistant secretary. "It's great to be part of something that *matters*."

Significantly, the administration's new superlobbyist spent seven of his first ten days in office testifying on Capitol Hill. Even such initially critical liberals as Senator William Proxmire yielded to the subtle flattery implicit in the Secretary's preparation and informed answers. Connally didn't relax in the witness chair, but sat straight on the edge of his seat for hours at a stretch, all business, alert, respectful, performing a ritual with due regard for the rank of the men facing him. He made them feel *important*. When Proxmire remarked on how glad he was to see the Treasury restored to "strong hands," it was a compliment from one guardian of an institution's integrity to another.

On the legislative track, Connally started from several laps behind as the result of the administration's disregard of the realities of power in the hostile Congress. Democrats such as Chairman Wilbur Mills of the House Ways and Means Committee owed a Republican President precisely nothing, but they were willing to get along with someone who showed proper appreciation of their role and influence. However, the Nixon men systematically neglected and thus affronted the proud barons of the Hill, who, in turn, exacted an entirely predictable revenge. The administration's most important legislative proposals, relating to welfare reform and revenue-sharing, could be ransomed from Mills's committee only by paying whatever price he demanded in the way of amendment. In effect, Mills was writing the program on which Nixon was campaigning for re-election, evidence of presidential impotence which the Democrats intended to keep before the voters.

But the habit of getting along, confirmed by more than three decades in the House, was stronger in Mills than partisan instinct, and he received Connally with the polite respect he accords a suitable emissary. ("It's the first shrewd move Nixon's made," Mills was heard to remark privately after Connally's appointment. "He won't let those *twerps* stand between him and the President.") In their first encounter, Connally announced to Mills at the outset that the Treasury simply had to have all the relief it was seeking in a bill to lift the interest-rate ceiling on long-term financing. There could be no compromise. Several hours later, at the close of the hearing, Mills held out a compromise and Connally, adroitly stating it in the most acceptable form, took it. A Treasury assistant described the thought process behind the pattern: "Connally realizes that if Mills is against you, you've got a problem. But he also realizes that Mills will be *realistic*. They'll not only talk, they'll comprehend each other and work out an accommodation — something for Mills and something for the President."

One might suppose that Connally would be tied down by the chore of acting as human bridge between the White House and the Hill. Not so. He was as independent here as in his broader arrangement with the President. In the late spring of 1971, immediately following the dollar-exchange-rate crisis in Europe, Connally planned to join other American officials at a meeting of international bankers in Munich. The telephone rang. Mills wanted the Secretary as the lead-off witness on revenue-sharing. The Secretary was sorry, but he was going to Munich. The telephone rang again. Senator Fulbright wanted the Secretary as a witness for hearings he was holding. Sorry, Munich came first. Again the telephone rang. Ehrlichman said the President was expecting the Secretary to testify for the administration's revenue-sharing proposal. The Secretary told him what he had told Mills. When Ehrlichman called back, Connally refused the call. He was going to Munich, by God, and he did. Nixon, Mills, and Fulbright waited while Connally, correctly assessing the priorities, told off the Europeans and Japanese, demanding that they pay their fair share of defense costs and lower their trade barriers against American goods. "It isn't a question of cutting the number of troops in Europe," he told a reporter on the trip. "It's a question of who the hell is going to pay for them."

II.

Plain, direct talk was in short supply within the Nixon administration, which preferred the cotton-wrapped vocabulary of public relations. Hard, attentive listening was equally uncommon. Of the resulting communications gaps, perhaps the most surprising was the one separating Nixon men from their seemingly natural constituency, the corporate business community. Here, no less than on Capitol Hill, Connally succeeded by recognizing and repairing a failure of politics.

Any administration that brought on near-panic by making money tourniquet-tight (together with a desperate profit squeeze by planning a recession that did little to slow wage and cost inflation) would be unloved by corporate business, but it would not necessarily be hated. Businessmen, on the whole, were willing to listen to a plausible political hardluck story, especially from a Republican administration, *if* someone in Washington would hold their hands and hear their sad stories in return. This the Nixon administration strangely failed to do. One found an almost stunning ill will among Republican big businessmen, a bitter feeling of betrayal and exclusion. The people who paid for the bubble around the isolated and insulated President had been shut out, left to press their noses against the plastic facade. "Businessmen simply feel lost when they come down here," the Washington representative of a major manufacturing company said. "Nobody at the White House seems to have any clout. If they can't get through to John Mitchell, and they usually can't, they're out — and as far as they're concerned, the Democrats might as well be in."

Assistant to the President Peter Flanigan was the White House aide responsible for receiving businessmen, seemingly an ideal role for a former vice president of the investment banking firm of Dillon, Read, & Company, and the wealthiest member of the Nixon staff. But Flanigan's blue-chip background did not seem to facilitate sympathetic listening. Businessmen went away both empty-handed and angry. "I'm not going down to Washington again and be pushed around by Peter Flanigan," ran a New York executive's not untypical complaint. Flanigan was well intentioned and briskly industrious, but his entire political experience had been confined to Nixon campaigns. An official who watched Flanigan closely diagnosed a severe case of congenital campaignitis. "Peter wants to lecture the people who call on him. He uses his meetings to propagandize them, and they resent it. He thinks he's got to make votes. But he *has* their votes. What he needs is their trust and support. If he would only *listen* to their problems and agree with them when they're right . . ."

What businessmen were searching for in Nixon's Washington was, as one described it, "a good, helpful address." They found it at Connally's Treasury. This was not the case when David Kennedy, a member of the banking fraternity, was Secretary. Even if he understood the message of his callers, which was doubtful, they had little confidence that he knew what to do about it.

The Republicanism of corporate business is a very long way from what it used to be in the days of the Liberty League,

153

Sewell Avery, and even George Humphrey. The difference was dramatically apparent when Barry Goldwater, that robust champion of unfettered enterprise, failed to command big-business support for the excellent reason that he scared non-proprietorial managers out of their wits. Not so much with the Bomb, it should be noted, as with the specter of instability. He threatened to upset the system which, for all its imperfections, was familiar and comfortably endurable. The complaint against "creeping socialism" died when businessmen accepted society's leftward creep as the predictable trend, on the basis of which they made long-term plans and commitments. In the heyday of the Great Society, when Johnson combined respectable leftism with soaring profits, businessmen flocked to Washington, many of them still Republicans at heart, but happy to jump into the pocket of the attentive President.

What such businessmen demand of the Republicans in power is *not* the restoration of the ideology (still less, the practice) of free and competitive enterprise. What is demanded is soothing rhetoric and first-name clubbiness, but even more the same deal the Democrats provided. Businessmen want competent, gentlemanly socialism for themselves up to the established standard. They want the federal government to do less where their interests would be adversely affected (for example, in consumer protection) and a great deal more where their interests supposedly merge with a "public interest" requiring subsidy by the taxpayers. Capitalists and their anxious bankers are now unembarrassed to approach the government as the banker of last resort and to press for public money in support of insolvent private ventures. To be sure, such selective socialism, entailing nationalization of losses while profits remain private, involved a bit of ideological back-

154

pedaling, but businessmen had before them Nixon's exemplary declaration: "I am a Keynesian," meaning *We're all Democrats now, boys.*

Connally's popularity with the business community, as well as his standing at the White House, stemmed from the assumption that he knew what was expected of the Treasury and how to provide it. He demonstrated the soundness of his doctrine in his approach to the possible bankruptcy of the Lockheed Aircraft Corporation, the nation's largest defense contractor (and, incidentally, a major California employer).

In May 1971 he laid before Congress proposed legislation authorizing emergency loan guarantees to "major business enterprises," defined as those whose failure would cause severe economic distress and unemployment, failure of suppliers and customers, increased costs to the government resulting from contract termination, and reduction of "competition" and productive capacity within important industries. The entire $250-million loan guarantee requested was to be committed to Lockheed, so that some 30,000 employees might continue with production of the L-1011 Tristar airbus. This might very well be just the beginning, not only for Lockheed (independent estimates of the cash needed to complete the L-1011 program ranged well above $250 million) but also for other strapped companies.

The Emergency Loan Guarantee Act of 1971, which eventually passed the Senate by a single vote, may prove to be the modest forerunner of an updated version of the Reconstruction Finance Corporation. The RFC was the New Deal's instrument of state capitalism that became at once the biggest bank in the country and the largest single investor in the U.S. economy.

Connally approached his task of lobbying for the Lockheed loan bill with an asset singularly lacking in the born-yesterday Nixon administration — a historical memory. He'd not only read the minutes of the last meeting; as secretary to that gawky young New Dealer, Congressman Lyndon Johnson, he'd kept some of the minutes. Arthur Schlesinger's *Coming of the New Deal* describes another Texan, Jesse H. Jones of Houston, the RFC's czar, in terms that apply equally well to Connally: "He . . . loved power, was indifferent to ideology, never read books, had no sentimental illusions about the underdog, and kept his word. He could do business with anybody. . . ."

As a young newcomer to Washington, Connally watched Jones operate, recalling him as "a large man, very dignified looking, with great poise and bearing. He didn't know me, but I stood in considerable awe of him. He had an awareness of the interplay between business and politics that was rare for those days." Connally possessed a keen awareness of those same interconnections, which accounted for a good part of his influence within the Nixon administration. He saw with perfect clarity, for example, that the old RFC's practice of direct investment in ailing companies and banks was unnecessary as well as unfeasible. He appreciated the principle of leverage: for little or no direct cash outlay, and therefore with minimal impact on the budget, the Treasury could underwrite a great many private loans. The old RFC was an independent agency; a new RFC-type function built into the Treasury would reverse the process of the past generation and shift responsibility for management of the economy from the White House to the Treasury.

Connally's face was expressionless, his tone matter-of-fact as he discussed the possibility of reviving the RFC ("Many business concerns have reached the size where the financial community can't meet their needs in time of stress"). He anticipated events and positioned himself accordingly, noting: "The time to lay plans is when you're *not* under stress." He would be ready if and when power sought him out.

Businessmen sensed this foresight and responded to it. When Connally addressed them at their watering places, proclaiming the administration's line on the economy, they applauded with newfound enthusiasm. If the cheerful forecast was in error, as many suspected, they believed he would be ready to help them. After his talks, many approached him to say, in effect, "You're the only one we trust." While Connally professed to notice no increase in limousine traffic to the Treasury's side door, his assistants reported with satisfaction that "everybody and his brother" had been coming around for get-acquainted chats.

"Businessmen have been bothered by a confusion of voices," Connally remarked. "There's been no single spokesman for economic policy." His manner left no doubt that that spokesman now resided in the Treasury.

III.

The origins of the Nixon-Connally arrangement went further back than many supposed. During the 1968 campaign, when Nixon spoke of bringing a Democrat into his Cabinet, he had Connally in mind as a likely Secretary of Defense. In return for such consideration, the retiring governor of Texas was expected to adopt an attitude of benign neutrality toward the Nixon-Humphrey contest — "to go in the woods," as conservative Texas Democrats have regularly done in presidential years. Until well along in the campaign, Connally made himself inconspicuously useful to the Nixon forces, giving advice, encouraging contributions from individuals, and even recommending a friend as chairman of Citizens for Nixon.

But the cement holding the arrangement together was, of course, Nixon's apparent strength in Texas and in the country at large. As his lead in the polls melted away, so also did the arrangement with Connally. At the eleventh hour, the governor campaigned hard for Humphrey, hard enough, some Nixon men judged, to tip the state narrowly to the Democrats. "When the votes were counted in Texas," one of them recalls, "we suspected, as always in Texas, that they weren't being counted quite right. If Connally had felt sure that Nixon would win, he might have passed the word around the courthouses and prevented that from happening. But it was too close for him to take a chance, and so he let them count the votes in the usual way."

Nixon, who blamed everyone but himself for the loss of Texas, did not hold Connally's desertion against him. Indeed, as a professional, he may have respected him for guessing right and protecting his base. In any event, there were no lasting hard feelings. When Connally visited Washington early in 1969 and told White House political operatives that he had done "all he could" for Nixon, the friendly signal brought a response in kind. The President appointed Connally to his Advisory Council on Executive Organization, headed by industrialist Roy Ash. Later, as an additional mark of favor, Nixon named the Texan to the Foreign Intelligence Advisory Board.

A prominent Democrat who recommended Connally to Ash recalls: "When the council presented its final report to the President, Connally dominated the meeting. He explained in a very articulate, confident, and forceful way the reasoning behind the recommendations. That meeting lasted more than three hours, and Nixon came away very impressed."

Evidently he was. The Ash council reported to the President in the fall of 1970. A couple of days later Connally received a call from the White House reminding him of the next meeting of the intelligence advisory group. And, by the way, the President would like to see him privately while he was in Washington. Not long before, Treasury Secretary Kennedy had tendered his resignation and offered himself to Nixon as the pre-election sacrificial goat for the economy's stagnation. Nixon postponed the offer and held up the announcement of Kennedy's departure, but he had the resignation on his desk when he sat down with Connally.

When they talked around Thanksgiving, the President told Connally that he wanted him in the Cabinet and that the Treasury position was available, a significant order of priority: the man, not the function, for once mattered to Nixon, who tends to "slot" people like parts of a machine. Connally asked for a few days to think it over. When he returned to his suite at the Madison Hotel late that Thursday afternoon, however, a message was waiting. The President wished to see him at breakfast the following Monday.

Connally is as susceptible as the next man to that sort of flattering hard sell, and that weekend he made his decision to accept the offer. An important factor, say friends in Texas, was Connally's boredom with the good, fat life of a rich lawyer and rancher. "After you've spent most of your adult life at the head table, it's a helluva letdown to be just another citizen." There were no more political worlds left to conquer in Texas. Over the horizon lay the important prizes, but there was no apparent way of moving toward them within the Democratic party.

He made his decision without consulting Lyndon Johnson, he explained afterward, "because I didn't feel that I was at liberty to tell him — the President had asked me not to talk about it with anyone." The Connally-Johnson connection was extremely complex, characterized by the strain of opposing emotions. Through the years, Connally had served Johnson with unquestioned loyalty and was always there when needed, but more than any other member of the Johnson inner circle, he remained his own man, with his own firmly held convictions. Johnson simultaneously valued and resented this independence. He referred to Connally as "a big man," a term of praise, but he sometimes found him a formidable critic for just that reason.

One day in the spring of 1960, Johnson, Connally, and House Speaker Sam Rayburn were driving along Pennsylvania Avenue in the then Senate majority leader's car. An argument was in progress: Connally and Rayburn were telling Johnson that he could not both run the Senate and run for President, and that if he had any idea of heading off Jack Kennedy, he'd goddamned well better get moving. Johnson was unwilling to commit himself. The argument grew louder and the profanity more explicit. Finally Connally lost all patience. *"Stop this goddamned car,"* he shouted at the startled driver. *"I'm getting out."* Rayburn, in spite of his girth and years, hurried after him while Johnson sat fuming. Rayburn caught Connally, reasoned with him, and brought him back to the car; the three rode on to the Capitol, arms folded and silent. Over lunch on Kennedy's Inaugural Day, a friend remembers, Connally showed more than a trace of displeasure with the man who had settled for second place. "Want to know what's wrong with Lyndon?" he said. "He's ashamed of being a Texan, and I'm not."

Contrary to the impression current at the time, Johnson did not promote Connally's appointment as Secretary of the Navy. "Speaker Rayburn initiated it," said Connally, crisply setting the record straight. In spite of much speculation (which he did nothing to discourage), Johnson did not figure in the Nixon-Connally arrangement. At first, the former President showed his pique at being left out by threatening to oppose both Nixon *and* Connally in 1972 if his faithless friend joined the G.O.P. ticket. Later, Johnson being Johnson, he complimented Connally's performance and bragged that *he* was the one who got John the job. One of the capital's many malicious habits is the reordering of history to accord with current realities of power, and so Washingtonians were heard repeating the quip that "Connally was never Johnson's protégé — it was the other way around." It wasn't, of course, but the fiction accurately depicted Connally's prospects.

When he arrived at the Treasury, Democrats in Congress — and elsewhere — frankly expressed their intense curiosity as to where he stood, for that would guide their relations with him and the administration. At Connally's confirmation hearing, Senator Russell Long brushed aside the customary question of financial conflict and raised the intriguing question of "potential political conflict." Recalling that he and Connally had campaigned for the Kennedy-Johnson ticket in 1960, Long drawled, "I think if you and I had stayed home, President Nixon might have been in the presidency eight years sooner. How do you explain being here under the present circumstances?" Connally drawled in reply that the President "convinced me . . . that I could contribute something to his administration and thus to the welfare of this country . . . And I suppose I was vain enough to believe it and silly enough to try it." The printed record does not show that the chairman and the witness exchanged winks, but they might as well have done so — it was a well-played scene, the kind that makes Congress the best theater in Washington. In this instance, Long received the assurance he was looking for: Connally was public-spirited, vain, and, at least for the time being, still a Democrat.

IV.

It was not difficult in the summer of 1971 to see how Connally served Nixon — as counselor, companion, upright advocate, clever lobbyist, and generalissimo to the worried captains of industry. And it was rather plain that the President's trust and favor satisfied Connally's own estimate of himself. Yet it was unclear how their arrangement might mature into a full-fledged deal.

If there is a thread of consistency running through Connally's career, it is his reluctance ever to make an irrevocable move. He is a devoted partisan of his present choice — until he changes his mind. "You should have a high regard for John's abilities," says one who has dealt closely with him. "But you should also have grave reservations about how far you can trust him. He's always loyal — to whatever he feels like being loyal to." A friend in New York who has known Connally for twenty years remarks: "He's the hardest trader you'll ever know, always calculating advantage for advantage."

At this stage of Connally's life and career, the only remaining prize is, of course, the presidency. John Connally *looks* like a President; indeed, he looks and sounds too much like a recent President for his own good. So what if his politics are not smart-left? At least he *has* politics. He is *alive,* this six-foot-two, blue-eyed, silver-haired Texan, and behind that strong smile and courtly-folksy manner he is thinking, scheming, calculating two responses ahead of his soft, easy drawl. He is at ease at the center. The hard fact is that Connally is equipped to be President; the harder fact for him to face is that he needs a break, an opening quite beyond his ability to force, if he is to gain a crack at the biggest prize before time runs out. The only strategy available seems the nonstrategy of patiently awaiting an opportunity that may not come.

One day in the spring of 1971, Connally received me in his spacious third-floor corner office overlooking the Ellipse. While he sat relaxed on the sofa and sipped black coffee, a sculptor worked unobtrusively in clay. From the likeness of Connally would be struck the Secretary's Medal, a vanity item the Treasury issues in honor of each new arrival. The first bills bearing his signature would roll off the presses the following week. In an anteroom, Flanigan and various minor assistants waited to be admitted. Connally, as he strolled past his secretary's desk, took a piece of candy from a jar.

"You know," he remarked, smiling expansively in the manner of a man well pleased with himself, "I thought I would be putting myself in a difficult position coming here. But I'm

163

not finding it difficult at all." He rolled the candy over his tongue. "I'm in the fortunate position of having been asked."

V.

Connally resigned from the Cabinet in mid-May 1972. Thereafter, through little fault of his own, his position became steadily less fortunate and his future less promising. Before the dimensions of the Watergate scandal became apparent, Connally assumed the chairmanship of "Democrats for Nixon," took due credit for the President's election sweep, and prepared for the next scheduled step in their evolving relationship, the announcement of his switch to the Republican party. But by then the dam of Watergate revelations had burst, and each time Connally scheduled a press conference, another wave of bad news forced him to postpone it. Not until the spring of 1973 did he officially cross the party line, just as the Haldeman-Ehrlichman White House apparatus was coming apart.

Connally then made a pair of mistakes. He allowed himself to be entrapped into becoming a part-time, unpaid "special adviser" to the beleaguered President, which forced him to resign his lucrative directorships and take a leave of absence from his Houston law firm. Then he made the greater error of telling Nixon in very blunt terms that he should clean out the White House staff from top to bottom, firing everyone tainted in the slightest degree by the Watergate cover-up. This was the kind of advice that Nixon, for reasons which became apparent, did not wish to hear. Connally received the familiar silent treatment. Finally, after a month spent mostly waiting around his Mayflower Hotel suite for the telephone to ring, Connally resigned again and went home to Texas.

The collapse of the Nixon administration discouraged other members of the Texas Democratic establishment from following Connally's party-switching example, at least until the full extent of the damage to the Republican party was known. In mid-1974, Connally was damaged by the allegations of a former lawyer for the milk producers' interest group, who claimed that he had given the then-Secretary of the Treasury a $10,000 bribe for helping to boost milk price supports. Connally denied any wrong-doing, but in the post-Watergate climate even an innocent Texas wheeler-dealer could not reasonably aspire to the Presidency. Connally seemed finished politically. This was ironic because the economy of the Corporate State was faltering, and the politician who best understood how the system worked would have been the logical choice to oversee its emergency repair.

Scoop Jackson:
The Last New Frontiersman

AT THE 1972 DEMOCRATIC NATIONAL CONVENTION, the cause of Senator Henry Martin (Scoop) Jackson was hopeless and he knew it. Yet he refused to withdraw. The final tally of the delegates showed 1,715 votes for the nominee, Senator George McGovern, and only 534 votes for the runner-up Jackson. What, many of the angry McGovernites wondered, was the die-hard Jackson trying to prove?

Similar question marks had hovered over Jackson throughout his belated, poorly organized bid for the nomination. To chic-left liberals, he seemed a faintly ridiculous figure as he loped through airports, a garment bag slung over his shoulder and a speech warning against the Soviet Union's missile buildup in his pocket. The idea of a defender of Nixon's Vietnam policy, the military-industiral complex, the SST, the FBI, and good old-fashioned patriotism campaigning to lead the "reformed" Democratic party struck these sophisticated observers as, well, funny, and they would have laughed out loud except that Jackson was basically a decent fellow. So, as a kindness, some of them included him among the very dark horses, a notch or two above Representative Wilbur Mills.

In mid-1974, however, the continuing Jackson candidacy is

no longer puzzling or amusing, but accepted as an increasingly serious enterprise. Only Senator Edward Kennedy and Governor George Wallace stand higher in the early polls, and Jackson is gaining on Wallace, whose constituency resembles his own. The point he intended to make at the 1972 convention is now abundantly clear: the McGovernites, by abandoning the broad middle of the American electorate, committed political suicide; and if the Democrats want to win in 1976, they will have to come home to the centrist position and philosophy Jackson upholds. When Senator McGovern declined to fight for control of the party's wreckage after his defeat, Jackson's aides and backers helped engineer the choice of a moderate party chairman, Robert Strauss of Texas.

Events since the 1972 election have given Jackson a powerful lift. The Vietnam war has faded from public consciousness, and so have home-front antagonisms. The October 1973 Yom Kippur War, launched with Soviet connivance, sent many pro-Israel liberal Democrats scurrying toward Jackson's corner. The erosion of American-Soviet détente confirmed the judgment of the man who had raised early warnings against its pitfalls. The Arab oil boycott against the United States suddenly made Americans aware of a potential energy crisis — and there was Jackson, on television and in the headlines, taking charge on the energy front. Almost single-handed, he pushed the stalled Alaskan pipeline bill through the Congress, an impressive display of legislative clout.

As Watergate devastated the Nixon administration and Congress regained authority, Jackson emerged as its single most influential member. Indeed, as Nixon and Kissinger and the Soviet leaders negotiated on trade, joint energy-resource development, limitations on nuclear weaponry, a

Middle East settlement, and other issues of the highest importance, they all felt another presence at the summit — Jackson,
whose demonstrated ability to command the Senate on such
questions gave him virtual veto power.

It is too early to judge whether Jackson will be able to trans-
late this "inside" power into national visibility and vote-getting
appeal in the 1976 primaries. Circumstances beyond his control — Kennedy's decision on whether to run, Wallace's
health — could have decisive impact on his candidacy. Yet
Jackson undeniably has come a long way since the summer of
1971, when I followed him on the campaign trail for the *New
York Times Magazine.*

I.

One day in the early spring of 1969, a high-ranking aide to
President Nixon and a trusted friend from Capitol Hill sat
talking in a West Wing office in the White House. The aide
lowered his voice and spoke, as politicians say, "within the
family." The President's proposed Safeguard ABM system,
the subject of this strategy meeting, was in trouble in the Senate, he said. Beyond that, he foresaw no end of trouble on a
wide range of defense and foreign-policy issues, especially the
Vietnam war. Soon, he said, it would be Nixon's War.

The visitor, who had the unique distinction of having declined *two* invitations to join the Nixon Cabinet, listened sym-
pathetically, then delivered an avuncular judgment. "Don't
worry about the war. You ought to worry about the economy — *that* will be your undoing."

Senator Jackson, the Nixon administration's favorite Democrat, gave that advice. He acted on it as a candidate for the Democratic presidential nomination in 1972, and he's still betting it will pay off. Jackson believes the Democrats will make "a serious mistake" if they count on Watergate to win the White House in 1976. The winning appeal, he is convinced, will be based on "bread and butter issues" such as jobs and inflation.

The seriousness of the Jackson candidacy is no longer in doubt. It goes to the nature of the man who has made up his mind he *can* be President, and to the nature of the challenge he poses to his fragmented party.

"Scoop" Jackson is a senator's senator, a studious and diligent member in good standing of the exclusive Inner Club. A trim, youthful sixty-one-year-old (he swims a quarter mile daily in the Senate pool), he thrives on an unusually heavy workload: chairman of the powerful Interior and Insular Affairs Committee, chairman of the Permanent Investigations Subcommittee on Government Operations, chairman of the same Committee's Subcommittee on National Security, third-ranking majority member of the Armed Services Committee (and chairman of the special subcommittee to monitor the U.S.-Soviet Strategic Arms Limitations Talks), and member of the Joint Committee on Atomic Energy. Jackson is the Senate's acknowledged authority on nuclear armament and strategy, and even those colleagues who disagree strongly with his hard-line views respect his detailed grasp of these uninviting subjects. He exercises similar authority in the field of energy policy, where his views are closer to the liberal consensus.

Jackson is also a professional's professional, with three full decades of shrewd and successful politicking behind him. In 1970 he won a fourth term in the Senate by the almost incredible margin of 709,000 votes in his small state, an 83.9 percent majority unmatched in the nation's two-party contests. The impetus of that victory led him with characteristic caution to test his belief that "an unclaimed constituency" lay within the broad middle ranks of his party, and that the efforts of the other candidates to appease the vocal left-wing opened up an opportunity for someone who was "different."

It says a great deal about the condition and prospects of the Democratic party after the Vietnam ordeal that Jackson should be so singular. For he is the very model of what the party's presidential nominees traditionally have been. He is a champion of continuity, who takes his foreign policy from John F. Kennedy's Inaugural Address, his domestic policy from Lyndon Johnson's Great Society, and his fundamental stance vis-à-vis the electorate from the New and Fair Deal tradition of speaking to and for the "common man," more recently known as "forgotten" and "silent." He acts as though he were the representative of a governing consensus, based on interests rather than ideology. He stands where the majority of the voters presumably stand: somewhat to the right on social issues, to the left on economic issues, and, withal, astride the commanding center of American politics.

In one of those curious reversals of role that occur periodically in our party system, the Republicans, against the undertow of cherished moralisms, have tried to behave the way Democrats used to behave. Simultaneously, the more energetic and well-publicized elements of the Democratic party have yielded to the compulsion to abandon interest politics for the heady delights of moral and ideological politics. In 1972, modishly leftist Democrats mouthed the 1964 slogan of the Goldwaterites: *This time,* we must offer a choice, not an echo.

Meanwhile, Republican politicians viewed Jackson with a mixture of admiration, approval, and apprehension. When dealing with the press, they invariably trotted out the story — true enough before Nixon was elected — that a charismatic opponent such as Senator Edward M. Kennedy would pose the greatest threat to the President's re-election. But the way G.O.P. professionals, especially the image-makers at Republican party headquarters, fairly purred as they mentioned "Chappaquiddick" gave the little game away. A highly visible and vulnerable opponent, particularly one pushed leftward, would provide what Nixon badly needed to divert attention from his record: a target. Jackson, in contrast, was much the same kind of low-key, low-profile personality as Nixon, though he prefers dark, conservatively cut Ivy League clothes rather than the executive-suite uniform of Nixonites.

It is not generally appreciated that a "centrist" Democrat could manage a plurality in a three- or four-man presidential race, while a "centrist" Republican very likely could not. Such a Democrat probably would cut deeply enough into the Wallace following on his right to more than offset defections and even a splinter-party insurgency on his left. If such a Democrat called for strong U.S. defenses, the main tenet of present-day conservatism, he would not only be invulnerable to right-wing attacks; he might also pick up a fair number of disaffected Republicans.

Such calculations were in the minds of Republican leaders across the country in June 1971, as they answered a query from the *Christian Science Monitor*. Although Jackson then stood near the bottom in the preference polls, they placed him at the head of the list, above Kennedy, Muskie, and Humphrey, as Nixon's "toughest" opponent. Obviously, these

Republican professionals feared the script enthusiastically projected by Sterling Munro, Jackson's chief of staff: "Jackson would neutralize Nixon's strengths — foreign policy and national security — and knock him out of the box on his weakness — management of the economy."

But Munro, who went to work for Jackson more than twenty years ago while still in high school, was as much a realist as his boss, and his enthusiasm subsided in the face of the inescapable sequence of events in 1971–1972. "The real tough — perhaps the impossible — thing is to get fifty-point-one percent of the delegates at the Democratic Convention. The election is easier." Another Jackson strategist admitted: "I can think of a dozen scenarios for winning the election, but I have trouble coming up with a really good one that gives us the nomination."

The only possible scenario, and the one Jackson pursued, was a frontal assault on the nomination through the primaries. Unavoidably, however, the victory scenario based on a string of hard-fought primaries aroused bitter intraparty antagonisms and increased the chance of a left-wing revolt. Typical of the attitude toward Jackson among antiwar Democrats was Paul O'Dwyer's dismissal of a Nixon-Jackson-Wallace choice: "No true Democrat could support any of them. Under the circumstances, we would need a new populist party." Frank Mankiewicz, press secretary for the late Senator Robert F. Kennedy and a key adviser to Senator McGovern, went further, declaring: "If Jackson gets the nomination, a fourth party is inevitable."

The even-tempered Jackson blasted off like a Minuteman missile at such threats: "Let those people go form a fourth party. I'm a liberal, but I'm not an extremist. There's a real danger in our party that a few will try to impose their will on the majority." In 1970, he pointed out, antiwar activists imposed their platform on the state Democratic convention in Washington. Running against the official party plank on Vietnam in the primary, Jackson rolled up 87 percent of the vote in crushing a "peace" candidate. "So let the extremists go," he says. "You gain much more than you lose."

II.

Behind these words lay genuine, deeply held conviction, for Jackson, in his own way, is ideologically committed. During his twelve years in the House of Representatives and twenty-one years in the Senate, he has supported every important piece of domestic liberal legislation. His claim to the "best" voting record on civil rights among the Democratic candidates goes unchallenged, and it is supported by the NAACP's Roy Wilkins, who describes the Jackson record as "very good." His credentials as a conservationist are outstanding: he was the chief sponsor of the National Environmental Policy Act, a landmark bill passed after three years of effort in 1969; and he is the only elected official ever to receive the Sierra Club's award. (To those who complain that "the senator from Boeing" tarnished his record as a protector of the environment by his support for the supersonic transport, he retorts that complaints against the SST were either unfounded or unconvincing, and he condemns the "environmental extremists" who would sacrifice economic growth on the altar of half-baked ideology.) Finally, in exasperated defense of his status as a progressive, Jackson recalls his outspoken opposition to Senator Joseph R. McCarthy in the McClellan subcommittee hearings of the early 1950s, and wears as the badge of his liberalism the enmity of "both McCarthys."

All that long, loyal, and productive service to liberalism, say Jackson's enemies on the left, doesn't count anymore. They brand him the "conservative" in the Democratic field because he has been frightfully "wrong" on what they regard as the paramount issues of Vietnam and the overall U.S. defense posture. Such left-liberal Democrats advance an exclusive and restrictive definition of liberalism (O'Dwyer's "true Democrat") as the test of a candidate's fitness to lead a party which has succeeded in the past by opening its doors to almost all comers. Only in the sense that he wants to continue that inclusive politics is Jackson "conservative."

The opposing tendencies pulling the Democratic party apart in 1972 were clearly apparent in the ratings of the Senate presidential candidates by Americans for Democratic Action and the AFL-CIO Committee on Political Education (COPE). In 1961–1963, Jackson's 92 percent ADA rating was the same as Eugene McCarthy's and slightly better than Muskie's. By 1969–1971, as the ADA included in its ratings votes on Vietnam and defense issues, Jackson had slid to a 56 percent mark, while Muskie shone as an exemplar of the new liberalism at 91 percent. Over the same ten-year period, Jackson's rating by COPE, with the exception of 1963–1965, stayed at a straight-A 100 percent.

"The ADA has nothing to do with the Democratic party," said Jackson in late 1971. That put his challenge to his party about as bluntly as it could be put. Those who shared the ADA's world-view expected to have a great deal to do with choosing the 1972 Democratic candidate and setting the party's course for the next decade.

In the epilogue to the 1971 edition of their book *The Real Majority*, Richard M. Scammon and Ben J. Wattenberg framed the "big question" for the Democratic National Convention to resolve: Is the Democratic party a movement or a political party? Arguing that "compromise and coalition are the essential tools of political action," the authors warned against heeding the siren call of "upper-middle-class elitists" who want to institutionalize their movement, and who have forgotten that "the man who chooses the Presidents of this country is the man who bowls on Thursday night."

In the spring of 1971, Wattenberg joined Jackson as a part-time counselor. He had served on Johnson's White House staff and assisted Hubert Humphrey in his 1970 campaign to recapture his Senate seat in Minnesota — a year in which the Scammon-Wattenberg thesis of the ascendancy of The Social Issue was proved as a number of liberal candidates made quick switches in their campaigning styles to get on the right side of the "law-and-order" line drawn by Vice President Agnew and other Republicans.

The fact that "Scoop" Jackson was a liberal who had long felt comfortable on the side of social order *and* measured social progress attracted Wattenberg. And the senator, then testing his belief that the "real" Democratic majority of moderates lacked a candidate, liked the stream of ideas and words the lively Wattenberg served up. Intellectuals and politicians do not see reality the same way, and shouldn't, but in this instance an unusual collaboration occurred.

It bore fruit in a May 1971 speech in that citadel of Nixon Republicanism, San Diego (the site originally chosen for the 1972 G.O.P. National Convention). The "different" Democrat brought a Jefferson-Jackson Day dinner to attention by going beyond the standard antiadministration fare. Jackson laced into "an absolute radical left fringe that is attempting to steal the Democratic party from the people," a faction "characterized by their total intolerance for other views." These radicals, he declared, have "a gloom-and-doom view of America that denies the existence of progress" as they engage in "the politics of the emotional binge." None of the Democratic party's leaders were in the ranks of this radical fringe, Jackson reassured his listeners. "But it is quite clear that some run the risk of marching to its drums. They are having trouble hearing the voice of the people because the noise from the absolute left is so loud. I'm afraid that by wooing this faction, by apologizing for it, by excusing it and glorifying it, the Democratic party can be dragged down to defeat."

Jackson, in cataloguing the excesses of the absolute left, sounded surprisingly like Spiro T. Agnew — as some liberal journalists remarked with horror — but he also struck a note of class and cultural empathy with "the little guy" missing from the keyboard of Republican abstractions. For example, on the "gut" issue of law-and-order, he said in San Diego:

"Who could possibly be against the preservation of law or the preservation of order in America? Well, first the absolute left said that law-and-order was a codeword for racism. Then they said it was a codeword for repression. Then they said cops are pigs. Meanwhile who takes it on the chin? Not the fellow in the new high-rise downtown. He has a twenty-four-hour security guard. Not the fellow in the exclusive suburb. Not the student at the cloistered university. No, it is the vulnerable little guy again who is victimized. There are elderly people, there are poor people, there are black and Chicano people in this country who are afraid to walk out in the street at night or during the day. Talk about repression!"

In his peroration, Jackson sounded the theme that recurred in his 1971–1972 speeches: "The absolutists . . . have lost faith in American universities; they have lost faith in the American system of justice; they have lost faith in America's foreign policy. *They have, in fact, lost faith in America.*"

Appearing before the convention of the New York State AFL-CIO in August 1971, Jackson came down hard on the antiwar left in a speech interrupted repeatedly by bursts of applause. "I do not want to see the Democratic party become a party which gives any aid and comfort whatever to people who applaud Vietcong victories or wave Vietcong flags. Our party has room for hawks and doves, but not for mocking-birds who chirp gleefully at those who are shooting at American boys."

From that forum Jackson went directly to a conference with the editors of the New York *Daily News,* whose politics seldom give union members much to cheer about. They too were delighted with Jackson's patriotic line, and listened apprecia-tively as he fielded questions for more than an hour. The next day the *Daily News* gave him a handsome editorial pat on the back. What the *Daily News* editors did not know was that Jackson had met a week earlier in Washington with nine members of the Young People's Socialist League, serious-minded campus foes of the New Left and admirers of the senator's no-nonsense progressivism. Though Jackson is no Socialist and told his visitors so, he welcomed their offer to contribute material on the plight of the abused workingman for his New York speech, which they did.

This easy passage between hostile camps illustrates Jackson's rare knack for winning friends and influencing people who don't have a kind word for each other. As his immense suc-cess in his two-party state attests, his appeal transcends his positions and philosophy. A Republican businessman in Seat-tle expresses a common attitude: "Hell, I don't agree with a lot of things Scoop stands for. But he's sincere, honest, and aw-fully hard-working. He wants to do what's *fair*. What more can you ask of a politician?"

The man whom *Time,* in its perplexity, calls "a perplexing study in political paradox" defies both the ideological labeling process, which requires liberals to be doves, and the conven-tional wisdom that a political "personality" must have a strik-ing image and lots of charisma. Jackson is almost devoid of color. Friends asked for anecdotes about him respond with head-shaking and pained silence. Nevertheless, the attrac-tions of personality are abundantly evident in his vote-pulling power. "I guess," says a long-time friend, "that the answer is that Scoop simply has a lot of old-fashioned virtues that peo-ple still admire." An image-conscious aide agrees, and adds: "We've been on such an antivirtue kick that maybe Jackson can make the old virtues seem fresh."

III.

Whether or not he can, he comes by his ways in the classic American manner of work-and-win. The son of Norwegian immigrants (his father worked in the lumber mills and later became a minor union official), Jackson was born and raised in the Puget Sound city of Everett, Washington. His older sis-ter, Gertrude, bestowed his nickname. She thought Henry resembled a comic-strip character named "Scoop, the Cub Re-porter," appearing in the Everett *Daily Herald,* who kept a jump ahead of the competition. As a carrier-boy for the newspaper in the 1920s, Jackson showed that quality. He had cards printed advising the readers on his route to call him, rather than the circulation manager, if they had any complaints. His enterprise paid off with a national award for three years' service as a carrier without a single delivery complaint — at least none that anyone in the *Herald* circulation office knew about.

In 1938, three years after receiving his law degree from the University of Washington, Jackson was elected prosecuting attorney of his home county, Snohomish. Two years later, at the age of twenty-eight, he was elected to Congress from Washington's Second District. When a young man from Massachusetts named Kennedy arrived in the House in 1946, Jackson, a contemporary who had learned the ropes, struck up a friendship with him that grew close and soon extended to other members of the Kennedy family. Jackson helped young Robert Kennedy get his first job in government, as Democratic counsel on the staff of the McClellan subcommittee. In the Georgetown touch-football games on Sunday afternoons, the wiry but compact Jackson carefully avoided collisions with the hard-charging kid brother, Teddy — something he may not be able to do in the future.

At the 1960 Democratic Convention, the nominee and his manager-brother wanted Jackson on the ticket, but Joe Kennedy, giving sentiment its customary low priority, insisted that second place be offered to Johnson, who astonished everyone by taking it. At John Kennedy's request, Jackson dutifully assumed the party chairmanship for the campaign. ("That wasn't the job for Scoop," says a friend. "It was an all-out partisan job, and he just isn't that way.") More than once during his White House years, Johnson remarked to the man the Kennedys had really wanted: "You might have been sitting here."

Through the 1960s Jackson enjoyed the satisfactions of the Senate, where his seniority steadily accumulated, and of family life. Long one of the most eligible bachelors in Washington, Jackson was in an elevator on his way to the opening session of the Senate in January 1961 when his good friend, Senator Clinton P. Anderson of New Mexico, entered with his new secretary, a striking blonde named Helen Eugenia Hardin. Just before Christmas that year, she and Senator Jackson were married. They now have a daughter, Anna Marie, and son, Peter Hardin, and Jackson includes among his titles "Father of the Year," bestowed in 1970.

Just a few days before he took his children on their "first sleeping-bag camp-out" in the Cascade Mountains in the summer of 1971, Jackson mused about rearing a family in a way that helps explain the kind of liberal he is — and the source of his nonpolitical, nonideological appeal. "You can't subcontract the job of being Poppa and Momma. Some people think you can solve every social problem by writing a check — that's ridiculous. The need running through our social legislation is the need to strengthen family life, which is weakening among the poor and the affluent alike."

Jackson sponsored the act creating the Youth Conservation Corps, which in its prototype phase employed 3000 youths in the national parks, and he insisted, over objections from other liberals, that the corps should include recruits from various social and economic backgrounds. "They wanted to know why we should send middle-class kids off to camp in the woods. Well, I think the Job Corps was a mistake because it failed to reflect the genius of our society — its diversity. You need a balance between the deprived and the affluent, so that they can help and learn from each other." Put so reasonably, the revival of the New Deal–era CCC could not fail to win over the most adamant reactionary.

In late 1968, President-elect Nixon tried to lure Jackson away from the Senate with the portfolio of Secretary of Defense. He wanted not only a prominent Democrat, but also one who understood the intricacies of the mammoth defense budget and the Pentagon bureaucracy. Jackon was eminently qualified and considerably tempted, but he finally declined. Later, as the scramble to complete the Nixon Cabinet became hectic, Jackson was offered the job of Secretary of State, which would have produced dancing in the streets of Tel Aviv, where the Senator is regarded as Israel's stoutest ally. Again he declined.

Jackson, out of respect for "the office of the presidency," refuses to disclose his reasons for staying out of the Nixon government. Friends and aides say that Jackson, after taking discreet soundings among senior Democratic colleagues, came to the conclusion, as one of them puts it, that "the thing wouldn't work politically." At the sacrifice of his powerful position in the Senate, Jackson would have acquired additional prestige, to be sure, but also demanding executive responsibility and very uncertain influence inside and outside the White House.

It wasn't enough, especially if entering a Republican administration meant abandoning all ambition for national office within the Democratic party. In any event, Jackson's high standing with Nixon remained unimpaired, and his steadfast support for the administration on Vietnam, the ABM, and other defense issues earned him a solid place within the "ideological majority" the President sought to build. During the 1970 election, the White House ignored the requests of the

Washington State G.O.P. and gave not the slightest assistance to Jackson's Republican opponent.

IV.

After his re-election, Jackson received pleas from many Democrats that he "take these people on" — that is, the anti-war left — and give the party's moderates a rallying-figure. Starting with "no plan at all," Jackson went on the speaking circuit, presenting a twofold message: the Democratic party should stand by the tradition of progressive liberalism; and it should link a strong domestic economy with a "prudent" defense policy.

As Jackson sees it, the highest priority of U.S. domestic *and* foreign policy is the avoidance of recession. "Without a healthy economy, we can't generate the resources to meet other priorities, at home and overseas." If that sounds too foreign-policy oriented, Jackson points out that "state and local governments lost some $3.5 billion in tax revenues alone in 1970 because the economy wasn't operating at the full employment level." Like other Democrats, however, he lost almost his entire prescriptive program for the economy when President Nixon announced his New Economic Policy in August 1971.

The Nixon bombshell from Camp David caught Jackson on the eve of an appearance before the Veterans of Foreign Wars Convention in Dallas. This is a Middle American and hard-hat audience combined, with the special twist that the hats are World War II and Korean War helmets. (Perhaps the flavor of the occasion is best captured by the recollection of a speechwriter for Lyndon Johnson: "We were on Air Force One and on our way to the VFW Convention, and the President finally got around to looking at the text. He didn't like it at all. He leaned into the aisle and hollered the length of the plane: 'Put some goddamned machine-gun bullets in it!' ")

That evening, by the time the proud recipient of the VFW's J. Edgar Hoover Gold Medal Award had said several hundred indifferently chosen words and Jackson was introduced, it was well past nine o'clock. Only a rat-a-tat speech could have roused the audience. But the machine-gun bullets had been left out of Jackson's text, and he plodded through it haltingly, as he often does with prepared material. Toward the end, however, he spoke off-the-cuff, and every line crackled through the room, winning applause that became a standing ovation.

"This is a good country, a great country, a country with un-limited possibilities if we have faith in the future based solidly on faith in ourselves," cried Jackson, echoing vintage JFK rhetoric. "All of us want an America — *not* first *if, when,* or *but* — but an America that is first *period.*"

Later, relaxing in his seat in the first-class cabin of a Boeing jet winging across the country toward Seattle, Jackson refused a cocktail when the hostess rolled the cart by, but, showing his thrifty Norwegian upbringing, he took the two small bottles of Scotch to which he was entitled and stowed them in a large zipper bag at his feet. (He has, by his count, about one drink a week.)

He spoke about his approach to politics. "I feel that I'm in a position to speak my mind on the issues. I have a lot of faith in the common sense of the American people. They want it told the way it is. They're looking for someone calm, cool, and sensible — for a steady hand in a very unsteady world. Most of all, they want someone who will level with them. I think the American people are a lot more sophisticated in making political decisions than many politicians give them credit for."

After Watergate, there are few, if any, national politicians who possess Scoop Jackson's solid moral credentials and long-demonstrated empathy for the concerns of the ordinary citizen. If he can be nominated in 1976, Jackson can be elected President, probably by a real old-fashioned Democratic majority.

PART THREE

What Happened, U.S.A.?

Migrations and Escapes

I.

"EVERY FRESH GENERATION," wrote Tocqueville, "is a new people." In the 1960s in America, a vastly greater number of "new people" appeared than ever before in our history, a demographic explosion of youth — persons aged fourteen to twenty-four — that sent shock waves through our society, culture, and politics. This upsurge in the young population was a natural, indeed inevitable, consequence of the nation's soaring birthrate after World War II, yet it took the suddenly overwhelmed adult population by surprise. In the best of times, the process of tutoring, socializing, and assimilating "new people" is difficult. The sixties was not the best of times, and the process went very badly.

This was not entirely, or even mainly, the fault of the young. Always and everywhere, even within rigidly controlled societies such as Communist China, young people get into trouble with authority out of all proportion to their numbers — the Red Guards, after all, wound up menacing their frightened masters. As many social scientists have pointed out, the time between a child's physical maturity and social maturity has steadily lengthened. Education in advanced industrial nations now extends into the third decade of life, forcing postponement of the individual's passage from dependency to independence. Frustrated, physically mature young people are naturally prone to rebellion, and this is especially true when they enjoy economic security and a sense of immunity from the consequences of their actions, as did the most privileged and rebellious youth in America in the sixties.

Now that the youth explosion is past, we have a better understanding of what caused it. Daniel P. Moynihan has offered statistics and a retrospective hypothesis. The numbers are startling. From 1890 to 1960, the total increase in the American population aged fourteen to twenty-four was 12.5 million. In the 1960s alone, the same age group increased by 13.8 million persons, a 52 percent expansion within a single decade, five times faster than the average of the preceding seventy years. In the 1970s, the youth population will increase only 11 percent, and in the 1980s it will *decline* by 8 percent.

What happened in the 1960s, according to Moynihan, "is that suddenly a new social class was created in the United States, so large in its number that it was fundamentally isolated from the rest of society. It was isolated on campuses, it was isolated in slums, it was isolated in a way in the armed forces. . . . A youth culture developed. Youth acquired its own music, its own forms of dress, its own grammar, all to a degree without precedent in the United States." Concentrated and isolated youth provided the combustible material, and the independently changing attitudes toward social injustice, racial equality, patriotism, sex, drugs, and authority in general provided the sparks.

Yet the youthful nation-within-the-nation did not give birth to itself. Adults created it. They provided ideas, publicity, and cash. They were at once patrons and exploiters of the youth rebellion. The parents who gave their son, the campus radical, air-travel and telephone credit cards, a generous allowance, and a Honda bike were obviously doing their bit for the "revolution." The record and tape producers and denim clothing manufacturers who supplied the ingredients of the "youth culture" obviously were also inventing it a step ahead of the market's fast-changing taste. And the middle-aged intellectuals, mass communicators, and politicians, who were determined to prove themselves still "with it," were obviously indispensable as explainers and rationalizers. Without their sponsorship, the rebellion would have died of incoherence.

Despite the extraordinary weight of numbers, the process of socializing youth should not have broken down so extensively in the sixties. If the young did what came naturally, many of their elders did not. Most unnaturally, they opted out of the crucial responsibility their generation owed the next. Primitive tribes hidden away in the mist-covered valleys of New Guinea's Central Highlands recognize that the mature must not merely provide for the physical well-being of the dependent young; they must also teach them the way the tribe lives, what it believes, its customs and taboos, and the meaning of adulthood. These Stone Age people understand the law of life perfectly well, and they heed it so that their tribe may continue. But highly educated, affluent, and sophisticated Americans failed to comprehend this fundamental truth in the 1960s. As a result, they proved themselves inferior to savages in the way they shortchanged their children.

The power to determine what is defined as moral, Max Weber wrote long ago, is the ultimate power in society.

189

Adults in authority, beginning with parents, have wielded this power over the young throughout history. In the 1960s, however, too many adults were unable or unwilling to perform the role of moral arbiter. They fled from judgment and recoiled from power. Many inverted the tutelage relationship between the generations and tried to adopt the lifestyle and "new morality" of the young. (Decadence, a contemporary observer remarked, is a grandmother in a miniskirt.) Why did these adults cop out? From emptiness, envy, boredom, dread of age, fear of appearing illiberal — the catalogue of motives is endless. Of the tumultuous 1960s, Dr. W. Walter Menninger has said: "The real subversion in the world is not external — it is the emotional rebel within us all, the unacceptable infantile feelings which we adults must disown and deny. Everyone is seeking a scapegoat, someone outside who is responsible for what is taking place." This was the truly wrenching discontinuity of the decade: the flourishing of an adult infantilism which reinforced and made legitimate the self-destructive violence of the young.

The "new people" in the sixties were not only denied moral example. They were also cheated of the resource of historical memory — the tribal story. The young, isolated in their generation-ghettos, did not realize, and few elders informed them, that the sixties was not entirely unique. The sixties was connected to the fifties and the seventies. The young were entering a stream of time which flowed ceaselessly, carrying the consequences of remote events and the fulfillment of beginnings made long ago. Much of what seemed distinctive in the sixties — the youth cult's music, dress, drugs — had actually first appeared well upstream. Indeed, the main trends and concerns of American life, though distorted by the peculiar circumstances of the decade, did not fundamentally change and probably will reassert their force in the 1970s and beyond. By then, most of the "new people" of the sixties will have completed their difficult passage to adulthood, and it will be their turn to cope.

A look backward, then, may also provide a glimpse ahead.

II.

Between 1940 and 1960, two great migrations occurred within the United States: the movement of poor blacks from the land, and the movement of newly prosperous whites from the city.

America had first become a truly urban nation only as recently as 1920, when the census-takers found a bare majority (51 percent) of the population living in cities. Although the movement of people from countryside to city seemed commonplace as it occurred, a thread of continuing change in the nation's life binding together the social fabric, it was in fact revolutionary. As war and postwar prosperity expanded the internal shifts of population, the character of the nation changed profoundly. In the twenty years after 1940, the net out-migration from the farms was 17.4 million persons. During the 1950s, urban areas absorbed more than 100 percent of the total U.S. population growth; that is, for the first time in history, rural population, including farmers and nonfarmers, declined absolutely.

Within the South and on its borders, blacks had been moving from rural to urban areas since the Civil War. Cities such as Atlanta, New Orleans, Memphis, Baltimore, and Washington had large, well-established black populations. During the late forties and the fifties, the black emigration spilled out of the South. By 1960, almost a million and a half Southern blacks had moved to the cities of the North, the Midwest, and the rapidly growing Far West.

Between 1950 and 1960, the racial composition of the nation's large cities changed dramatically: the black population of New York rose from 10 percent to 14 percent; Chicago, from 14 percent to 23 percent; Philadelphia, from 18 percent to 26 percent; Detroit, from 16 percent to 29 percent; Los Angeles, from 9 percent to 14 percent; Cleveland, from 16 percent to 29 percent. Behind these impassive statistics lay an endlessly repeated biography of flight, hope, and, too often, at journey's end, disappointment. Everything outside the South was strange to the migrants, except the familiar vantage point of the underdog.

During World War II, when untrained white housewives were becoming riveters in defense plants, blacks moved relatively easily from field to factory because industry was willing to break the work down to the level of skills available. But in the postwar years, industry became more interested in holding down costs than in raising production. The jobs most readily automated were those requiring the least skill. To protect its increased investment per employee, both in capital equipment and benefits such as pensions, industry upgraded job qualifications, sometimes needlessly so. The unions, terrified by the specter of automation, protected the job security of those already employed and rigorously enforced seniority rules governing hiring and layoffs, which discriminated against the black newcomers. Other more subtle forms of union discrimination also were practiced with the employers' connivance.

By 1960 about 12 percent of the nonwhite labor force was unemployed, more than twice the rate for white workers. Among young blacks between the ages of eighteen to twenty-four, the jobless rate was estimated at perhaps five times that of young whites. The idleness of the black teen-ager was an urgent social problem, but even more ominous was the condition of working black adults who seemed to be on a treadmill. From the outbreak of World War II through the Korean War, blacks had surged ahead, lifting their median income from 41 percent to 61 percent of the white median. During the fifties, however, they stopped catching up and began losing ground.

As blacks flocked into the cities in the 1950s, whites moved out. New York lost 50,000 a year; Chicago, 15,000; Cleveland, 3,000. Suburbia grew more than *ten* times faster than the cities. The factor of race accounted for much of this exchange of population, but it was very far from the whole explanation. Even if the racial composition of the cities had remained stable, a large-scale white exodus probably would have occurred. Henry Ford, that mirror of the American mind, had once predicted: "We shall solve the city problem by leaving the city." In the 1920s and 1930s, cities grew along the expanding lines of public transportation, but many of those who rode streetcars and subways dreamed of buying an automobile and escaping beyond the city. Postwar prosperity made their escape possible. Within ten years after V-J Day, there were twice as many motor vehicles in the United States as before the war. Those who had been city-dwellers by necessity — especially young people — now had the means to flee the city.

Individual motives for moving to suburbia were countless, yet two trends were visible and related: as more Americans entered the economic middle class, more of them left the cities; and as they arrived in suburbia, they underwent social and cultural transformation, shedding distinctive ethnic and religious identities in an attempt to be assimilated into the majority way of life.

Attempts to define with precision the resulting new mass, middle class, were bound to fail. Income alone was too crude a measure of who belonged. The difference between the office worker and the skilled machinist was less a matter of earnings than of outlook. Noneconomic factors that helped determine class outlook included the individual's level of education, the birthplace of his parents, their schooling and occupation, and their experience in the upheaval of the Depression. In a way *their* children would never comprehend, young parents setting up households in the suburbs in the 1950s bore "the invisible scar" of their families' experiences in the thirties, a heritage of a thousand dinner-table laments and small daily deprivations.

As the flight to suburbia grew, intellectuals wondered how anyone could give up the city's excitement, diversity, and cultural richness for a desert like Levittown, Long Island. The critics ignored the fact that, with a handful of exceptions led by Manhattan, American cities were neither exciting nor attractive; those who could afford it had been leaving them since the 1920s. A strain of snobbishness ran through the criticism of the new suburbia. In a supposedly middle-class country, one might have expected that the effort of the sons and daughters of workers to rise would have aroused satisfaction among social observers rather than scorn. The critics, though typically "progressive" in their social attitudes, disliked the practical effects of democracy and especially the rise of the tasteless mob closer to *their* privileged station. Those who extolled the rewards of the city usually had the income and insulation from social change necessary to enjoy urban life. Critics who condemned the alleged pressures for "conformity" in the suburbs were under the influence of a romantic, literary ideal of nonconformity. The new suburbanites who had conformed to the standards of their families and working-class neighborhoods for most of their lives now conformed without complaint to the demands of what seemed a better way of life.

The old city neighborhood had served the new suburbanite's parents and grandparents well enough, usually admitting them after a difficult initiation to a modest portion of America's bounty. The process that turned a European peasant into an American was called "acculturation," and the demands on the first generation were brutally clear-cut. But what lay beyond a measure of material prosperity? In the suburbs the children underwent a second initiation. There they found a ready model of middle-class life, a pattern of behavior and consumption fully American. Not infrequently a family moved into its tract house almost without furniture, partly because the old was worn out and would make the wrong impression on their neighbors, partly because they felt as their fathers and grandfathers had felt on stepping ashore in the United States — they were launching a new life and taking on a new identity.

In popular fiction, suburbia was sometimes confused with upper-income exurbia. The true middle-class suburb was not a bedroom for adult commuters; it was a nursery, elaborately organized around the primary function of rearing children. The suburban public school was the secular church of the aspiring middle class, and attention and tax dollars were lavished on it throughout the fifties. The city public school had been abandoned physically, economically, and spiritually by fleeing white parents because it was "changing." It was ceasing to be an institution that indoctrinated the young in "community" values and standards. The reason was obvious. More and more of the children in attendance were poor, neglected, and infected with the virus of despair. They were also black.

In the mid-nineteenth century, when the public school was assuming the mission of "Americanizing" immigrants, Horace Mann had defined education as the "great equalizer of the conditions of men." But the era of the school as the "melting pot" had ended by the 1950s, even though an optimistic mythology persisted. Education had become the chief means by which Americans were differentiated and separated and their inequalities perpetuated. Because of economic and technological changes, education conferred and protected social status in a way unknown only a generation earlier. An unreckoned gulf separated the black child whose mother could not read his report card and the white child whose liberal but aspiring parents drove him to achieve to the limit of his ability and beyond.

The new suburbanite looked back only to congratulate himself on "making it" and getting out of the city. When he looked ahead, he did so mainly in terms of planning his children's future. They would go to college, which for him represented the climactic stage of assimilation and the apparent guarantee of "success." During the sixties, as the bumper crop of post–World War II babies raised in the suburbs came of age, college enrollment doubled — and parents suddenly discovered they could seal off every danger except the rebellion and ironic desire for escape of their own bored, rootless, and aimless children.

III.

> I saw the best minds of my generation destroyed by madness,
>   starving, hysterical naked,
> dragging themselves through the negro streets at dawn looking
>   for an angry fix . . .

Thus began a long poem called *Howl,* written in 1955 in a seedy San Francisco furnished room by an innocuous-looking young man named Allen Ginsberg. The poem was an intensely personal bellow of rage and protest, a hymn to heroin and a celebration of homosexuality in particular and perversion in general — in short, a gob of spit in the eye of the respectable, square world. After a widely publicized obscenity trial in 1957, *Howl* was unleashed upon its target with court sanction and Ginsberg became a minor celebrity, the poet laureate of the so-called Beat Generation.

The early, unselfconscious Beats were misfits and drifters, mostly in their late twenties and thirties, who lived on the fringe of the affluent society in places like Greenwich Village, San Francisco's North Beach section, and Venice West in Los Angeles. They worked irregularly or not at all. Some were jazz musicians, others talked about writing novels and poetry, but most were without even seriously pretended artistic ambitions. They were lumpen Bohemians, highly individualistic fugitives from commitment and responsibility and, in many cases, themselves. They wanted to be left alone to drink cheap wine, smoke marijuana, listen to records, and talk end-

197

lessly; and for a while after they were noticed, they were. Then a wanderer named Jack Kerouac wrote a disjointed novel about his adventures, *On the Road,* and coined the name "Beat" for people like himself. Ginsberg's *Howl* followed. And close behind were the novelty-seeking mass communicators and fascinated intellectuals, all determined to "discover" the hapless Beats.

The Beats were not only voluntary fugitives from square prosperity — living proof that bountiful America could provide for those who chose not to make it in the conventional world. They were also, and more importantly, the first substantial link between the white majority culture and the newly urbanized black minority subculture. The link was cemented by music and narcotics, which blacks had long used to escape the circumstances created by white dominance. Now, whites acting from quite different motives appropriated these means of escape and sought the "natural" freedom they romantically identified with blacks. The lust of the civilized for pseudo-primitive states of existence was familiar in Western society. What distinguished this latest manifestation was the absence of civilized qualities among those who condescended to immerse themselves in the inferior culture. The immature, ignorant, and unbalanced, who scarcely knew what they were forsaking, formed the dubious avant-garde on the black man's doorstep.

Ginsberg, a wildly articulate and utterly shameless exhibitionist, was in his glory in the spotlight, shouting his self-pity and self-admiration. The Beats supposedly aspired to withdraw and to be "cool" — one of the many words borrowed from the street slang of the black whom they idolized at a distance. At the same time they felt an infantile compulsion to shock, to "bug" the white squares. As the Beat phenomenon caught on and was inevitably commercialized, Ginsberg was booked into coffee houses and jazz cellars for poetry "readings" — actually, belligerent harangues — which hecklers interrupted at their peril. At a performance in Los Angeles, a man stood up and demanded to know what Ginsberg was trying to prove. "Nakedness," he replied. "What d'ya mean, nakedness?" asked the customer. Without a word, Ginsberg shucked his clothes.

Many of the exhibitionist Beats, it developed, were mentally unbalanced. As a youth growing up in Paterson, New Jersey, Ginsberg was confined for several months in a mental institution; his mother had spent her declining years in an insane asylum. A young San Francisco psychiatrist, after conducting an extensive study of the inhabitants of North Beach, came to the conclusion that at least 60 percent of the Beats whom he interviewed were so psychotic or paralyzed by tensions, anxieties, and neuroses as to be incapable of making their way in the square world, and that another 20 percent were just barely hanging on to emotional stability.* This finding highlighted the culpability of the news media. If Americans had taken up the sadistic practice of baiting the physically crippled, the press would have delivered outraged rebukes. Yet the press saw nothing wrong with exploiting commercialized masochism, and so the emotionally twisted Beats were given the media-amplified opportunity to bawl against society's "sickness."

The flood of publicity alerted and instructed impressionable squares who donned old clothes on weekends and went prowling the quarters where Beats reportedly hung out. The disguised tourists and voyeurs who milled around looking for

* Paul O'Neil, "The Only Rebellion Around," *Life*, November 30, 1959.

the "scene" were influenced less by the Beat propagandists than by the films and media cult of James Dean, the aimless loner in *Rebel Without a Cause*. Dean, who killed himself speeding nowhere, became the symbol of inarticulate adolescent discontent. The Beat rebellion could take any form the individual preferred, from wearing long hair and dirty clothes to dabbling in Zen and beating on drums. Directed against everything from the Bomb to split-level housing, the rebellion demanded nothing of its adherents except their plentiful resentment. If *everything* was awful, one could strike a pose of rebellious superiority without the necessity of explaining or justifying it.

At the same time, among the great satisfied and politically inert mass of the young, something new was loudly in the air. Just as they deserted their dull babysitter, television, for James Dean movies, so the young returned to another older technology, radio, for their rebellious music: blaring, hot-blooded rock 'n' roll. Rock 'n' roll was aggressively different from existing popular music; it marked a break, a discontinuity, and it revealed that the culture had become a battleground. The adults were not in charge anymore.

The singer who launched rock 'n' roll was a hillbilly from Tupelo, Mississippi, named Elvis Aaron Presley. In less than two years, he rocketed from a $35-a-week truck driver's job to an income well above $500,000 a year. To adults, the way Presley sounded was bad enough: he howled, bawled, mumbled, and cried his way through hits like *I Want You, I Need You* ("Ah Wa-ha-hunt Yew-who, Ah Nee-hee-heed Yew-who"). As for the way he looked — long hair, sideburns, motorcycle boots, tight pants, and a surly expression — and the way he sinuously rotated his hips and frantically quivered his torso —

many thought he ought to be locked up. "I don't do no dirty body movements," Presley protested. Perhaps not, but he was undeniably "subversive." As Eldridge Cleaver later put it with black radical satisfaction, Presley and his imitators and successors poured negritude by the ton into the souls of white America's teeny-boppers, disconnecting them from restraints that went far beyond music. When Ed Sullivan, the impresario of television's top-rated family variety show, paid $50,000 for Presley to bump and grind on three Sunday evenings, the subculture was triumphantly on top. After that breakthrough, the commercial mechanism of mass marketing did the rest.

Adult missionaries more malevolent than Sullivan, filled with their own resentments, were prepared to certify the deep significance of the "movement." The Beats were conscripted as shock troops in a cultural war they were unaware of. The media-myth of the Beat was falsified again to serve polemical ends. Novelist Norman Mailer offered a "hipster" ideology in a celebrated essay in *Dissent,* "The White Negro." The Beats and hipsters, he announced, were trying to emulate the Negro's "primitive . . . joy, lust, and languor," as racist a line as any "progressive" intellectual ever wrote. Mailer glibly invented a new Noble Savage in the guise of a sexual outlaw whose life centered on the quest for the perfect, apocalyptic orgasm. "One is hip or one is square (the alternative which each new generation coming into American life is beginning to feel), one is a rebel or one conforms, one is a frontiersman in the Wild West of American night life, or else a Square cell, trapped in the totalitarian tissues of American society, doomed willy nilly to conform if one is to succeed."

In time, Mailer fully politicized his fantasy and identified

John Kennedy as a "hipster" who would answer America's deepest need: "to face into that terrible logic of history which demanded that the country and its people must become more extraordinary and more adventurous, or else perish . . ." Kennedy's reaction on reading the Mailer piece was to remark drily that the author certainly ran on.

The Beats were scrutinized to death. Meanwhile, the blacks, through their own heroic suffering, showed that they wanted what Mailer and so many others comfortably pretended to reject: the right to choose to be square.

IV.

In May 1954, the United States Supreme Court decided the landmark case of *Brown v. Board of Education* and held racially segregated public schools unconstitutional. Thurgood Marshall, then chief counsel of the National Association for the Advancement of Colored People, expressed the optimism of the moment by setting September of 1955 as the target date for abolishing segregation in all public schools throughout the country. The Court subsequently directed that desegregation should proceed with "all deliberate speed." Thereafter, as bitterness mounted, the Negroes waited largely in vain for the law of the land to prevail. By the end of the 1950s, despite the Court's decision, nearly three fourths of the biracial school districts ruled unconstitutional remained unchanged.

President Dwight D. Eisenhower maintained a public attitude of noncommitment, refusing to say whether he agreed with the Supreme Court's decision. The governor of Arkansas, Orville Faubus, forced the President's hand. He interfered with a court desegregation order and white mobs in Little Rock attacked black children on their way to school. Reluctantly, the President sent paratroopers of the 101st Airborne Division to Little Rock to enforce the federal judge's decree. "If the day comes when we can obey the orders of our courts only when we personally approve of them," he wrote afterward to a friend, "the end of the American system, as we know it, will not be far off." Eisenhower personally believed that integration was not the most promising way to achieve racial equality. He said privately that disregard of the deep-rooted beliefs of white Southerners could lead to "social disintegration."

As 1960 began, all but 175,000 of the 3 million black children in the South were still in segregated schools. In Scott Hall, a dormitory on the campus of North Carolina Agricultural and Technical College in Greensboro, the state's largest school for blacks, four freshmen met regularly in the evenings during the winter of 1959–1960 to sip Cokes and talk. "We talked about everything," Ezell Blair, an eighteen-year-old social studies major, recalled. "We talked about the rights of the individual in modern society, and what it was moral for him to do and not to do." Inevitably, the talk turned to race and discrimination. Unlike their parents who had ducked their heads and kept silent, the four young men were conscious of belonging to a new generation. But what could they do?

One evening in late January 1960, inspiration came. The Jim Crow lunch counter was a daily, humiliating reminder of the past that would not die; the descendant of the slave could not sit and eat next to the descendant of the master. After classes, the boys entered the F. W. Woolworth store in downtown Greensboro, made a few purchases, carefully collecting the sales slips, and then advanced to the lunch counter and sat down.

"I'd like a cup of coffee," Blair told the startled white waitress.

"I'm sorry," she said, "we don't serve colored here."

Blair produced the sales slips.

"I beg to disagree with you," he said. "You just finished serving me at a counter only two feet from here. This is a public place, isn't it?"

The boys asked to speak with the manager but he did not appear. Expecting to be arrested at any moment, they sat silently as the waitresses served white patrons around them. At five o'clock, sales clerks began shutting off the lights and closing the store. The boys left quietly, resolved to return each day until they were served.

The next day the four were accompanied by fifteen other students who had heard about the sit-in. After a story appeared in the local newspaper, white students at Bennett College and the State Women's College asked to join the next demonstration. Waitresses started to serve them and then refused after discovering they were with the blacks. As the seats filled up at Woolworth's, the demonstrators went to nearby stores. The sit-in technique spread rapidly. Within a few days, demonstrations were occurring across North Carolina, then in neighboring states, and then throughout the South. A spontaneous gesture had become a movement. An editorial in the Greensboro *Daily News* declared: "An idea whose time has come is sweeping the South today . . . The idea's moral force — that colored men no longer will tolerate being served at nine counters and rejected at the tenth — cannot be denied."

Within six weeks, sit-ins had occurred in sixty-five communities in twelve Southern states, leading to approximately 1500 arrests. Arrests, fines, and imprisonment only raised the morale of the movement. Filling the jails would not quench this spirit, for a jail sentence had become a badge of honor. While serving a sixty-day sentence in the Leon County Jail, Patricia Stephens, a junior at Florida A. & M. University, wrote in a letter: "We are all so very happy that we were (and are) able to do this to help our city, state and nation. This is something that has to be done over and over again, and we are willing to do it as often as necessary." *

White college students in the North and South rushed to enlist in the crusade. At New Haven, thirty-five Yale medical students picketed local variety stores in four-hour shifts, and at Saratoga Springs, twenty Skidmore College faculty members and two hundred students staged a demonstration. Marion Wright, a senior at Spelman College and a leader in the Atlanta sit-ins, was invited to speak in the chapel at Agnes Scott, an exclusive white girls' college. Afterward, scores of her listeners crowded around. Tears streaming down her face, one girl said: "You're suffering so much. What can we do?" Marion told her: "Stand up for equality." Later, as I spoke with her, she recalled the exchange with visible distaste. "I'm almost thankful to have been born with a cause, with something to *do*."

The students saw themselves as liberated from the patronage and direction of well-meaning white liberals. Their tactics of direct, nonviolent action also broke with the established strategy of the older generation, who patiently relied

* Quoted in Helen Fuller, "We Are All So Very Happy," *The New Republic,* April 25, 1960.

on the courts. If a law was "immoral" in their eyes, the students would violate it, depending on physical confrontation to crack the segregationists' conscience and produce swift justice. And they would take the consequences, no matter what.

The disarming strength of the students in such confrontations arose from their *unrepresentative* character. They were the children of the black middle class — studious, determined, utterly unwilling to conform to the stereotype in the white man's mind. "You keep asking yourself: when do I tell my child he is inferior?" a sophomore at Tennessee State College in Nashville told me. Eyes blazing, she added: *"I won't."* The emergence of the militant students, poised and self-disciplined exemplars of middle-class values and ideals, startled many whites in the North and South alike. These young blacks were already the intellectual and moral superiors of their antagonists; they could not be denied the full legal equality they asserted.

But what of those more representative of the condition of black Americans? An elitist student movement, guided only by a sense of righteousness and drawn to potentially violent confrontations, could endanger the prospects of the black population as a whole. The social advance of black Americans depended absolutely on continued respect for the rule of law among the white majority. By the early 1960s, this respect was eroding under increasing pressure for "order." Soon, this would become a shorthand expression for halting and even reversing the great social and political advance toward equality in the postwar era.

V.

For most Americans, the fifties was a decade of catching up and getting ahead. Jobs, money, and goods at last were available simultaneously. Between 1950 and 1960, despite inflation, real family income rose by 37 percent. The consumer began with essentials — 14 million one-family homes were built in the fifteen years after World War II — and went on to luxuries which swiftly became necessities as the standard of living rose. As late as 1948 television was an expensive novelty, and the first family on the block to own a round-screen Dumont found its living room filled nightly with silent, gaping neighbors. By the end of the 1950s eight out of ten of the nation's 53 million households owned a television set; it had become as ubiquitous as the telephone.

World War II had ended large-scale unemployment and lifted the country out of the Depression. In the postwar era, ordinary citizens and experts alike expected the economy to be thrown into reverse. But the massive deficit spending by which the war had been financed created a vast pool of pent-up purchasing power. And when wage and price controls ended, the dam of consumer demand burst. The boom rolled on, occasionally slowing, but never losing forward momentum. Gradually, most Americans, especially young adults entering the labor market, assumed the inevitability of prosperity.

Consumer debt rose from $21 billion to $55 billion during the 1950s. This dizzying pile-up of paper alarmed many who recalled the credit spree of the twenties and its dismal hangover. In the early 1950s, the great merchant, J. C. Penney, a firm believer in cash-and-carry retailing, paid a visit to his regional manager in California and heard a detailed explanation of the necessity for offering credit. "I guess we must," the old man finally admitted. "But I want you to know I'm still against it in *principle*."

Many Americans shared Penney's worry about the staying power of recognized principles in the undertow of a new mass prosperity. The enjoy-now, pay-later economy seemed to subvert established truths. And the growing dependence on the government in the postwar scheme of things appeared to violate basic assumptions of individualism. Nevertheless, although argument raged on the advent of "socialism" in American life, not even the most rightward Republicans wanted to return to the bad old days of the Depression when individuals were free to starve.

The New Deal–World War II generation had experienced crisis on a scale which overwhelmed the resources of voluntary social cooperation: economic collapse, total war, and permanent mobilization for war. The federal government was the only collective instrument barely able to deal with such political and economic emergencies. As emergency became permanent, so did the expansion of government. What remained of nineteenth-century capitalism was mainly the folklore of individualism that people carried around in their heads. But few of the people had yet formed a portable philosophy describing the mixed system under which they lived; and they had not yet gained much confidence in its ability to deliver on its promises.

The ordinary citizen at once esteemed himself a sturdy individualist and applauded attacks on "big government," yet behaved as a practical collectivist. He believed in individualism yet assigned responsibility to large bureaucratic organizations

208

for ordering his daily life, protecting his interests, and assuring his security. Many such organizations were "private" — the corporation, the union, the trade or professional association, the farmers' cooperative. But all, in fact, were bound up with the federal government, which the citizen did not quite trust. So it was that many Americans enjoyed prosperity with their fingers crossed and looked for some means to resolve or at least escape the contradictions they felt between the way things were and the way they were supposed to be.

VI.

But there was no escape — not for lower-middle-class collectivists who hated the government that subsidized them, not for hippies who hated the parents who underwrote their wanderings, not for blacks who believed too ardently the promises of speedy deliverance under the Great Society and its bountiful subsidies. By the latter 1960s, acute contradiction was encountered at every turn in American life. The most progressive and enlightened government in the nation's history sat in Washington — and it could not extricate itself from the most pointless and unpopular war Americans had ever waged. The boldest and most costly social reform programs ever attempted were whooped through the Congress — and the attempt to uplift minorities somehow resulted in their violently resentful uprising. Freedom — "doing your own thing" — led to self-entrapment in drugs, promiscuity, and aimlessness. Rock music festivals celebrated love and ecstasy — and ended in mayhem and murder.

The people on top — the educated, liberal-minded, prosperous urban elite — saw their optimistic illusions coming apart and fell into despair. *Not* about themselves, of course. They despaired of America, which was failing them. In 1972, this attitude was crystallized in the presidential candidacy of Senator George McGovern. It attracted the scrutiny of futurist Herman Kahn, the director of the Hudson Institute and a 350-pound gadfly of the intelligentsia. In the summer of 1971 he was interviewed by *Intellectual Digest,* very much a publication of the angst-ridden elitists. His reflections are worth quoting not only because they are typically unqualified and provocative, but also because they express the essence of the growing reaction against the sixties.

Asked about "the mood of hopelessness in the nation today," Kahn unloaded:

> That mood is not as deep as it looks to the upper middle class in the city. The upper middle class, the group running the media, educators, city planners, some students — all are basically out of touch with reality. It's a very specific illness of a very specific group . . . The average American is extremely concerned about the future of the country. He also feels that something is going wrong, but what's going wrong is the upper middle class . . . There's an enormous hostility toward the upper middle class. People like Wallace talk about a guy with a briefcase, the professor with the pointed head. That's me he's talking about and you . . . We're part of the class that has failed . . . We gave [ordinary Americans] the war in Vietnam. We gave them the wrong programs and then didn't answer when they questioned us. We didn't defend the programs, and that is a tragedy . . . The upper middle class insists on misunderstanding all of the central issues of American life.

Kahn wound up in typical fashion with a devastating statistic and a flat prediction: "Remember 67 percent of America is quite square and getting squarer. I call this . . . the *counter-*counterculture. It is the biggest thing going in America today and it will either dominate or heavily influence the next decade or two."

Evidence of this trend — away from experiment and back to time-tested basics — is everywhere. Fundamentalist religions are flourishing among the young (the "Jesus freaks") as well as the old, and liberal denominations are waning. White ethnic consciousness and pride are rising, and the enormous commercial success of movies such as *The Godfather* guarantees future emphasis on selling the ethnocentric market. Romantic sentimentality is back in style too, as witness *Love Story* and its imitators. The colleges are quiet and undergraduates are returning to traditional concerns and pursuits: getting a job, beer-drinking, and pranks (co-ed "streaking" has replaced politically motivated public coupling). ROTC has reappeared, even on once radical Ivy League campuses. The blacks, many of whom made a great leap forward during the 1960s in income and status, seem preoccupied with getting ahead and exerting their political muscle. Trend-setting Los Angeles has elected its first black mayor. Southern black Democrats looking toward 1976 openly speculate on the possibility of supporting a regional favorite son — Governor Wallace. Wallace, who once stood in the university's door to prevent integration, now proudly crowns the University of Alabama's black homecoming queen. There is a boom in nostalgia, especially for the fifties. Longer dresses, shorter hair-styles, romantic music reflect it. Radio stations are switching back to the hits of the fifties (the "golden oldies"), and country music is the in-sound far from Nashville.

Money, which seemed so crass in the free-spending sixties,

is now uppermost in the minds of Americans. Inflation, taxes, and worry about the cost of living head the list of concerns in every opinion poll, far ahead of Watergate. (The news media does not understand inflation or the actual workings of the complex U.S. economy, and so they persist in giving public morality priority over private money concerns, which widens their credibility gap.) In the hyperinflated economy, the retired old and the just-starting young face a special problem in finding decent housing they can afford — and many within both age groups solve it by buying relatively inexpensive "mobile homes" that don't go anywhere. These immobile trailers, a compromise between a cramped city apartment and an impossibly costly suburban house, perhaps symbolize the way it may have to be in the seventies — a scaling down of expectations, a settling for the attainable, a coming to terms with a less-than-perfect reality.

The "new people" who stormed through the colleges in the sixties are now old enough to be pairing off and eventually getting married. (Regardless of how long couples live together before matrimony, the bride usually wears white and sales of gowns rise annually, another sign of return to traditionalism.) But the young families are in no hurry to have children, and thanks to modern birth-control technology and readily available abortions, they can with certainty postpone the arrival of children indefinitely. The results are apparent in the dramatic turnaround in the fertility rate. At the peak of the baby boom in 1957, the typical American woman who had children had almost four of them (3.7), but by late 1973 she typically had less than two (1.8). As the social demographer Ben J. Wattenberg has pointed out, the current birth rate is now well below "replacement" (2.1) and, exclusive of immigration, ultimately would lead not only to Zero Population Growth, but also to Negative Population Growth sometime in the twenty-first century. While some couples offer ideological justifications for remaining childless, skeptical marketing experts discern a new self-centeredness and unwillingness on the part of young marrieds to surrender the lifestyle made possible by two paychecks. Playing Mom and Dad has less appeal to the grown-up products of suburbia than playing with undiminished discretionary income.

Among those predicting a more "conservative" society in years ahead is the liberal Moynihan, "simply on the ground that a society whose population is barely growing tends to be curiously straitened and strict in its behavior." Relative to the numbers competing, there will be fewer places at and near the top, particularly in the fields most attractive to the highly educated and ambitious. The myth of endless, ever-expanding opportunity will be seen by the coolly realistic next generation as just that — a myth, at odds with the stratified society of a mature America. Yet, in Moynihan's vision, this will not necessarily produce an encompassing social conservatism. He generously gives his fellow liberals a bit of hope: they may have their ideology and their cake too. "The French indeed have a phrase for it: 'Think left, live right.' I incline to think we're going to see a lot of both."

Perhaps we will. If so, the hostility of those below toward the moralizing, comfortable upper-middle class may intensify, unless it is contained and dissolved by a genuinely conservative government reflecting a broad cultural as well as political consensus. Considering what we have experienced in reaching the seventies, the prospect is inviting.

The Automobile-Centered Society

DURING THE WINTER of 1973–1974, the Arab oil sheiks turned off the tap and Americans at last began to comprehend the true cost of their long and impassioned affair with the automobile. To be sure, we had been warned repeatedly against Detroit and its subtle deceits, and we were vaguely aware of environmental damage caused by our insolent chariots, and some of us, the second or third time around, had even taken up with skinnier, less demanding love objects imported from overseas. But we were a long way from breaking off.

Then we were given time to think about it as we waited in seemingly endless lines at gasoline stations for the few gallons that would keep us going another day. Suddenly and anxiously, we thought of almost nothing except access to gasoline. We argued and fought over it. We read with compassionate understanding of those prepared to kill for it. The more timid among us devised strategems that in retrospect seemed pathetic and ridiculous, such as trailing tank trucks and alerting neighbors to after-dark deliveries.

Could it be that the automobile utterly dominated our lives? It was true. Without wheels we were literally nowhere, cut off from commerce, sociability, and spiritual sustenance in our

214

suburban Siberias. Everything we needed and wanted seemed to require driving to get it. (Our preadolescent children, unconsciously transported daily, could have told us as much; they impatiently awaited a driver's license as immigrants awaited citizenship papers — only then would they be full-fledged Americans.)

As the shadow of doubt fell across our beloved automobile, we suspected third-party malice and intrigue. The major oil companies, partners of the Middle East monopolists, were prime suspects. They struck many as likely co-conspirators and obvious profiteers. Perhaps the "energy crisis" was a gigantic fraud to compel the gullible consumer to pay much higher prices. In the age of the rip-off, the oil companies presumed too much with their bland explanations as they reported skyrocketing earnings.

But this confused cause and effect. We were vulnerable to the unforeseen gasoline shortage because the automobile had become indispensable. Our ever-increasing consumption of gasoline was the least part of what we used up in order to keep moving, alone with the radio, encapsulated in the rolling metal womb. We did not foresee or realize until we belatedly thought about it that the automobile was using up America.

I.

The distinctive and shaping feature of man-made America is the road. A people restlessly on the move, we have built a mile of road for each square mile of land on the continent. Highways and their rights of way cover 15 million acres, or the area of the state of West Virginia. By the usual yardstick of American concern, the amount of money spent, we care extravagantly about roads. The 41,000-mile Federal Interstate Highway System, now almost completed and likely to cost more than $110 billion by the mid-1970s, will link 90 percent of our cities with populations of 50,000 or more. It is the greatest public-works undertaking of all time — more ambitious than TVA, the pyramids, or the Great Wall of China.

Roads are needed, of course, because America is a nation on wheels, the first society based on the assumption of universal personal mobility. Four out of every five persons old enough to drive have driver's licenses. More than 100 million motor vehicles of all kinds — including more than 85 million automobiles — are currently being operated. Eighty-three percent of the nation's 65.1 million families own an automobile, and 28 percent own two or more cars. Automobile transportation, as a nationwide survey concludes, is "a deeply ingrained way of life that Americans wish to continue."

Quite deliberately, we made a choice more than a generation ago: the automobile comes first. In the superhighways curving through the countryside and the stilt-legged expressways striding across the cities, this choice has been fixed in concrete. Suddenly we are appalled. To lay pavement, we have willfully ravaged scenic wilderness, farmland, historic sites and landmarks, parks, waterfronts, churches, schools, shops and businesses, suburban towns, and city neighborhoods. And the automobile-centered way of life seems to require that more and more of America disappear under the bulldozer. "We *know* that we encourage more traffic by building more highways," says a federal planner with a trace of despair. "In a hundred years, the whole damned country will probably be paved over."

216

Although scores of millions of acres of wild and unspoiled land still exist on the American continent, our attitude toward this priceless national treasure lends support to such gloomy predictions. More and more Americans want to use and enjoy the open spaces, which is perfectly understandable, but they want to do it on their own terms of ease and comfort, which means getting back to nature by automobile. Unfortunately, the highways that open up the wilderness also tend to assure its rapid destruction. At pavement's end, motorists seeking nature find only other motorists, all searching futilely for what was pushed out of the way so they could get there.

In more than a score of communities across the country, especially where proposed highways collide with cities, determined citizens have resisted encroaching concrete. About a third of the 6000 scheduled miles of urban highways in the Interstate System remain unbuilt because of intense opposition. These are more than scattered local protests; these are signs of a radical shift in national priorities. The demand is for a new choice: *people* should come first. The protest against an environment created for the automobile reveals one of the essential crises of man-made America — a crisis of values.

Edward H. Holmes, former director of policy planning for the Federal Highway Administration and a veteran of fifty years of road building, gazed out his window over Washington and tried to sort out the rights and wrongs of the antihighway rebellion. "We've been trying to build for the city as it *now* functions. But we've been pouring concrete into a mold that may be breaking up. Highways last for fifty years or more — they're the most permanent things we're building these days. But what kind of cities do we want? Do we *know?*"

We have only begun to define the kind of cities we want —

cities built around the needs and desires of their inhabitants — and we find that we cannot escape redefining ourselves. For the failing cities we have and deplore are what we accepted when we eagerly embraced the automobile.

Nothing remotely like our mobile society exists elsewhere. California alone has more cars than either England or France. Los Angeles has more than 1300 miles of freeways built, under construction, or planned. The automobile-centered way of life emerged quite suddenly, in little more than a generation. Since the end of World War II, the number of automobiles on the road has more than tripled. And 28 percent of the area of the nation's cities has been surrendered to the automobile. "It's amazing, but we built all those highways without the slightest idea of their long-term impact on our way of living," remarked a Department of Transportation official responsible for mass transit, which died as the automobile thrived.

As automobile ownership spread, only the motorist seemed affected, and he was gaining a measure of personal freedom unknown anywhere, at any time. He was free to change his place of work and residence, free to seek out distant services and pleasures, free to throw off constraints of custom, manners, and morals. Further, this personal transportation system, operated according to the motorist's whim and convenience, satisfied a national nostalgia. Simply by stepping on the gas and taking off down the highway, the American could reclaim the frontier.

The long-term impact of the automobile became evident as a nation of freewheeling individualists chose the same destination. Freed from rural isolation and limited opportunity, Americans headed for the city. More than seven out of ten in the population now live in and around cities. This convergence of 145 million Americans on barely 2 percent of the land came about through blind, headlong momentum.

In ways we are just beginning to understand, our accidental environment — crowded, polluted, wasteful, inhuman — makes victims of us all. Ironically, the same automobile that freed us now enslaves us. We drive less and less for satisfaction, more and more because our way of life permits no other choice. By the late 1960s, for the first time, motor vehicles in the U.S. were rolling up an estimated *trillion* miles of annual travel, and more than half of it occurred in urban areas, where traffic is growing twice as fast as population. The pressure for more pavement grows as the results of past mistakes become intolerable. "We build roads now to accommodate what's there and what the planners say the future will be," a federal highway administrator observes. "The planners are usually wrong."

Consider the hopeless case of the Long Island Expressway. One morning after heavy overnight rains had flooded parts of the expressway, commuter traffic bound from the suburbs to Brooklyn and Manhattan was backed up bumper to bumper for twenty miles. It took several hours — and countless wasted man-hours — to unsnarl the expressway. Even on a clear day, the nation's most congested urban highway earns its nickname, "The World's Longest Parking Lot." The planners of the expressway failed to predict Long Island's booming growth, and they chose an inflexible right of way through densely populated Queens that skirts apartment houses and bisects cemeteries, creating a permanent bottleneck. New York's late Traffic Commissioner Henry Barnes proposed laying another six-lane deck atop the elevated expressway, but his critics pointed out that this costly and unsightly expedient would merely transfer congestion westward to the clogged Queens-Midtown Tunnel. Of course, at further enormous cost, another tube could be built under the East River, but that would merely dump more cars into Manhattan.

In spite of contrary evidence and experience, federal highway researchers continue to offer reassuring claims. "Urban residents today," declares a study prepared by the Department of Transportation, "can reach in an hour's travel time or less an area 25 times as great as they could 50 years ago." (Nothing is said about *what* hour of the day this splendid journey occurs.) Statistics aside, the reality of the automobile-centered way of life is mounting human frustration. The suburban housewife stuck without a car is a prisoner; in her more characteristic role of chauffeur, she possesses the same freedom to keep moving as a squirrel in a cage. Her husband, inching homeward behind 280 mocking-horsepower, has reason to envy his grandfather who drove a single horse — at least from the seat of his buggy he could breathe fresh air. (A person consumes about 30 pounds of air a day; the average automobile, 160 pounds. A person exhales a microscopic amount of carbon monoxide; an automobile throws off 6 pounds.)

II.

Frank C. Turner, who joined the Bureau of Public Roads as an engineer straight out of Texas A. & M. in 1929, belongs to the generation for whom the interests of motorists are overriding. During his years as director of the BPR he supervised a vast domain: the BPR routinely has in progress some 20,000 projects worth upward of $10 billion. Turner was proud, and rightly so, of the skill with which his agency carried out its mandate to pave America, but he also felt winds of change rattling the windows of the closed world of the highway professionals. "There is a lot of talk about us being old men out of tune with the times," he conceded before he retired. "But we sleep well at night because we feel that we're performing a service that the public appreciates."

Turner naturally meant the *mobile* public. The "highway users" are the people who count, in the engineer's view, for they pay for new roads and ultimately pay his salary. To finance the Interstate Highway System, Congress created in 1956 a self-perpetuating Highway Trust Fund, into which flow revenues from federal taxes levied on gasoline, tires, spare parts, and other travel-related purchases. Prior to 1956, the Federal Government paid about 50 percent of the costs of building federal-aid highways; in the Interstate System, the federal share has soared to 90 percent. The states select and plan routes, acquire rights of way, and award and supervise construction contracts, paying for work as it progresses and then claiming reimbursement. The BPR, which must approve each step in the process, doles out money to the states at a rate of around 5 billion dollars annually.

What is remarkable about this great public spending program, financed outside the federal budget, is its insulation against changing social and political realities. Until recently, it has been nearly immune from serious criticism in Congress, where rurally dominated public-works committees of the House and Senate regard the officials of the BPR as old friends and benefactors. The hard-pressed states and cities, able to build roads with ten-cent dollars, are submissive before the lavish federal handouts. Around the federal highway program lies a protective web of influence and interest spun by the heavy construction firms, allied unions, material suppliers, consulting engineers, truckers, automobile and tire manufacturers, petroleum companies — all those who have a stake in preserving the automobile-centered way of life.

The BPR's first and formative mission was to get the nation's farmers out of the mud. Nowadays the farmers remaining among us hop off their tractors at day's end and drive to the supermarket like everybody else. Although the highway engineers have literally paved the way for social and economic revolution, they have been slow to shift the basis of their road-building decisions away from a formula which belongs to vanishing rural America. They are still concerned with the "costs" and "benefits" to the all-important "highway users," as though a highway, particularly in an urban area, affected only the mobile population.

In 1966, Morris Ketchum, Jr., then president of the American Institute of Architects, resigned from a federal advisory committee on highway beautification because he did not want to appear to tolerate the building standards being used. "Although standards for highway design . . . between cities are well developed and in general well utilized," he said, they are "blindly applied to highway design within cities with disastrous results."

Such subversive ideas have firmly taken hold among reform-minded federal officials. "The whole theory of highway building has been to build it the cheapest way per mile," says a youthful planner in the Department of Transportation. "Now we've discovered that knocking down neighborhoods may be

222

the most expensive thing you can do." A close observer in the private sector, James Kise of Urban America Inc., a Washington-based research organization, hails the new official awareness that "social costs" are involved in highway construction. "The problem is that all decisions have been left in the hands of engineers. You can't just cost-account for the highway user; you have to cost-account for the whole city the road enters. Otherwise the highways that have built cities will destroy them."

Originally barred by law from intruding upon built-up areas, where state and local governments were responsible for road building, the Bureau of Public Roads was directed in the 1950s to catch up with the unmet highway needs of the exploding metropolises. The agency encountered little or no opposition from urban planners for the simple reason that few were around. "We developed most of the processes that so-called urban designers have recently taken up," said a veteran road planner. "I think we invented the theory and concepts of urban planning more than anyone else." The engineers, as they chose their rights of way, assumed the incidental task of reshaping the urban scene. The eight-lane John F. Fitzgerald Expressway, mostly elevated, was sent barreling through the heart of old Boston, sealing off the historic waterfront. The Dan Ryan Expressway cut a sixteen-lane swath through miles of Chicago. In Baltimore, the city's loveliest park, designed by the great landscape architect Frederick Law Olmsted, was buried beneath the Jones Falls Expressway.

In 1959, the highway builders ran into a city with a strong sense of identity, San Francisco, and there they suffered their first major rebuff, symbolized by the unfinished Embarcadero Freeway, which stops in midair. The freeway would have blocked much of the view of the magnificent bay, a threat to civic pride that caused citizens from forty-one protest groups to assert the heresy that a vista was worth more than a motorist's convenience. In a series of stormy city council hearings, they ultimately prevailed by a six-to-five vote. Since that victory, antifreeway forces have defeated an attempt to complete the Embarcadero and a plan to tunnel under Golden Gate Park, even though it meant rejecting $250 million in federal funds.

Much of the antihighway feeling abroad today springs from the same city-saving spirit. These rebels are mostly white, well-educated, middle- and upper-class citizens, running heavily to activist housewives, civic-minded lawyers, and other professionals who are alarmed by the destruction of surroundings they cherish. They possess political power and influence; their problem is to make it effective against remote and elusive foes.

There is another side to the antihighway rebellion, which is not conservative, but increasingly radical. It has little interest or stake in saving the cities as they are. This rebellion attacks the "system" through its highways, and it enlists the special victims of our automobile-centered environment — the nonmotorists. The automobile that brought us together in metropolitan centers now separates us in a new social division. Transportation expert Wilfred Owen of the Brookings Institution has said, "The person who for a variety of reasons has no car is increasingly barred from enjoyment of what the city has to offer." This applies to the young, the old, the infirm, and the poor — especially the black poor concentrated in the cities.

The city now extends far beyond the central business district. In the first stage of the transformation of America made possible by the automobile, the white middle class abandoned city neighborhoods for the greener pastures of suburbia, but returned downtown during daylight hours to work and shop. The raw suburb of the 1950s has become the satellite city of the 1970s. While many old core cities are almost stagnant, the expanding outer rings of the urban complex are enjoying rapid growth in jobs and income. Not only familiar shopping centers but new plants and office buildings are being located where parking space is ample. It is taken for granted that employees will drive to work.

This pattern of metropolitan growth leaves behind the unemployed living in the inner city, who often cannot qualify for the downtown white-collar jobs or reach the blue-collar jobs in the new factories on the outskirts. Since 1945, as auto registrations tripled, the use of public mass transit has declined by 80 percent. What remains is usually tied to the downtown core, and it serves the expanding suburbs poorly or not at all. Uniquely spread-out Los Angeles provides an exaggerated illustration of the penalties imposed on the nonmotorist. "When we talk about jobs here," says William Hibbard, director of the Transportation-Employment Project in Watts, "we are talking about distances of twenty and thirty miles." The project gathered statistics for travel from south-central Los Angeles to several employment centers: Santa Monica, for example, is sixteen miles away by the most direct route, and involves a travel time of one hour and fifty minutes on four separate buses.

Thus the automobile has ceased to have only personal meaning in America's failing urban environment. The mobile population, mistaken for the "public" by the road builders, has been making a heavy and largely uncompensated social claim

225

upon the passive and immobile population in urban highway construction. Under the engineer's rule of building at the cheapest-cost-per-mile, the "best" right of way often lies through inexpensive housing, which is likely to be low-income black housing. Urban highways have not suddenly flared into racial battlegrounds; the opposition has long been smoldering unseen. All that has changed is that at last the victims are raising their voices.

III.

Looking to the years 1973–1985, state highway departments have already estimated that they will spend a staggering $17.4 billion *annually*. Planners in the federal highway establishment talk of a program to build high-rise parking garages in cities at a cost of $7 billion. Even those who see the necessity of a truly balanced transportation system are fatalistic about the prospects for change. "It's hard to see anything closer than twenty-five years away. We're pretty much totally committed to the private transportation system we have — and we can't pin our hopes on a brave new world," says a pessimistic federal planner.

But the crisis overtaking the automobile-centered society will not wait a quarter century. The uprising of the victims of our accidental environment is happening *now*. Human and social values are being destroyed at an intolerable rate *now*.

An attempt has been made to reform highway building in the cities without tackling the highway establishment head on. So far, the results have not been encouraging. Under the Federal Aid Highway Act of 1962, the BPR is empowered to withhold highway funds from any city of 50,000 or more population that does not undertake "a continuing, comprehensive transportation planning process," which means planning not only expressways but mass transit as well. The act, however, does not apply to highways planned before 1965. Hence the reformers are reduced to seeking ways of making harmful highways a little more acceptable. Two techniques are used: joint development and the urban design concept team.

Joint development aims at correcting situations in which urban highways often depress the value of surrounding property. A city acquires a wider corridor than necessary, sells the right of way at cost to the BPR, and then develops the rest under various federal programs. To the extent that land can be developed for private use it will stay on the local tax rolls. Joint development has been used in Philadelphia and New Orleans, chiefly to preserve what is already there. It remains to be proved, however, that a desirable environment for people can be created around and above a highway.

The urban design concept team has a great virtue — it ends the engineer's monopoly in highway planning. But its flaw is almost as great — the team of architects, city planners, sociologists, economists, and other specialists can go to work only after the engineers have fixed the route of a highway.

It is hard to believe that racially divided and faltering cities will be revived by running highways through them. But the money is available for highways, not for low-income housing, and so those affected by roads must be grateful they are remembered at all. What makes the whole approach suspect is its objective of seaming together, not broken neighborhoods, but strips of federally subsidized pavement. "Everywhere, there's a search for expedient solutions that will enable us to

227

complete the freeways in the Interstate System," a bureaucrat admits. "Is access to the center of a city really necessary or desirable? We could connect the interstate highways without going through cities."

The government could — and it certainly *should*. The right of interstate travelers to tear through the heart of a city can be revoked if it is seen for what it is — a violation of the rights of those who live in the city. So, too, can suburban commuters be asked to respect the city and those who live there. We are not obliged to allow every motorist to drive to within a few steps of his office door, and to yield more and more of the city's space to storing his car. In the few places where it has been seriously tried, such as Cleveland, fringe parking and rapid transit do the job perfectly well. The object is not to move vehicles, but people. Just 45 buses, each carrying 50 persons comfortably seated, can deliver as many bodies to their destination as 1500 automobiles, each carrying an average of 1.5 passengers.

"America is a crisis-oriented society," says an official of the National Highway Research Board, an affiliate of the Academy of Sciences. "We always wait until almost too late — look at our air, our rivers, our cities generally. Then, when the situation becomes unbearable, we demand *immediate* solutions. But the costs of a rational transportation system, when we get around to demanding one, will be enormous, much greater than Vietnam, and the lead times will be measured in generations. Perhaps planning just isn't possible in our society. What we call planning is often a way of trying to perpetuate something that is already out of date."

By spending thirty times as much annually on highways as on all forms of mass transit, the federal government has perpetuated an obsolete and increasingly destructive system. Late in 1973, proponents of a balanced transportation system finally won a small but potentially immense victory over the fierce opposition of the highway lobby. The 1973 Highway Act permits some money in the Highway Trust Fund to be used for highway-related urban mass transportation — such as the purchase of buses; eventually, funds will also be available for rail transit.

It should be possible to halt construction of urban highways, not by violent protest in the streets but by rational decision in the halls of Congress, until plans can be drawn and resources allocated within the framework of the late President Johnson's dramatic forecast: "In the remainder of this century, urban population will double, city land will double, and we will have to build homes, highways, and facilities equal to all those built since this country was first settled."

This is America's second chance, the necessity and the opportunity to rebuild itself. To redeem the accidental environment and create the second America, we need not just a highway or mass transit trust fund but, even more, an urban trust fund. Planning is needed, not merely to expedite the movement of highway users but mainly to enhance the lives of city users. The need, in short, is to cast off a cramped self-definition in terms of our mechanical means, and to redefine ourselves and our environment in terms of our human ends. Our highways are the uniquely enduring artifacts of our civilization, and their planning and construction should call forth the highest expression of our civic genius. If we heedlessly build only to go from here to there, we may arrive to discover nothing there — and leave nothing to mark our passing.

Who Owns America?

I.

WHEN THE ORIGINAL JOHN JACOB ASTOR was past eighty, he was so weak his exercise consisted of being tossed gently in a blanket. His delicate stomach could tolerate only the breast milk provided by a wet nurse. The old man spent the days brooding upon his career as merchant, fur trader, and investor. His fortune of $20 million made him the wealthiest American of his time, but he was not content. Astor finally announced a regret. "Could I begin life again, knowing what I now know and had money to invest," he said wistfully, "I would buy every foot of land on the island of Manhattan."

Astor was not lamenting a missed opportunity — he was already famous as landlord of New York — but even he, as a young man, had grossly underestimated the riches to be gained from real estate. The same thought occurred to other successful capitalists who came later. John D. Rockefeller and Meyer Guggenheim wrested fabulous wealth from beneath the soil in the form of oil and minerals, and they too were surprised by the capacity of the earth to enrich them. Generation after generation, while the economy and the country were being transformed, the land — as real estate and as the source of oil, minerals, and raw materials — endured as the most important source of great American fortunes. And so it remains even today.

Of course, wealth is no longer simply on and in the land. In present-day America, wealth exists in a seemingly endless variety of forms. And it is owned in ways that reflect both the changing needs and constant ingenuity of the American people. The wealth of modern America is, first of all, paper — billions of pieces of paper in the form of currency, bank checks, stocks and bonds, insurance policies, and other easily exchanged claims upon goods, services, assets, and, to close the cycle, cash. Our prosperity depends upon the highly sophisticated circulation of precious, symbolic paper. What we truly *own,* our individual and collective wealth, consists of what lies beneath this immense, shifting sea of paper.

As stockholders, millions of Americans own claims upon such physical assets as factories and steel mills. The most common tangible asset — the residential dwelling — illustrates the difference between having and owning. The American householder usually does not own his house outright. Yet the equity in his house is a form of wealth, and so are the abundant possessions in and around it: the automobile, the television sets, the furniture, the tools in the basement workshop, even the paintings on the wall and the stuffed bird on the mantel. Roughly 93 percent of all homes in America have basic plumbing facilities and 71 percent have washing machines; *96 percent have TV sets.* The fast-paced home-building boom of recent years has upgraded the nation's housing stock. One in four houses, for example, is less than ten years old. Fewer homes are crowded — that is, holding more than one person per room (there were 5.2 million such homes in 1970 compared with 6.1 million in 1960).

All this and much more comes under the definition of wealth as "an object of human desire." Wealth need not be tangible in order to be real. An airline's franchise to fly a particular route, a television station's license to use the airwaves, a few hours' access to a costly computer — such rights exist on paper only, but their exercise has a large dollars-and-cents value.

The aggregate assets of America, tangible and intangible, have never been inventoried. A few years ago, before the double-digit inflation of the early 1970s, Dr. John Kendrick of the National Bureau of Economic Research estimated these assets at $4.5 trillion. But even this huge sum underestimates our wealth, and the dollar sign is misleading. Paper money, after all, is an imaginative product of human necessity, and our trillions of dollars worth of assets and possessions would be worth very little without the intellectual resources of the people who create and use wealth.

II.

Who owns America? The answer, superficially, is governments, corporations, institutions, and individuals. The federal government's role is crucial: it creates the money that symbolizes the nation's wealth. It is by far the largest single owner of the country's physical assets. State and local governments have grown at an explosive rate, responding to public demands, particularly for improved education. The tax laws have inspired a continuing boom in philanthropy and a massive transfer of wealth. *The Foundation Directory* lists 6803 foundations holding total assets of some $20 billion. Church and church-related institutions hold land and buildings alone — aside from securities — worth $80 billion. The Roman Catholic Church, the largest religious institution in the U.S., has assets estimated at around $50 billion, or more than the *combined* assets of General Motors, RCA, General Electric, U.S. Steel, and Standard Oil of New Jersey. The total assets of all U.S. corporations are well above $1.5 *trillion.* In 1972, the 500 largest corporations had total assets of $486 billion. By far the largest corporation was AT&T ($60 billion), almost $26 billion ahead of next-ranking Prudential Insurance Company of America. The Prudential, it may be noted, is our largest private financer of home and farm ownership in America, holding the mortgages of some 335,000 homes and 35,000 farms.

In an economy where even cash is going out of style (business executives' wallets are stuffed with credit-card receipts), it seems a long time since capitalists distrusted any asset they could not touch. But change has not swept away certain essentials. Underlying the transformed economic landscape is the land itself, which remains the most basic commodity and the proper starting point of any attempt to discover who owns America. The total land area of the U.S., some 2.3 billion acres, is worth more than $726.5 billion,* and all the buildings on it are valued at more than $1 trillion. These are the most tangible of income-producing assets, the very essence of what we mean by *capital.* The federal government owns fully one third of the total U.S. land area, and corporations (especially

* Latest figure available, from Federal Reserve research (1968).

the railroads), foundations, and institutions are also large landowners. It is the individuals, however, who reveal most clearly that, for all the change in America over the past century, the great wealth is intrinsically in the ground.

Ownership and capital go together — this fact has not changed. The truly wealthy Americans, millionaires and better, number an estimated 120,000, according to Internal Revenue Service data. Not surprisingly, these large holders of capital, comprising less than .05 percent of the population, own a disproportionate share — about 12 percent — of America's private wealth. Corporate business dominates the modern economy, and the rich, who have fully half their collective assets in the form of stock, are the leading owners of industry. They hold an estimated one fifth of all stock in U.S. corporations. (Eight out of ten American families own no stock.) To escape the federal tax-collector, the rich typically carry much of their wealth in tax-exempt state and local government securities.

Such portfolios would seem strange to an Astor or even a Rockefeller, but these capitalists of a simpler day would approve the continuing enthusiasm of the rich for the land. Oil and real estate account for at least one fifth of the assets of the typical American worth a million dollars. The more millions he has, the more likely that his wealth came originally from the ground.

The distinction of being the wealthiest American, though he mildly disputes it, belongs to expatriate John Paul Getty. Now in his eighties, Getty, a lifelong Anglophile who was educated at Oxford, lives in baronial splendor in a Tudor manor house in Surrey, England. He is a noted art collector and something of a philosopher. In a book he wrote, he offered this insight:

"Great wealth is due to imagination, ability, and a successful risking of capital." In 1903, Getty's father, a prosperous Minneapolis lawyer, visited Oklahoma on business, imaginatively saw the long-term prospects beneath the oil boom, and, for a starter, risked $500 on a lease in what was then Indian territory.

From that beginning has risen a huge international company, Getty Oil (assets: $2.1 billion). Including income from his other investments, John Paul Getty receives some $100 million annually. He is worth perhaps $2 billion, yet he protests against making his wealth a personal matter. "The companies in which I own shares are rich enterprises," Getty argues, "but I am not wealthy. They hold the property. They control me. In terms of extraordinary, independent wealth, there is only one man, H. L. Hunt."

Haroldson Lafayette Hunt of Dallas is worth more than $1 billion, and in contrast to Getty he loves to talk about his wealth. Hunt is the largest independent oil operator in the world. During World War II, Hunt's company controlled more oil reserves than all the Axis nations combined.

Hunt was born on an Illinois farm in 1890, and could read before he was three, but he left school after the fifth grade and drifted from Canada to Arizona, working as a lumberjack and a cowhand. An immensely successful gambler (he has had private wires to the major tracks and has cleared as much as $1 million a year from his wagers), he may have won his first oil lease in Arkansas at the poker table. In 1930 he came to East Texas and obtained leases on 4000 acres in what was to become the world's largest producing field. Since then, he has expanded throughout the Southwest, and has invested in timberland, canning factories, citrus groves, pecan farms, food-

235

processing plants, and drug-producing laboratories. His favorite product is a digestive tablet called "Amaze Aids." Using lyrics he wrote, Hunt's children once sang the praises of Amaze Aids from the H.L.H. Co. booth at the Texas State Fair, while the proprietor beamed.

A simple, unpretentious man, Hunt is nevertheless a caricature of Texas wealth. He has pursued his eccentric, right-wing politics through *Life Line* radio broadcasts, supported for many years by his own foundation. He publishes tracts and writes endless letters to newspaper editors. Yet his mountainous fortune has brought him little influence. In 1960 he went to the Democratic National Convention in Los Angeles to muster support for Lyndon Johnson (and the oil-depletion allowance), but hardly anybody noticed him as he walked the hotel corridors — a rumpled, wispy-haired, and lonely billionaire. Tucked away in his sparsely furnished downtown Dallas office, Hunt eats lunch from a brown paper bag which he carries daily from his home, an overblown reproduction of Mount Vernon. He has found no real purpose for his enormous substance except further accumulation.

As a group, the oil-rich of the Southwest own a large portion of America's wealth, but they are little known to their countrymen. Personal fortunes ranging from $100 million to $500 million have been amassed by such independent operators as R. E. Smith, George W. Strake, John Mecom, and James Abercrombie of Houston, but these names do not resound among the American public. Most of the big rich prefer it that way; they are intensely private accumulators.

The very rich men who control publicly held oil companies are somewhat better known. Getty, of course, is in a class by himself. Those who have amassed personal fortunes above

$200 million include Jacob Blaustein of Baltimore (American Oil), William Keck of Los Angeles (Superior Oil), A. H. Meadows of Dallas (General American Oil), and the late J. Howard Pew of Philadelphia (Sun Oil). These men are capitalists who have gone beyond accumulation to proprietorship. They are individualists, however, and the instinct to direct the companies they have built does not vanish with advancing age. J. Howard Pew, whose family owns 56.5 percent of Sun Oil, became president in 1912, upon the death of his father and company founder, Joseph Newton Pew, and he remained chairman until his death at eighty-nine years of age.

The best known of the contemporary American rich are the truly dynastic families, those favored not only with shrewd nineteenth-century founders but also with an abundance of able sons. In this respect, the Mellons of Pittsburgh have been singularly fortunate. Each of the principal members of the family — Mrs. Ailsa Mellon Bruce of New York, Paul Mellon of Upperville, Virginia, Mrs. Sarah Mellon Scaife and Richard King Mellon, both of Pittsburgh — enjoyed a personal fortune of around $500 million. The aggregate of Mellon wealth, held personally and in trusts, is at least $3 billion and perhaps considerably more, making them the richest family in America.

The founder, Judge Thomas Mellon, went into private banking at an extremely propitious time. The golden era of Pittsburgh's industrial development was beginning, and he backed such men as Henry Clay Frick, the coke king. His sons, Richard and Andrew, expanded the family's holdings across a range of growing industries: the Mellons own about 20 percent of both the Koppers Company and the Carborundum Company, and about 30 percent of the Aluminum Company of America. Andrew took a leading role in raising the Mellon National Bank & Trust Company (about 40 percent family-owned) to the first rank of finance, and later served as Secretary of the Treasury under Harding, Coolidge, and Hoover. The present heirs have conserved and added to their immense wealth. Yet, for all the diversity of Mellon investments, the taproot goes deep into the riches of the earth: the family's 25 percent ownership of Gulf Oil Corporation alone is worth better than $2 billion.

Wealth in the ground is a secure base for family eminence, provided male heirs are plentiful. The waning of the proud name of Guggenheim makes the point. The immigrant Swiss peddler, Meyer, was blessed with eight sons (seven of whom survived). They joined him in building a $5000 investment in two flooded mines into the American Smelting & Refining Company and a fortune of some $200 million. But there the luck ran out. The sons of the founding line failed spectacularly to reproduce themselves. By the fourth generation, only two male heirs had survived. The sturdy family tree planted in America by Meyer Guggenheim had been drained of vigor, and its limbs were dried and ready to fall.

The most solidly established American name and fortune belongs to the Rockefellers, who are collectively worth upwards of $2 billion. The family has a distinction surpassing mere possession: through their pioneering foundations, the Rockefellers have given away more money — more than $500 million — than any other family in American history. In the Standard Oil empire, the original John D. Rockefeller raised a monument to the crude capitalism of his time, integrating production, refining, and distribution. To outcries against his methods, John D., a pious Baptist and a no-quarter competitor, offered a classic reply: "God gave me my money." His son, John D., Jr., conceived a filial duty to give much of it back, declaring, "I regard it as my responsibility to see that the vast amount of money [my father] accumulated is used for the good of humanity."

In their philanthropy and desire for public service, the Rockefellers have been a pace-setting family among the very wealthy. Even where they came relatively late, as in their investment in Manhattan real estate, they left a distinctive mark. By far the most valuable buildings on the most valuable land in America are in Rockefeller Center in midtown Manhattan. The center came to be built, ironically, because John D. Rockefeller, Jr., was unable to give some land away.

In 1929 the patrons of the Metropolitan Opera wished to relocate it. John D. Rockefeller, Jr., took a long-term lease from Columbia University on a three-block site further uptown, intending to donate part of it as a public square in the opera project. With the stock market crash and the coming of the Depression, the Met decided to stay put, and Rockefeller had what appeared to be a white elephant on his hands. Nevertheless, he decided to raze the stores and brownstones on the site, and build offices and theaters. The National Broadcasting Company and RKO (which soon went into bankruptcy) were persuaded to locate in the complex, which was to be named Radio City. One of John D., Jr.'s five sons, Nelson, became the leading spirit and chief renting agent of the unpromising venture. With 5 million square feet of office space to fill in a Depression-busted market, Nelson realized he needed more than clever advertising. He proceeded to buy up long-term leases at other buildings and moved the kidnapped tenants to what was finally called Rockefeller Center.

The name was changed to help the shaky undertaking, although John D. Rockefeller, Jr., was at first opposed to "plastering the family name all over a piece of real estate."

It turned out to be an extraordinary piece of real estate, and a very profitable one. Built at a time of low construction costs for $125 million, the Center, according to Laurance Rockefeller's ultraconservative estimate, could not be duplicated for three times that amount. Once rented, the buildings stayed filled. Land values in the vicinity soared. In the late 1950s, a boom of hotel and office building began in the surrounding blocks which still shows no signs of abating. (To complete this tale of semiaccidental good fortune, when the Met finally moved uptown to its new home in the Lincoln Center for the Performing Arts, the chairman of Lincoln Center's board, appropriately, was John D. Rockefeller III.)

Steelmaker Andrew Carnegie once observed, somewhat ruefully, "More money has been made in real estate than in all industrial investments combined." This was certainly true of investments made in Manhattan island, which sometimes seems to exist solely to be bought and sold. The Rockefellers had the daring to violate the rule laid down by John Jacob Astor: "Buy and hold. Let others improve." Astor preferred to lease land, rather than sell it. When the lease expired, he had the right to buy, at its estimated value, any building his tenant had erected, or to grant another lease at much higher rent. The pressure of rapidly growing population on the fixed land area of narrow Manhattan thus became the force behind his mounting fortune, while he did little but pour rent money into the purchase of more land. At his death, he owned thousands of residences, scores of commercial buildings, acres of vacant lots, miles of waterfront.

The American Astors faded with the death of Vincent Astor in 1959, but the absentee British branch of the family subsequently owned valuable property in New York City — the land beneath the New York Hilton Hotel and the Park Avenue lots occupied by the headquarters of the First National City Bank, which administers the Astor Trust. In 1963, Tiffany & Company wished to purchase from the Trust the ground beneath its building at the corner of Fifth Avenue and 57th Street — a mere 85 feet by 125 feet. The heirs were pleased to heed another of John Jacob's rules: "Buy the acre and sell the lot." Tiffany paid $2.8 million.

The heirs of lesser Manhattan landowning families — the Rhinelanders, the Roosevelts, the Beekmans, the Schermerhorns, and the Goelets — still live very comfortably on their ancestors' foresight. A leader of the landed New York aristocracy, Robert Goelet died in 1965 at the ripe age of eighty-six, leaving an estate worth an estimated $50 million. The foresight in this family belonged to Peter Goelet, an ironmonger during the Revolution, who bought farmland north of the small but growing city. His sons acquired more land, and so did their sons. In time, the Goelet holdings, which included fifty-five acres stretching along the East Side from Union Square to 48th Street, were valued at more than $140 million. The Goelets helped found the Chemical Bank, allied themselves with other important financial institutions, and skillfully practiced the art of conserving wealth. The elderly Robert, though he did not stint the pleasures of Europe and Newport, was true to his obligation, as his ample estate showed. If the heirs apply themselves, old New York wealth based on the land can go on practically forever.

III.

Manhattan real estate not only sustains wealth; it also attracts great capital in search of speculative gain. The du Ponts have been active there. The estate of William Randolph Hearst still holds some of the properties he bought with open-handed abandon. For a time, John Paul Getty owned, among other things, the elegant Hotel Pierre; when he sold it, he kept a lease on the ballroom and banquet facilities. And, of course, Joseph P. Kennedy, though a celebrated moviemaker and whiskey-importer, made the bulk of his fortune dealing in Manhattan real estate, most of which was sold before his death.

Speculators seek the rapid turnover of property. In contrast, Mrs. Geraldine Dodge displayed a stubborn sense of ownership and refused to part with what has been called "the choicest residential plot in New York." It lies on the northeast corner of Fifth Avenue and 61st Street, and a boarded-up private home occupies one corner of the 28,000-square-foot site. Luxury apartment house builders coveted the land, but Mrs. Dodge enjoyed the view from her nearby window and preferred to leave the lot unused. She could afford to ignore the fact that it would bring her around $16 million. At her death in 1973 at the age of ninety-one, Mrs. Dodge left an estate estimated at $80 million.

Land prices in Manhattan — more than $400 a square foot along Park Avenue at the peak of the boom in the late 1960s — are fantastic, to be sure, but they seemed no less fantastic to the men who bought at a fraction of the present prices twenty years ago. And so knowledgeable men such as

Lawrence A. Wien and Harry B. Helmsley, the leading real-estate operators in the city, continue to buy. They have acted as partners since 1949, and have holdings, mainly in New York, which they value at around $1 billion.

In the early 1950s Wien, a lawyer, pioneered the creation of public real-estate syndications, in which hundreds of small investors combined resources to buy very large properties (and their share of tax advantages). In 1961, a syndicate of some 3000 individuals led by Wien and Helmsley bought the Empire State Building. Later, the partners bid for the $150-million real-estate holdings of hotelman J. Myer Schine. The deal collapsed when the then seventy-three-year-old Schine read that he was selling because he was "old."

Undaunted, Wien and Helmsley next put together an even bigger deal, one of the largest involving a single property in New York's history. In order to build a fifty-two-story office skyscraper on an extremely desirable square block, they agreed to lease the ground from the owner, the Bowery Savings Bank, for a whopping $200 million in rent over a period of fifty years. The biggest prior deal for a single property was the $100 million purchase of "air rights" above Grand Central Station for the hulking Pan Am Building. Wien and Helmsley, whose income amounts to several million dollars annually, are not speculators and rarely sell. "Our business is owning," says Wien.

In New York and other long-settled cities, professionals like Wien and Helmsley are destined to replace all but the most resourceful of the old landlords. Unless each generation guards the family capital after the fashion of the Goelets, fortunes are reduced and dispersed through inheritance. In the mid-nineteenth century, one of the largest owners of city real estate in the U.S., ranking close behind Astor, was a colorful lawyer, Nicholas Longworth of Cincinnati. Longworth bought up hundreds of lots for as little as $10 apiece when Cincinnati was still on the edge of the frontier. But the Longworth property was soon dispersed, and other large owners arose, such as the Tafts. In Chicago, Marshall Field became the merchant prince of the prairies and bought vast stretches of the city. These holdings, too, have been fragmented. The most conspicuous structure in Chicago linked with the Field name, the huge Merchandise Mart, was sold in 1945. The buyer, Joe Kennedy, paid under $13 million for what proved to be the outstanding bargain of his real estate career. The Mart, now valued at about $100 million, is the largest single part of the Kennedy fortune.

Great landowners still flourish in the open spaces of the Southwest and Far West. Texans who have real estate fortunes above $100 million include Robert Kleberg, Jr., of the famed King Ranch, and William Blakely and Leo Corrigan, both of Dallas. One of eight children of an Irish immigrant family, Corrigan left school in St. Louis after the fifth grade and did not get into real estate until he was twenty-eight. He moved quickly thereafter. He owns scores of shopping centers scattered throughout the U.S., several thousand apartment buildings, ten hotels (The Biltmore in Los Angeles, The Adolphus in Dallas), and several large office buildings. Corrigan is another professional who believes in buying and holding: he still owns all but a handful of the hundreds of major purchases he has made.

In the South, Florida real estate millionaires are somewhat suspect. Too many have claimed wealth on the basis of their visions of shining cities arising from alligator swamps. The first true developer was Henry Morrison Flagler, a partner in the original Standard Oil Company and a very rich man when he arrived in Florida around the turn of the century. He needed to be rich. Flagler poured millions of dollars into construction of the first luxury hotels and the Florida East Coast Railway to Key West. The state legislature rewarded him by granting 8000 acres of land for each mile of railroad he constructed south of Daytona. His Model Land Company eventually owned some 2 million acres in the state.

After the wild land boom and bust of the twenties, Florida slumbered until another very rich man, Arthur Vining Davis, came on the scene in the late 1940s and began buying everything in sight. Davis made his money in the Aluminum Company of America, of which he was board chairman. The story goes that he came to the attention of the Mellons when he asked for a small loan at the family bank in Pittsburgh. "I will tell you the worst," the young Davis said. "I am a college graduate and the son of a minister, but I mean to pay." The loan was made, repaid, and the Mellons chose Davis to manage the company they formed to try Charles Martin Hall's new process for aluminum-making.

Davis was eighty years old when he made his first land purchases in Florida, and he acted as though he had no time to lose. Within six years, he spent $50 million and became one of the state's largest land owners, holding 125,000 acres which included one eighth of Dade County. He moved in deep secrecy, but a reporter once managed to get him on the telephone and asked what his aims were in Florida. "Making money," roared Davis. "What else?"

Though cantankerous, Davis respected a man who stuck to his job. "I've had to work sixteen hours a day to make a good

245

living," he once told an interviewer. One day, he was out overseeing a development he owned, and he found his path blocked by a bulldozer, which was clearing away brush. He shouted to the driver to stop and let him by. The driver knew who the visitor was, but he replied: "I ain't about to stop work until my foreman tells me." Davis waited patiently. The next day he gave the driver a $100 check.

In 1962, Davis died at the age of ninety-five in his pink oceanfront mansion, Journey's End. Until forced to his bed, he had insisted on operating his own wheelchair, as though he still had some distance to go toward an unspecified goal. He died, according to the newspapers, the richest man in Florida.

On the other side of the continent, two little-known families are among the more important land owners in America. The Weyerhaeusers of Tacoma, Washington, are descended from a German immigrant, Frederick (Dutch Fred). In the early years of this century, he became the biggest lumber man in the world. On his death in 1914, his company owned almost 2 million acres of timberland, four fifths of which had been purchased from the Northern Pacific Railroad. When he struck the bargain with James J. Hill, paying only six dollars an acre, Dutch Fred, who once cut the virgin forests ruthlessly, said: "This is not for ourselves and our children, but for our grandchildren." His great-grandson became chief executive of the company, which has extended its timberland to some 3.6 million acres. This is an average of one acre for every square mile in the U.S., and a total area larger than Connecticut.

The Irvine family of Orange County, California, owns — and has fought bitterly in public about — what is probably the most valuable tract of land under development in the U.S.

The Irvine Ranch, assembled by the late James Irvine, Jr., consisted of 138 square miles stretching from the Pacific Ocean to the Santa Ana Mountains. The original ranch lay in the path of southward expansion of one of the fastest-growing metropolitan areas in the world, and its development may eventually bring as much as $1 billion.

Before his death in 1947, the dictatorial "J.I." deeded the majority of the stock in the company which owned the ranch to the Irvine Foundation, a precaution that did not prevent turmoil among his heirs. At the center of it was his favorite granddaughter, Joan Irvine, who owns the largest (one-fifth) interest outside the foundation. Hot-tempered Joan has battled in and out of the courts to have the ranch sold off in a way satisfactory to her.

In recent years, the leading mystery among those who know the land and the men who own it was unfolding in Nevada. Howard Hughes, whom everybody has heard of and nobody knows, appeared to be buying the city of Las Vegas. The legendary recluse, whose fortune is near $1 billion, answers to no one. His industrial empire, built on Hughes Aircraft (estimated sales: $500 million) and Hughes Tool Company ($400 million), is entirely his — no stockholders, and only he gives commands over the telephone to a few trusted executives.

During the late 1960s, Hughes, who already owned an estimated $100 million in real estate, bought or took options on another $100 million worth of property in and near Las Vegas. His agents always paid cash and gave no explanation. Hughes bought or had options to buy half of the hotels along the "Strip"; in the others, everyone from the bootblacks to the managers awaited the phantom's call. He took over undeveloped land in the city and a ranch twenty-five miles west.

He bought the local CBS-TV affiliate and expressed a desire to buy the second station as well. He discussed buying a newspaper and an advertising agency. He had an option to buy the North Las Vegas air terminal. It was as though Hughes were an unseen visitor from another planet, who had sent scouts ahead to establish, quite legally, a colony in the desert.

IV.

The image of Howard Hughes alone in the cockpit of a plane, roaring through the night sky to a city purchased for his secret purposes, is the absurdly heightened reality behind the American dream of possession. *Every man can own and rise; everything is possible.* The great fortunes no longer excite much envy or even attention. Capital has lost its power to awe. It is forty years since the mood of the nation was reflected in Ferdinand Lundberg's famous accusation: "The United States is owned and dominated today by a hierarchy of its sixty richest families . . ."

Yet not as much has changed as we like to imagine. The rich in America own one fifth of the corporate stock, regardless of the comforting estimate that there are 31 million stockholders. Contemplating the extent of poverty in the United States, Gunnar Myrdal, the Swedish economist and social philosopher, has declared: "I draw the conclusion that the common idea that America is an immensely rich and affluent country is very much an exaggeration." There are plenty of statistics tending to show that Americans are not as well-off as they suppose. The median family income in 1972 was $11,120, barely enough to support a "unit" of four persons. The

Bureau of Labor Statistics estimates that a typical city worker's family of four needs more than $11,000 to live "moderately," an increase of 75 percent over the estimate in 1959.

In four out of ten families with incomes above $10,000, both husband and wife are working, and she brings home as much as 30 percent of the total income. What would happen if she had to quit? The wife is the chief breadwinner in 7.4 percent of the 44 million families in the U.S. — up from 5.7 percent in 1960. A University of Michigan survey of liquid family assets — checking and savings accounts and nonnegotiable savings bonds — reveals median holdings of not much more than a month's income. One family in five had *no* such assets, and one in three had under $200. Such evidence indicates that the deceptively expansive American way of life is actually lived close to the margin.

More than a generation after the New Deal, the nation as a whole is much wealthier, but the cause is sustained economic growth rather than redistribution of wealth. The relative shares of the national income remain stubbornly constant: the lower 40 percent of families continue to receive about 17 percent of overall income, while the families in the top 5 percent receive 15 percent. Except among the ghetto poor, however, economic inequality appears to have subsided as a political issue. At least until the stagflation of 1974, the majority of Americans seemed convinced they had gained a place in the middle class, and they expected to stay there and climb higher.

It is true that a large majority of American families (approaching 70 percent) now earn incomes between $5000 and $15,000, but "middle class" is not a definable economic status. It is a state of mind. It ignores abstract statistics or vast aggregates and concentrates on down-to-earth sums the size of weekly paychecks. These pay the mortgage, put a child through college, finance a second car, and perhaps even justify the impulse to fly-now to Forida in midwinter. Heavily taxed and vulnerable to inflation, the typical American family does not measure its well-being in terms of capital, although it has respectable equity in pension funds and insurance policies, and in its house. (The personal net worth of the population, to note a truly vast aggregate, is above $1.5 trillion.) The family judges its prosperity by the income it earns — and it lives a step or two ahead on the reasonable expectation it will soon earn more.

Who owns America? The answer cannot be found in statistics or be reduced to lists of large property owners. Even if the possessions of the entire population could be totted up, the ownership of every asset nailed down, it would not be sufficient. The answer lies with the American people, and it changes as their sense of equity in America changes. It consists not so much of what they possess now as what they *hope* to own.

The U. S., Japan, and the
New Economic Era

I.

ON A HOT WEEKEND in August 1971, President Nixon and his principal economic advisers met at Camp David, the official retreat in Maryland's Catoctin Mountains, and adopted a set of measures called the New Economic Policy. All that was truly "new" was Nixon's sponsorship, for he took over and made his own almost every proposal of his Democratic opponents. This was a definitive instance of Nixon playing pre-emptive politics. With his eyes fixed on the election fourteen months away, the President was determined to deny the opposition every possible inch of ground on which to attack his mismanagement of the economy.

For almost three years, the Nixon administration had attempted to bring under control the serious inflation inherited from the Johnson years. It succeeded only in slowing down the economy, boosting unemployment, and reducing corporate profits. Prices were still rising sharply. Once, Nixon men had spoken confidently of a "game plan" that would produce noninflationary full-employment. Now that talk had ceased. "There isn't any game plan," said a ranking economic adviser privately, "and it's ridiculous to go on pretending." Conventional, neo-Keynesian economic theory provided no prescription for the situation. The federal budget, the supposed stabilizer of the economy, was largely beyond the control of the would-be managers. The American Welfare State had come to maturity, and it was fantastically expensive. Nixon saw nothing to lose in trying almost anything.

The New Economic Policy consisted of a freeze on wages and prices, suspension of the U.S. guarantee to redeem dollars in foreign hands at the rate of thirty-five dollars per ounce of gold, imposition of a 10 percent surtax on most U.S. imports, and various tax measures intended to stimulate consumer spending, investment, and employment. The officials who posed for photographs outside the Camp David lodges appeared well pleased with themselves and their work. Their host certainly was. He shook hands, distributed souvenirs of the meeting — drinking glasses etched with the presidential seal — and then returned to the White House to deliver the speech that he knew would confound the Democrats and shake the world.

The weekend was historic, as everyone agreed at the time, but the significance of the New Economic Policy was somewhat obscured in the reaction to the President's dramatic self-reversal. Nixon's decision to bury more of his avowed beliefs in a shallow, hastily dug grave was unimportant. Much more significant was his decision to abandon the perspective and practice established by American Presidents since World War II. For the first time in a generation, the U.S. had made decisions of the highest international importance secretly and unilaterally on the basis of domestic self-interest. None of the allied nations directly affected by the new policies was consulted in advance. What lay buried at Camp David was the remains of America's commitment to internationalism.

Few Americans mourned its passing. As they saw it, the U.S. had unselfishly carried a mounting burden for prosperous and ungrateful allies who were now bruising trade competitors. It was time for "Uncle Sucker" to begin looking after the U.S.'s neglected national interests, and let the foreigners look out for themselves. The popular perception was not entirely accurate — the U.S. had reaped great trading and investment benefits from the special status of the dollar — but the sovereign democratic will demanded "domestic emphasis" and the politicians translated the popular desire into economic nationalism. The retreat from international responsibility was made unavoidable by another consequence of democracy: chronic federal budget deficits financed through inflation. Rather than accept the discipline of fiscal tightening-up at home, which would risk recession and increased unemployment, the U.S. had flooded the world with dollars. When foreign holdings of depreciating paper dollars reached a figure that would clean out Fort Knox several times over, the U.S. simply closed the gold window.

As the surtax on imports revealed, the new international economic policies were aimed chiefly at a single nation — Japan — with which the U.S. suffered a trade deficit approaching $4 billion. Devastated during World War II, the former enemy made a miraculous recovery and embarked on a phenomenal record of economic growth. In the 1960s Japan's gross national product grew at the astonishing rate of 11.3 percent each year, far outdistancing all other major industrial countries. Productivity rose at the awesome annual rate of 11 to 13 percent during the decade. In 1968, Japan moved ahead of West Germany to take third place on the world's GNP ladder behind the U.S.S.R. and the U.S. Japan was a vast workshop. The Japanese were without natural resources, and they prospered by efficiently converting imported raw materials into finished goods. Although exports amounted to under 10 percent of Japan's GNP, these grew three times as fast as total world exports in the 1960s. Japan's extraordinary trade expansion and resulting huge surpluses lay at the heart of the continuing international monetary crisis.

II.

The basic ingredient of Japan's economic success was the character of the tightly knit and culturally homogeneous Japanese people, with their capacity for hard work, ingenuity, aggressiveness, and diligence, and their propensity for savings and investment. Because Japan's welfare programs were modest and retirement benefits skimpy, workers were forced to be savers. As a result, Japan enjoyed a very high rate of capital formation and allocated a larger part of its GNP to investment than any other industrialized country. The government-directed banking system channeled this capital into high-priority growth industries. Productivity and output also were promoted by exceptionally stable labor-management relations. In Japan's favor too was the availability from abroad of the proven modern technology necessary to rebuild the war-ravaged industrial base.

The U.S. contributed greatly to Japan's recovery and growth, providing sound economic policies during the Oc-

254

cupation and a subsequent flow of raw materials, services, grants, and loans. The one-sided U.S.-Japan defense arrangements enabled the disarmed Japanese to devote only a tiny fraction of their resources to unproductive armaments. American technology was exported and helped increase Japan's competitive strength. Traditional U.S. free-trade policy gave high-quality Japanese consumer goods far more liberal access to our domestic market than American products received in Japan. Finally, Japan enjoyed the trading advantages of a substantially undervalued currency. In the minds of many Japanese, the 360-to-1 yen-dollar exchange rate was as fixed and immutable as the American "big brother's" obligation to defend Japan.

By the end of the 1960s, rising Japanese imports had created intense resentment and opposition from threatened American industries and unions. A unique communications gap, arising from cultural, language, and racial differences, already separated the two nations. (Prior to World War II, both sides consistently misread each other's political temper, and in some instances diplomatic exchanges between Washington and Tokyo were literally misinterpreted, with disastrous results.) The flow of current information between the countries was woefully one-way. The Japanese press, with its huge circulation and English-language editions, carried a great deal of political and economic news about the U.S. — more, in shameful fact, than many U.S. papers carried — while the American press ignored Japan. Americans were uninterested in foreigners generally, and the Japanese were too remote and alien to be worth the effort of understanding.

The World War II–era, racially biased stereotype of "the Japs" prevailed at all levels of American society. A South

Carolina representative inserted in the *Congressional Record* a song that he said was popular with the unemployed textile workers in his district. Called "The Import Blues," it included this verse: "Buying Japanese products so sleazy to see/ Is a damn fool thing for you and me/ And I'm fighting back because I won't run/ From the slant-eyed people of the Rising Sun." In New York City, the ultraliberal International Ladies' Garment Workers' Union sponsored blatant anti-Japanese propaganda in the form of subway-car advertisements: "Has your job been exported to Japan? If not, it soon will be." By the fall of 1970, under pressure from politically powerful unions, some 300 members of the House (out of 435) had introduced or co-sponsored bills that would impose quotas on imports, principally from Japan. "The retreat from free trade is part of a broad national retreat from international commitments," observed a veteran staff member of the House Ways and Means Committee. "You can feel the blast of the wind blowing in this country — and you can be sure these politicians feel it."

When the Japanese, perplexed and themselves resentful, asked why the U.S. was so adamant about restricting their textile imports, which in 1970 amounted to only 1.3 percent of the total value of American domestic consumption, they asked the right question. The highly charged textile issue was only the tip of a political iceberg, of which trade issues as such formed a much smaller part than the public realized. President Nixon had promised import protection for the textile industry to Senator Strom Thurmond of South Carolina, whose support had been decisive in Nixon's 1968 campaign for the Republican nomination. Looking toward 1972 and coveting the South's electoral votes, Nixon intended to keep that promise. Democrats in the Congress and their union allies also had their sights on much bigger targets than the textile invaders. "Congress can get tough with the Japanese and get the textile industry off its back, but that doesn't affect the much more serious problems," an AFL-CIO official privately declared. "We aren't nearly as concerned with the Japanese as we are with the runaway U.S. multinational corporations."

From 1969 to 1971, the Americans and the Japanese talked about the textile problem but failed to communicate. At their first meeting, President Nixon hinted at a deal to visiting Premier Sato — the U.S. would return occupied Okinawa in exchange for "voluntary" Japanese textile export quotas. ("That way," said a White House staff member, "both Nixon and Sato could save face with their constituencies.") But Sato, if he understood the message, failed to act on it. Other figures soon entered the confused picture, and as inept emissaries shuttled between Washington and Tokyo, misunderstanding grew.

When Sato visited Washington for a second time in the fall of 1970, the White House issued a positive-sounding communiqué and officials voiced optimism. The true situation was quite different. "All was sweetness and light on the surface," a Nixon insider recalled, "but it was darker than ever underneath. Things weren't better, they were worse. Nixon had tightened the screws on Sato, telling him that we had moved on Okinawa — so what was holding up the textile question? Sato withered right there in the President's office. Here he was catching political hell at home, dancing around the fires set by his own textile and union people — all of them screaming that Sato had sold them out to the scheming Yankees who always treated Japanese as second-class citizens — and now here was Nixon face to face, giving Sato another scorching."

257

This encounter poisoned the personal relations between the two leaders. "When the Japanese allowed the textile question to drag on and on, Nixon became angry because he felt let down and embarrassed," according to a top-ranking presidential adviser. "That was the main reason why he didn't inform Sato in advance of the proposed trip to Peking."

When Nixon concluded Sato would not deliver on their deal, the White House began lobbying hard in the House Ways and Means Committee concerning the President's supposedly critical need for new textile quota legislation. The U.S., it was emphasized, couldn't get Japan to agree to anything without a blackjack in the President's pocket — the threat of a restrictive trade bill that would almost surely be drafted to include scores of other industries claiming damage from import competition.

Eventually, amid much needless bitterness, the Japanese submitted to the American demands and adopted textile export restraints. Ironically, within two years, as a result of several factors including the denim jeans craze among Japanese youth, Japan became a net *importer* of American textile products. And Japanese and American textile manufacturers were complaining to their respective governments about "cheap labor" competition from Hong Kong, Taiwan, and South Korea. Moreover, some of the big textile companies began forming trans-Pacific joint ventures to operate in third markets where they could not prosper separately.

In truth, the U.S. and Japan, though very different and apparently fated to suffer perpetual misunderstanding, had too much in common economically to go their separate ways. The U.S. was Japan's biggest customer, and Japan was second only to Canada as a U.S. export market. In third markets, they were each other's suppliers, partners, and bankers as well as competitors. A cause of conflict, arising from similarity of commercial instinct, was that the two nations continually ran into each other in the world marketplace.

America's turn toward so-called protectionism, however, was much more than an expression of an economic attitude. The threat of protectionist trade legislation which American bargainers held out when dealing with the Japanese could not be eliminated by their concessions alone. That left unresolved the psychological conflict within the Japanese-American relationship.

In a candid speech to the Japan Society in New York, then Secretary of Commerce Peter G. Peterson looked beneath the oft-cited ignorance and resentment of Japan among Americans. He found "an element of envy as well; the patronizing envy of the teacher equaled or even surpassed by his pupil; there is an element of shock — not since the Industrial Revolution have U.S. commercial interests had to reckon with an economic superpower outside of Europe. Finally, there is the element of sublimated anger, the anger of the profligate, who, suffering some guilt from the charge of having squandered a major part of his treasure, makes his more prudent neighbor bear the brunt of the irritation he feels with himself."

There was much truth in this statement, unhappily. America's own self-image would have to improve in order to brighten Japan's image in the U.S.

III

When I visited then Secretary of the Treasury John Connally in his office in mid-April 1972, the economic scene was brightening. Housing starts and capital investment were rising, and the stock market was soaring. *Business Week* summed up the emerging mood in a headline: "It Really Looks Like the Boom is Here." From Connally's spacious corner office, he could look out the window over the Ellipse and see the cherry blossoms surrounding the Tidal Basin.

But the view from the Treasury, with the huge public debt extending into the next century, is necessarily longer than today and tomorrow. Quite apart from that, Connally, as a prudent politician, was intent on using this period of calm to get ready for the seemingly inevitable instability ahead.

The previous December, he had engineered the Washington Agreement that enabled the U.S. to gain a substantial devaluation of the dollar in return for a nominal increase in the official price of gold — which the U.S. continued to refuse to sell. The world's major currencies were now "floating" rather than tied to fixed parities. Connally was optimistic that the makeshift monetary arrangements would hold through the fall of 1972 and the presidential election. After that, however, he foresaw a much darker and more difficult time for the U.S. and its political-military allies and trading rivals.

Serious negotiations on reform of the monetary system could not begin, Connally said, until the major trading nations "accept the fact that the United States must run a balance of payments surplus for a period of years." The Europeans were still a long way from accepting this unpalatable "fact." Instead, they suggested that the U.S. strive for the payments goal of "equilibrium," the fuzzy concept put forward a decade ago. The Secretary had asked the Europeans: "What does that mean?" So far, he had received no satisfactory answer. In the absence of such an answer, he saw no alternative but to demand conditions which would permit a solid, honest U.S. payments surplus for at least three consecutive years.

Many foreigners regarded the demand that the U.S. be allowed to run a surplus as unreasonable. Some of them suspected that, when Connally made such a demand, he was bluffing and trying to improve his ground before the bargaining started. In part, this suspicion was well founded. Right up until the eve of the Rome meeting of the Group of Ten nations which paved the way for the Washington Agreement, the Secretary had adamantly refused even to consider a devaluation of the dollar. And then, suddenly, he had sprung the idea, causing mouths to fly open and, one participant recalled, a full ten minutes of extremely thoughtful silence before some of the ministers excused themselves to seek instructions from their governments.

John Connally was completely unlike his recent predecessors at the Treasury in many important respects. For one thing, he was relatively uninterested in narrow monetary questions and intensely concerned with overarching questions of U.S. foreign policy. He naturally assumed the perspective of a President. "What kind of world will we be living in ten or twenty years from now?" he asked. "That's what we're really trying to determine." Even in our frank conversation, Connally did not answer that question. But what he deliberately did not say was sometimes as eloquent as what he said. Connally ignored the slogans of the past generation of international relations, based on a U.S.-centered world, and he used the new slogans of the Nixon era with visible restraint, for he realized very well how much uncertainty lay beneath the confident-sounding words.

Nevertheless, through the combination of his words and his silence, Connally conveyed an unmistakable impression of what he foresaw in the longer term, and answered his own question about the kind of world the U.S. could expect within the 1970s. *It would be a world dominated by considerations of economic necessity, and the U.S. and other industrially advanced nations would be forced to put national interests far ahead of sentiment in calculating complex and interacting balances of power.*

During the Vietnam decade of the 1960s, in spite of all the splendid one-sided alliances created during the previous generation, Americans discovered that the world was a lonely place. Not a single nation in Western Europe gave a moment's thought to sending troops, supplies, or other tangible assistance to Southeast Asia, even though these same nations based their own defense on the ultimate willingness of the U.S. to risk nuclear war on their behalf. Now the American people, as the shortsighted Europeans failed to see, were attracted by the seeming escape from responsibility offered by a policy of national loneliness ("neo-isolationism").

Connally, if he did not share this attitude, surely sympathized with it. He had not the slightest economic or cultural affinity for Western Europe. His world view was that of the landlocked Texan, who recognized neighbors and strangers only. Foreigners fell into two categories: cooperative and uncooperative. In his view, NATO (or any other alliance) rested entirely on the willingness of some foreigners to "earn" U.S. support by cooperation on key issues vis-à-vis other foreigners. Connally, like the British strategists of the nineteenth century, believed that the U.S. has no permanent friends or enemies, only permanent interests which must be served.

Many Europeans and more than a few Americans who did business in Europe professed to be unable to "understand" Connally. There was no difficulty in understanding him if one understood America, for his view was much closer to that of the ordinary citizen than the pious falsehoods of the Department of State. What the Europeans found incomprehensible was an American whose nationalism was as deep and selfish and tenacious as theirs. They were accustomed to American officials who had a well-bred internationalist outlook, and who took America's obligations toward the rest of the world more seriously than the balancing obligations of America's negligent allies. These Europeans were accustomed to denounce America's global power and simultaneously to depend on it. They had not yet adjusted to the end of America's attempt to assert global hegemony. Connally easily adjusted to it, for he never believed that his country should assume the proper burdens of other countries in the first place. The worst thing that could happen to a man or a country, in his eyes, was to be taken advantage of, to be played for a sucker. Connally plainly felt that America's generosity had been abused, and he proposed to do something about it.

"We should not deceive ourselves that we can have a single, worldwide policy on trade or money or what-have-you when other countries don't," said Connally. "We've seen that other governments in other countries don't operate the way our government does. At the time when we were a so-called superpower, we could write and enforce rules for world trade and exchange rates. And we were rich enough not to care that the rules we wrote worked out to our own economic and financial detriment. But no more. In the future, it will be necessary for us to have different policies toward different countries."

What about the traditional U.S. commitment to certain ideal concepts presumably having universal application, such as the ideal of liberalized trade?

The Secretary almost snorted his contempt. "Oh, ideals are

fine, but we have to pay more attention to realities. This world of luxury and ease is over and done with. From now on, we will have to *work*."

Hard work was easier preached than accomplished in the new American culture. A Gallup poll showed that a majority of Americans, including skilled and unskilled manual workers, believed that the U.S. labor force was not turning out as much work each day as it could. The manual workers, by a 58 percent majority, expressed the belief that they could do at least one-fifth as much more work than they now did. Whether or not they would actually do so, given the necessity and/or incentive, was highly uncertain. "Success relaxes the hard discipline of necessity," wrote Professor Henry Wallich of Yale University, the Treasury's senior private adviser, in his *Newsweek* column. "Today, if we want to observe the Puritan ethic, we must turn to Japan, and soon perhaps to China."

Connally agreed completely with that view and showed a healthy respect for the Japanese. He played down the seriousness of the so-called Nixon Shocks ("I never thought we had much trouble with the Japanese, and that trouble is behind us"). The bilateral problems between the U.S. and Japan were fairly clear-cut, he believed, and consisted mainly of negotiating an early end to various Japanese restrictions on imports and capital flows. For example, the Japanese exported more than 700,000 automobiles annually and imported only some 5000. "Obviously," said Connally, "the Japanese cannot go on doing what they are doing — other nations can't live with this one-sided way of doing business. The more self-restraint the Japanese show, the better it will be for them in the long run."

In the long run, the Secretary speculated, the U.S. and

Japan were likely to find themselves in the same position vis-à-vis Western Europe: that of outsiders effectively barred from the Common Market. They would surely be excluded if the economies of the non-Communist nations entered a period of persistent inflation and sluggish growth, resulting in high unemployment. Then a turn toward extreme protectionism and "beggar thy neighbor" trading and monetary policies, as in the 1930s, might be inevitable. Should severe worldwide recession develop, Connally foresaw swift popular demand for radical changes in national economic and political systems, including the U.S.'s.

The world of the late 1970s might be a more equitable and orderly place, but John Connally was not making an unhedged bet that it would be. "All the talk about money rates and parities and reserves is beside the point. You must tie your economic and monetary formulas to your ability to produce and sell goods. That's where we're badly in need of improvement."

Connally's attitudes survived his tenure at the Treasury because they arose from America's altered circumstances. His successor, George Shultz, came to the Nixon administration from the University of Chicago, and was a convinced advocate of the free-market economics for which the university was celebrated. But Shultz was powerless to apply his libertarian, free-trade philosophy to the crisis besetting the U.S. at home and abroad. It was politically impractical.

As Connally had privately warned before his departure, the dollar devaluation underlying the Washington Agreement was too small. In early 1973, when the dollar again came under attack in European money markets, the Agreement was abandoned and the dollar again devalued. Shultz, in defending the unilateral U.S. action, said without apology that domestic necessity, rather than the interests of other nations, took priority. In mid-1973 the President was compelled to announce further anti-inflation measures, including controls on exports of agricultural products. Nixon justified these steps in blunt nationalistic terms: "In allocating the products of America's farms between the markets abroad and those in the U.S., we must put the American consumer first . . ." Even though the U.S. urgently needed to expand exports in order to achieve a trade and payments balance, domestic politics dictated keeping the farm products home on the voter's dinner table.

Soybeans under export contract to Japan, a trade Washington had actively promoted in prior years of agricultural glut, were abruptly cut off in a time of unexpected scarcity. The dependency the U.S. had encouraged — soybeans, imported almost exclusively from the U.S., were a staple of Japan's diet — was used to exert pressure on an ally moving too slowly on trade and monetary concessions.

"The people in Europe and Japan who thought they saw a difference between Connally and Shultz were only fooling themselves," a high Treasury official said privately. "Shultz takes the same line Connally did, although he does it a little more quietly. The people overseas will finally have to realize that it wasn't Connally's personality that upset them. It was a dramatic new turn in American policy. We intend to upset a great many arrangements that work to our disadvantage."

But upsetting existing international arrangements, however outmoded and inequitable, would do little more than buy time for Washington. Unless the U.S. revitalized its faltering domestic economy, laying the basis for long-term prosperity at home *and* enduring international cooperation, the policy of expedient unilateralism would accomplish little. Concealed beneath the slogans of aggressive economic nationalism lay the fact of internal weakness and the imperative necessity of the new era: reform of the American political economy.

IV.

America's domestic and international economic problems — inflation, unemployment, balance of payments deficit, loss of trade competitiveness — are obviously related, but our system forces us to tackle them separately, in uncoordinated, piece-meal fashion. These are public policy problems, yet only private resources and initiative can solve them. In the light of new international competitive realities, is our "mixed" economy mixed *enough?*

Business leaders who ponder such questions have begun to examine Japan's unique partnership between business and government. "The Japanese were once taken lightly in the West as imitators and copiers," Donald T. Regan, chairman of the board of Merrill Lynch, Pierce, Fenner & Smith, told the leaders of America's 500 largest corporations in a speech in May 1972. "But we all respect their drive and ingenuity today. Now it is the Japanese who are the innovative pioneers and we Westerners who must be the imitators, in order to maintain our own way of life and accustomed well-being."

Commerce Secretary Peterson, the first high government official systematically to study Japan's business-government relationship, prepared a briefing paper for President Nixon that drew the contrast between the U.S. and Japan. He declared: "Japan's bureaucracy is not an 'umpire of private business,' as in the U.S.; it is a partner and shares its goals. This partnership in planning has helped give Japan the world's largest steel mill and its dominant role in world shipbuilding. It is now stimulating future growth in computers, petrochemicals, aluminum, aircraft, and space. Thus, by a combination of free enterprise and national planning, resources are allocated to strategic growth areas — including exports." Peterson recognized the limitations imposed by the all-important cultural dimension, observing: "We cannot nor would we want to graft the Japanese business culture in the U.S. soil. But we can learn from its remarkable record of growth, and the foresight in its planning for modernization."

One lesson to be learned, surely, was a certain humility, which came more easily now that the once almighty dollar was toppled. American businessmen, who pride themselves on having invented marketing, are often poor salesmen abroad, partly because they arrogantly insist that the customer ought to want what we have to sell, the way we choose to sell it.

Akio Morita, the brilliant maverick who built Sony Corporation into a global marketing phenomenon, spoke with blunt though friendly candor to a group of foreign correspondents in Tokyo in June 1973. Said the president of Sony:

> In order to sell products in a foreign country, it is necessary to learn in detail the situation of that country. American enterprises, therefore, need to take more time to study the market situation in Japan and manufacture products that the Japanese people will want to buy, instead of expecting too quick results.
>
> To put it more frankly, Americans often assume that their philosophy is always right any place in the world and that anyone who does not understand their philosophy is wrong. Even in advertising we see examples. I know of some American companies that

268

bring to Japan advertising prepared for the American market by American advertising agencies. They merely change the wording into Japanese, and assume that the Japanese public will respond in the same favorable way as Americans. Common sense should tell a person that he cannot appeal to another person's mind or heart without first understanding the other's psychology and environment that changes with the times.

We must not assume that all peoples in the world are the same as Americans. We always hear Americans telling us to be fair. Of course fair play is absolutely necessary. But being fair does not mean that all nations should do things the American way. Being fair, I believe, means that if I go to another country, I must understand the way things are done in that country and abide by that pattern of local behavior.

The Japanese approach, which may be called "sponsored capitalism," combines far-ranging interventions in the country's economic affairs, including controls over foreign trade, domestic and foreign investment and financing, with the essential characteristics of a competitive capitalistic system. Japan's government-business relationship, though highly structured and legalistic, is marked by informality. There is little direct and overt compulsion. The partnership expressed in the phrase "Japan Incorporated" is a subtle and flexible blending of many direct and indirect methods by which the Japanese government provides "administrative guidance" and incentives primarily to big business, encouraging the shift of resources from mature and slower-growing industries to young and dynamic ones. The government partner does not stifle but stimulates entrepreneurial skills and energies.

Japan is a uniquely well-wired information network, and the information is shared by bureaucrats and businessmen alike. (It helps enormously that they are often old friends who attended school together. Japan is an elitist meritocracy — almost anyone can make it to the top, but he must do it according to well-defined rules and abide by the hierarchical structure within which he makes his career.) Both government and business make extensive use of planning and sophisticated analysis and forecasting, and use a wide array of special institutional arrangements for solving specific problems. Planning in Japan, however, is generally short-term (up to five years) and indicative rather than authoritative. Economic plans devised by the government are not formally binding on the business community. The government does not assign quotas or set rigid targets for industry. Blueprints are sufficiently elastic to allow for innovation and improvisation. Much planning is done on an ad hoc basis. A chief characteristic of the Japanese government's behavior in managing key economic sectors, including planning activities, is its tendency to react to situations and challenges with programs created for the occasion — for example, a program to meet a shortage of petroleum, to build aircraft and large ships, or to develop computer technology.

Still, the government's role in the management of the economy and its leverage to insure that its goals are met is penetrating and comprehensive by American standards. Part of the reason for this intimate co-management lies in the nature of Japanese society. Group identity and group loyalty are particularly strong forces. Formal confrontations and visible exercises of power are generally avoided. As a result, business and government in Japan are not the adversaries they often are in this country, both by circumstance and by the nature of the U.S. regulatory system. Because they can assume a profound convergence of basic national values and interests, government and business are usually able to reach consensus through a complex but efficient procedure of consultation. Government consults with industry even when it has the power to act alone. For example, such consultation occurred on the difficult question of establishing quotas for steel production. In this instance as in most others, the businessmen cooperated in government decisions that favored their competitors. Japanese businessmen are not only more willing than their American counterparts to respond to the government's wishes regarding production and marketing policies in the national interest. They are also far more dependent on their government's favor and future good will, although this difference is clearly narrowing.

Much more often than in the U.S., business in Japan expects government to share the risks of industrial expansion and market development. (This is another difference that probably must begin to narrow in years ahead.) Agreement on the necessity of continued growth is the essential foundation of the government's solicitude and the businessman's cooperative attitude. The goal of expanding markets to assure national as well as corporate prosperity draws government and business into strategies calling for the closest possible cooperation. On occasion, to be sure, consensus might be elusive — for example, when the government attempted to consolidate the Japanese auto industry and block U.S. investment in the industry. But reason or exhaustion usually prevails and unity is achieved.

"Japan Inc." rests on the foundation of government control over investment. Industry requires a high percentage of loan capital, which puts the fate of business in the hands of the government-controlled banking system. By U.S. standards, the loan indebtedness of Japanese firms is an extremely high proportion of capital — as much as 80 or even 90 percent. In the U.S., business usually obtains capital through the sale of various types of equity-related securities — *if* there is a market for them. In Japan, a company's leading banker is the source of most capital, and therefore he has a powerful voice in basic decisions, including selection of management personnel. Interestingly, the U.S. government, as the banker of last resort for the aerospace industry and bankrupt railroads, exercises similar prerogatives, but only *after* bad managers have run companies into the ground. In the public interest, government might be more attentive *before* the fact.

Recently, under the pressures created by rampant inflation, the energy crisis, and almost incredibly selfish business profiteering, the collaboration between government and business in Japan has sometimes broken down. Public opinion — itself a new phenomenon in Japan — is increasingly critical of secret dealings at the expense of the consumers. New attempts are being made to define the difference between legal and illegal cartels. But even critics admit that the government's "administrative guidance" is an integral part of the modern Japanese economy, and that it must continue although the ground rules may change.

Much as they may envy the support their Japanese counterparts receive from government, American businessmen probably are unwilling to pay the price of similar assistance in terms of reduced autonomy and decision-making authority. But it is not an "either/or" proposition. There are widely varying degrees of business-government partnership, and the one suitable to the American character, experience, and culture will differ from the Japanese model. The essential point to be

grasped is the necessity of *some* form of partnership or Nip-
ponization between America's private and public sectors in the
contemporary economic setting. Clearly the Japanese are
more at home than we are in the increasingly competitive
trading world of the 1970s, and we are under rising pressure
to adapt our attitudes, methods, and institutions to the changing international environment.

V.

The adversary relationship that developed between U.S.
business and government more than two generations ago
lingers, even as it has become a wasteful and harmful anachronism. In spite of hostile rhetoric and public posturing by
businessmen as well as politicians, their ad hoc cooperation is
commonplace. But it lacks visibility and continuity and therefore, especially after Watergate, it raises suspicions of one-shot
private bailouts at public expense. The public interest in the
prosperity of the private sector should be openly acknowledged by government. Without business profits, Washington
cannot conjure up prosperity. At the same time, government
and business should acknowledge that some problems affecting the economy as a whole are too important to be left to the
private sector alone to solve, and too complex for government
to tackle in detail. Would the U.S. confront a serious energy
crisis if joint planning and business-government cooperation
had been the rule? Without it in the future, we run the risk of
national economic disaster.

Surely a prime subject for sustained business-government

273

cooperation is *productivity* — how to measure and improve it in our postindustrial economy. Another subject for intensive consultation and new forms of cooperation is the marketing of American high technology products overseas, an effort in which government and business have little choice but to become full partners. Most customers cannot afford it — for example, the Russians — unless the government provides the necessary large-scale financing.

In some fashion, we are bound to adopt an approach similar to the Japanese and encourage the transfer of national resources from mature and inevitably obsolescent industries to more viable, higher-growth industries with a far brighter competitive future. We shall be bound, as the Japanese are, to minimize the human and economic consequences of such shifts of resources, through job retraining and relocation programs and regional redevelopment efforts. These are scarcely novel concepts in our society, but we have yet to apply them with the vigor and seriousness of the Japanese, who have made what amounts to a total national commitment to economic efficiency and maximum growth.

Our greatest challenge, however, does not depend on shifting resources, but on recovering values. The Japanese are successful in large measure because they believe in the virtues of work, self-discipline, and thrift — the same virtues, significantly, that built America's industrial primacy. The root of our competitive problem is the erosion of those values summed up in the so-called work ethic that made us formidably productive. Contrary to fashionable belief, these values are not obsolete in the postindustrial society, but must instead be redefined in terms of a complex new economic environment, which is at least as demanding and competitive as the former era of industrialization. Therefore, we do not need to imitate the Japanese to regain lost ground. We need to be more ourselves.

The Second Cold War

I.

By MID-1974, it had become appropriate to describe the Watergate-crippled Presidency of Richard Nixon in the past tense. Although he continued to maneuver, especially in foreign affairs, his ability to lead had been destroyed. The time had come to assess his accomplishments and his failures. Perhaps the greatest of the latter was characteristic of the man and his manner: he had withheld the truth from the American people.

As Nixon understood it, the principal task of the President was to conduct U.S. foreign policy. He was fascinated by foreign affairs and mostly bored with domestic problems. He enjoyed the grand sweep of strategic thinking and the high drama and visibility of personal diplomacy. He was determined to leave his mark on American history as the President who adjusted U.S. foreign policy to the passing of the post–World War II era and the opening of a new era characterized by the interaction of several powers of the first and second rank — the U.S., the U.S.S.R., China, Japan, and Western Europe.

276

Nixon weighed questions of strategy carefully, but, once he made a decision, he too often described it to the public carelessly. He exaggerated and falsified as he attempted to "sell" his policy. An excellent example of such salesmanship was to be found in Nixon's interview with *Time* in January 1972, which accompanied the "Man of the Year" cover story. In this interview, Nixon said:

> I am confident that the United States right now is on the brink of exercising its power to do good in the world. Such good as never has been done in the history of civilization because we now can muster our moral force, our economic force and we, of course, have the military power to back up our words. Our aim is to build a structure of peace such as we could not dream of after World War II; we couldn't dream of this when Eisenhower was President. It wasn't the right time. It wasn't the right time when Kennedy was there. But now the time may have come, and we must seize the moment — seize the moment in our relationships with the superpowers.
>
> We must remember the only time in the history of the world that we have had any extended periods of peace is when there has been a balance of power. It is when one nation becomes infinitely more powerful in relation to its potential competitor that the danger of war arises. So I believe in a world in which the United States is powerful. I think it will be a safer world and a better world if we have a strong, healthy United States, Europe, Soviet Union, China, Japan, each balancing the other, not playing one against the other, an even balance.

That is surely among the more incredible statements ever made by an American President. If it were taken literally, it would not merely mark the rejection of the policy of "containment" that guided the U.S. during the postwar period. It would also mark the embrace of the opposite policy of unqualified "coexistence" without a shred of evidence to support the assertion that the world will be "better and safer" as Soviet military strength increases.

In private, Nixon made it perfectly clear that he did not believe anything so naive about a "strong" Soviet Union. But he felt bound to tell the American people what they wanted to hear. And so he described his goal ("an even balance") in a way that falsely reassured a people who hope the time of trial and sacrifice is ending and a more peaceful, less demanding era beginning.

Behind the Nixon administration's determinedly optimistic rhetoric about a "generation of peace" is the reality that the U.S. is slipping. The President personally believed in U.S. primacy, but he was deterred from following his instinct by the popular and political forces on the side of America's opting out. Even if he were to make the politically costly effort to recover military ground lost during the Vietnam decade, he would confront the massive unwillingness of Congress and the American people to risk becoming mired in "another Vietnam." Of course, the reason for having conventional and nuclear superiority over a rival is to reduce the dangers of pursuing an interventionist foreign policy. But the U.S. does not intend to pursue such a policy in the future — hence there is no apparent need for the exertion and sacrifices required to maintain superiority.

Nixon saw clearly that the U.S.-centered world is disappearing in large part because the American people will no longer accept the role and its heavy burdens. In every foreign policy statement, he tried to put the passing of U.S. global primacy in a positive light. He did not call attention to the ominous implications of the determined Soviet effort to seek power and influence on a similar scale. He emphasized the apparent advantages for the U.S. of ceasing to be Number One, but did not acknowledge the possibly grave disadvantages.

Yet he thought and sometimes talked about such matters within his circle. As much as he publicly declared the Cold War "over," Nixon continued to hold a Cold War view of the world. He still assigned the U.S. what he called "the central position." Sometimes his suppressed concerns appeared. "If the U.S. were somehow to be taken out of the picture," he said in such moments, "the rest of the world would live in terror." In terror of *whom?* Why, the same Soviets the President publicly described with radiant optimism.

At heart Nixon held essentially the same world view that John Kennedy expressed in his ringing Inaugural Address. Scattered through Nixon's 1968 campaign speeches and statements were approving references to Kennedy's conduct in the Berlin and Cuban missile crises. But Kennedy had at his disposal the unquestioned U.S. superiority inherited from Eisenhower, while Nixon had only the doubtful margin inherited from Kennedy and Johnson. Within the limits imposed on presidential action as the result of Vietnam, Nixon maneuvered with skill and effectiveness in threatening situations. But he operated from a position of increasing relative weakness.

Practically none of Nixon's original 1968 campaign promises concerning U.S. foreign and defense policies and nuclear strategy were kept. As a candidate, Nixon took the conventional Republican view that the U.S. should seek to maintain "nuclear superiority" over the U.S.S.R., thus maintaining the proved basis of international stability during the preceding generation. On October 7, 1968, Nixon declared: "At this time I do not believe that the United States can afford to accept the concept of parity with the Soviet Union." After his election, he not only accepted it, but also bargained with the Soviets to limit if possible the extent of the U.S.'s approaching inferiority. He and his emissary, Henry Kissinger, were unsuccessful. The Soviet advantage in nuclear and non-nuclear strength grew steadily.

While the U.S. consistently and stubbornly underestimated the U.S.S.R.'s strategic weapons deployment, as we shall see, the balance of nuclear power tipped in Moscow's direction. By 1974, the U.S.S.R. had surpassed the U.S. in the number of intercontinental missiles — 2090 ICBMs and SLBMs compared to 1710. More important, most of the Soviet land-based ICBMs were much larger and more powerful, and therefore were capable of delivering a far greater number of nuclear-tipped warheads — as many as 7000 re-entry vehicles, each carrying one megaton. If the Soviets decided to equip their missiles with small warheads (the size of the U.S. Polaris), they could deploy perhaps *three* or *four* times as many re-entry vehicles. The American-Soviet agreement negotiated by Nixon and Brezhnev permitted the U.S. 1000 small silos for light missiles, while the U.S.S.R. was allowed 1618 silos, including 300 large ones for their giant missiles. The U.S. sought an agreement limiting missile "throw-weight," but the U.S.S.R. flatly refused and said, in effect, take it or leave it. Nixon, wanting an agreement to present on his return to Washington from this "journey for peace," took it.

Kissinger, in rationalizing the U.S.'s disguised acceptance of inferiority, made it sound as though the nuclear superpowers could escape the gravitational pull of history. After the initial SALT agreements were signed, he told congressional leaders: ". . . throughout history, the primary concern of most national leaders has been to accumulate geopolitical and military power. It would have seemed inconceivable even a generation ago that such power once gained could not be translated directly into advantage over one's opponent. But now both we and the Soviet Union have begun to find that each increment of power does not necessarily represent an increment of usable political strength . . ." Kissinger failed to produce, then or subsequently, any evidence of the alleged Soviet "discovery" that their increasing power is politically useless.

Ironically, the Soviet overthrow of American nuclear superiority has produced much activity carelessly described as "peace-seeking." In fact, the U.S. and its apprehensive allies are engaged in competitive deal-seeking with the Soviets. The reality is not "peace," but gradual accommodation to emerging Soviet dominance and phased capitulation to Soviet demands. The hope is that the U.S.S.R. will be "reasonable," once its primacy is acknowledged. The further hope is that the Soviets, having secured their European borders on less than brutal terms, will turn eastward and succumb to their fearful preoccupation with China.

"We're going to be the broker between Russia and China," Nixon told the guests at a White House dinner in the winter of 1971–1972. "They will remain rivals even after Mao dies, because Communism can only recognize one leader and one leading nation." As for U.S.-Soviet relations, Nixon said, the U.S. would continue to have the Soviet Union as a "competitor" because of ideology, but it would not necessarily confront an enemy. He held out the hope of adjusting opposing interests through greatly expanded trade, which pleased the businessmen present. In more private settings, the President was more skeptical that such an adjustment would actually occur, but he believed that Moscow and Washington gained much from the appearance of détente and the postponement of conflict over ultimately irreconcilable differences.

Certainly, as the Watergate crisis deepened, Nixon gained from the appearance of détente — his most prized and appreciated accomplishment. Responsible White House sources reported in the winter of 1973–1974 that the President and Secretary of State Kissinger believed the Soviets had violated at least the spirit of the SALT I Agreement. They were preparing to place large new missiles with multiple warheads in existing silos. The Soviet bad faith as proved by satellite photographs fully justified American repudiation of the SALT I Agreement. But the desperately weak Nixon could not afford the further embarrassment of having hopes of détente cruelly deflated. Our children would pay for his deception and our self-deception.

II.

As we lived through it, the period after World War II seemed a time of unprecedented national peril. America emerged unscathed and much strengthened from the uniquely destructive war, but the nation was unprepared for the subsequent politico-military and psychological struggle. For the first time, technology put within an enemy's grasp the means of dealing America a devastating blow. For the first time, too, America found itself the target of unceasing threats by an enemy imbued with a sense of ideological mission and an avowed confidence in history's inevitable verdict. As the result of a series of shocks in Eastern Europe, particularly the takeover of Czechoslovakia and the Berlin blockade, and the outbreak of the Korean War, America accepted the challenge of Cold War.

After the Korean War, the U.S. embarked on a permanent "peacetime" mobilization. The society adjusted to the novel circumstance of war-in-peace. The Cold War reshaped political institutions, vastly expanded the military establishment, transformed the economy, and enlisted the nation's technological base and educational system. The danger of Communist aggression and subversion abroad, seen in perspective, was real enough. But the American response, arising from dashed hopes for lasting peace and from the trauma of the Korean War, revealed an immature and inexperienced people's susceptibility to extreme shifts in attitude.

The tone of America's reaction to the Communist threat was set in President Harry S. Truman's message to the Congress in March 1947, announcing the emergency program of aid to Greece and Turkey. The President announced what would afterward be known as the Truman Doctrine: "I believe that it must be the policy of the United States to support free peoples who are resisting attempted subjugation by armed minorities or by outside pressures." This declaration of universal responsibility became at once the foundation of U.S. foreign policy and the basis of a uniquely American ideology. It was not enough for the U.S. to extend economic aid and military protection to friendly nations out of national self-interest. The idea was established that democratic institutions and principles, which Americans assumed to be universally valid, were under universal assault. The extension of U.S. military power first to Europe and then to Asia, while necessitated by local power imbalances, was justified on ideological

283

grounds as America embarked on a global crusade for political reform and economic progress.

Rearmed and vigilant, the U.S. moved onto the great stage of world politics in the mid-1950s and found it empty of true competitors. World War II had destroyed the old European and Asian power systems. Even the victorious Soviet Union, which had suffered staggering losses, was at best a regional power, strong only by contrast with its prostrate neighbors. The U.S. was not only the most powerful nation in the world, but also the most powerful by a margin unmatched in history. Its advantage over the Soviet Union in nuclear weapons, the new measure of power, was absolutely commanding. Once the U.S. fixed and defended the line between East and West in Europe, the expansion of Stalin's Russia halted. The Soviets began the long process of absorbing their conquests and rebuilding their strength.

Meanwhile, the fall of China to Communism and the Korean War seemed to require a parallel U.S. policy of containment in Asia as well. But there, too, the reality behind Communist threats was weakness. As the U.S. signed "mutual security" treaties and extended economic and military aid to scores of "allies" that were in fact dependents, American power and influence encountered no obstacle. As the U.S. waged the Cold War strenuously, forging a system of alliances to check potential Communist expansion, the foe prudently declined engagement.

The Cold War, though it seemed risky at the time, appears peaceful in retrospect, perhaps the most peaceful period Americans will enjoy in this century. The vast imbalance of power between the U.S. and its rivals provided a degree of security and a freedom of action that can be appreciated only as these disappear. As the one truly global power, America exercised the prerogative of isolating crises. Washington could devote to a single trouble spot almost its entire attention and a disproportionate share of its resources, all in good confidence that such commitment would not jeopardize the overall balance and upset the order resting on it. As late as 1958, the U.S. could afford to mobilize an armed force to stabilize relatively quiet Lebanon without worrying unduly about the rest of the world. Nor were Americans concerned about such involvement. There was no panic when President Eisenhower dispatched the Marines, because there was no prospect of opposition. The Marines waded ashore in battle dress and were greeted by ice-cream vendors and giggling girls in bikinis. This is what being Number One in the world meant psychologically: the homefront remained calm when forces were committed in peripheral situations, and those affected by the intervention did not contest the assertion of overwhelming power.

A decade and a half later, the margin of U.S. power has narrowed, but the scope of U.S. commitments has not. Suddenly, the stage of world politics has filled up and the U.S. confronts rivals and competitors large and small. Now U.S. action is inhibited by the very real danger of counteraction. There is no longer a single, monolithic, and conveniently weaker enemy, to be dealt with from strength, one crisis at a time. The U.S. faces multiple, simultaneous, and interacting crises.

Even in the years of headlong, crusading expansion, Americans, to be sure, recognized certain limits on their power. For example, after Korea everyone seemed to accept General Douglas MacArthur's dictum: "Anybody who commits the land power of the United States on the continent of Asia ought to have his head examined." When "de-Stalinization" led to popular revolts in Eastern Europe, climaxed by the heroic 1956 rising in Hungary, the rebels' appeals to the U.S. were unanswered. General Eisenhower and the man in the street saw with equal clarity that ideals could not alter the map of Europe. U.S. military intervention in the center of the Continent was impossible without secure access to the sea.

But American awareness of unyielding geographic and strategics realities grew slowly in the years when the U.S. commanded the empty world stage. Only as the Soviet Union became stronger did we begin to recognize the limits of U.S. power. Thereafter, as the danger of direct conflict assumed catastrophic proportions, the U.S. sought ways to recruit the Soviet Union as a collaborator in preserving world peace. Another great and sweeping shift in American attitude occurred. As we came to fear Soviet power, we told ourselves that Russia was "changing."

Russia has indeed changed. And the Cold War, as we knew it even in the late 1960s, is "over." Through forced-draft investment, the Soviet Union has built an economic, industrial, and technological base justifying the rank of superpower. In the most advanced fields of nuclear and space weaponry, the Soviets now match and can hope to outstrip the U.S. The Soviets enjoy nuclear "parity" with the U.S., and they possess the means and momentum to aspire to politically useful superiority if they so desire.

A body of influential opinion within the U.S. dismisses nuclear superiority as a meaningless concept. In terms of assured mutual destruction, it is said, "enough is enough." True, when the Soviet nuclear capability was markedly inferior to that of the U.S., mutual deterrence existed, but the

U.S. and the Soviet Union then were restrained only at the level of general war. In local conflicts remote from Russia, the margin of U.S. overall superiority had decisive effect. For example, in the Cuban missile crisis of 1962, the Soviets backed down before President Kennedy's fully credible threat of nuclear retaliation.

But the "Cuban power environment," as the U.S. Joint Chiefs of Staff describe it, has passed. The new environment of essential parity, precisely because it is new, holds grave dangers, for neither side can calculate with confidence the likely counter to its moves, especially in peripheral areas.

III.

In the perspective of history, the events of a year or even a decade lose much of their significance. What matters is the decisive event, the turning point, and the new trend it points.

According to the conventional wisdom, such a decisive event occurred in October 1962, when, under the American threat of nuclear retaliation, the Soviet Union removed its offensive nuclear missiles from Cuba. Out of this crisis supposedly came a tacit understanding, not only between President Kennedy and Premier Khrushchev but their successors as well, that neither side would again push its ambitions to the brink of nuclear war. Their common, overriding stake was survival.

The Cuban missile crisis did represent a turning point, but the conventional wisdom was wrong. The Soviet leaders were frightened by the risk of nuclear war, but no evidence has yet come to light that they and their successors were converted to the cause of peace. True détente still eludes us. Meanwhile, the Soviets — and this is the actual turning-point — have gained a position from which they can grasp overall military superiority if they are willing to make the effort.

The haze of instant myth obscures the way in which the Cuban missile crisis was actually resolved. In the fall of 1962, the Soviet Union had fewer than seventy-five intercontinental ballistic missiles and all were vulnerable to attack. Even if the Soviets had been irrational enough to attack first, and Khrushchev was no madman, the U.S. had the means utterly to destroy the Soviet Union as a modern nation. The threat of such destruction, as Secretary of Defense Robert McNamara later told a congressional committee, was the only reason for the humiliating Soviet withdrawal of their missiles.

President Kennedy carefully saw to it that Khrushchev's humiliation was not complete. By agreeing to retreat, Khrushchev gained, as he later boasted, an American guarantee that no further attempt would be made to overthrow Fidel Castro's regime. This, then, was the concrete outcome of the missile crisis: an American agreement permanently to tolerate what had earlier been branded intolerable — a base for Soviet military power and Communist subversion within the Western Hemisphere.

Thus, while we respected the Soviet sphere, the Soviets were no longer bound to respect ours. While we took as the objective of our military strength the maintenance of stability, the Soviets took as theirs the overthrow of the status quo. While we identified nuclear war as the greatest danger, the Soviets identified nuclear inferiority as the greatest obstacle to their freedom of action.

Immediately following the missile crisis, Soviet leaders stated their views plainly. The Soviet Minister of Defense, the late Marshal Rodion Malinovsky, declared that the U.S.S.R.

288

had to accelerate its efforts to exploit the strategic potentials of modern science and technology. He promised: "We do not intend to fall behind in development or be inferior to our probable enemies in any way . . . In the competition for quality of armament in the future . . . [our] superiority will ever more increase."

As the opponents drew back from the brink following the Cuban missile crisis, the Kennedy administration believed it detected a sigh of relief from the Kremlin. There began a groping across the abyss for an accord that would prevent another confrontation. Washington's hopes for progress toward a détente were urgent and honorable, based on the conviction that the necessity for human survival transcended all earthly political differences. In his memorable speech at American University in June 1963, President Kennedy recognized the main threat to peace: "The Communist drive to impose their political and economic system on others is the primary cause of world tension today." But he saw a promising ground for agreement in the common peril of Communists and non-Communists — "our most basic common link is that we all inhabit this small planet." In view of the suicidal destructiveness of nuclear war, he identified peace as "the necessary rational end of rational men." Kennedy believed the U.S. could influence the Soviet Union by example. "We must conduct our affairs in such a way that it becomes in the Communists' interest to agree on a genuine peace." This would not come about immediately, he concluded, but "at least we can help make the world safe for diversity."

The Wilsonian flourish was appropriate, for this speech was another landmark in the dauntless twentieth-century march of American idealism. The emphasis on human reason was itself

289

an expression of idealism. From Wilson's day to the present, Americans have never relinquished their belief that inherent harmony exists among all men and nations, if only they can *understand* each other. Their vision has been one of nations tending toward peace and justice, rather than toward war and conquest. Such optimism contradicts history, but the Americans, children of the Enlightenment, disregard the evidence and avow man's perfectibility. The thrust of Kennedy's speech, which has been the principal aim of U.S. policy ever since, was to offer the Soviets an understanding that would leave the world divided but keep the nuclear peace intact.

For seven years, under Presidents Kennedy and Johnson, Robert S. McNamara served as Secretary of Defense, becoming one of the most influential Cabinet members in U.S. history. Curiously, his misconduct of the Vietnam war continues to be explored in detail, but little attention is paid his simultaneous and even more fateful miscalculation of Soviet strategic intentions. While Vietnam diverted and drained the U.S., it was the shifting equation of nuclear power that changed the balance of power in the world. McNamara believed the U.S. could influence the strategic policy of the Soviet Union by its example. The U.S. stabilized its force of land- and sea-based offensive missiles and steadily reduced strategic spending by one-half between 1962 and 1966. Many advanced projects were scrapped and others stretched out. The aim of U.S. research and development effort shifted away from innovation, which was deemed provocative to the Soviets, and toward refinement of existing weapons. The U.S. announced its determination not to lead an arms race, which was praiseworthy. But prominent scientists, who aggressively ventured into politics, also declared that even a *technological* race was futile.

Weaponry had reached a "plateau." Events soon proved this assertion to be dangerously untrue.

Thus the objective of U.S. foreign policy, preserving stability, filtered back into defense policy, which took as its goal nuclear stalemate. Yet it was only the effort to preserve a margin of superiority, through technological innovation, that made possible and reasonably safe a U.S. foreign policy aimed at preserving stability.

During the 1960s, while the U.S. declined to exercise the initiative in strategic weapons, the U.S.S.R. bent every effort toward seizing it. The Soviets developed and deployed as rapidly as possible not only offensive missiles but also the first antiballistic missile system in the world. Secretary McNamara reacted with approval. It seemed obvious to him that the Soviets were seeking what we already possessed: an Assured Destruction capability — that is, the ability to ride out a first strike and then retaliate so devastatingly that the enemy, weighing the damage that could not be prevented, would be deterred from striking. No one knew what level of damage the Soviets would deem "unacceptable," but Secretary McNamara ventured what seemed to him a "reasonable" assumption. The destruction of one fifth to one fourth of the Soviet Union's population and one half to two thirds of its industrial capacity, he declared, "would certainly represent intolerable punishment."

McNamara, an able and intelligent man, was also an intellectually arrogant man. Because he was so thoroughly persuaded of the logic of Assured Destruction, which he could "prove" by using statistical tables, he assumed that Soviet defense planners would also be persuaded. Indeed, he lectured the Soviets directly on their military posture in his public statements. "If our assumption that the Soviets are also striving to achieve an Assured Destruction capability is correct, and I am convinced that it is, then in all probability all we would accomplish by deploying ABM systems against one another would be to increase greatly our respective defense expenditures, without any gain in real security for either side."

The Soviets leaders, under men like Marshal Malinovsky, weren't listening — and why should they? *They* alone were responsible for defending the Soviet Union. If technology promised to make their nation stronger, they would commit resources unstintingly. The American Secretary of Defense, so intrigued with his brilliant logic, became a man in the grip of a fixed idea. His well-known fixation may have influenced his subordinates' view of the Soviet Union. According to newly declassified Pentagon documents, the U.S. underestimated the U.S.S.R.'s strategic weapons production and deployment in forty-two of fifty-one top secret intelligence estimates during the 1960's. Because McNamara believed there was no point in the Soviets' attempting to achieve nuclear superiority, he predicted flatly that they would stop building offensive missiles. As late as 1965, he said they had given up the attempt to match our missile force in size. But the Soviets disappointed their American tutor. They not only continued their build-up, they accelerated it.

Within a decade of the Cuban missile crisis, the Soviets surpassed the U.S. in the number of land-based missiles. This build-up is the result of having outspent the United States by better than two to one on strategic nuclear forces during the 1960s. Just as important, the Soviets are very close to achieving technical parity. While our expenditures on research and development remained stable during the past decade, theirs grew by more than 10 percent a year. In a period of extreme

THE SECOND COLD WAR

inflation, U.S. budget stability actually meant serious loss of ground. "U.S. strategic budgets," according to the respected analyst Albert Wohlstetter, "have declined nearly exponentially from the high plateau of 1956 – 1961."

From the mid-1960s, as the Soviets stubbornly continued to deploy both offensive and defensive weapons, Secretary McNamara tried to hedge against growing uncertainties by improving the quality of U.S. offensive missiles. The multiple independently-targetable re-entry vehicle, known as MIRV, introduced a radical new element into the strategic nuclear equation, for the number of missiles alone no longer determined the strategic balance of power. Now, each launcher became merely a vehicle to carry a number of warheads capable of striking widely separated targets.

MIRV, it should be noted, was being developed in highly secret U.S. laboratories in the early 1960s, at the very time when scientists were announcing that weapons technology had levelled off, perhaps permanently. Also under secret development at that time were future improvements in the guidance accuracy of missiles which disarmament-minded scientists not only failed to predict, but flatly said were impossible.

IV

It was the judgment of Nixon and Kissinger that the Soviets, in Kissinger's words, had come to accept "a certain commonality of outlook, a sort of interdependence for survival between the two of us." To gain Soviet assistance in the American withdrawal from Vietnam, President Nixon paid a very heavy, perhaps open-ended price. The American concessions made in the initial strategic arms limitation agreement were symbolic of Washington's resigned acceptance of a position of nuclear inferiority after the mid-1970s made inevitable by the diversion of resources during the Vietnam decade.

From such a posture of second-best, certain consequences follow for the U.S. and its allies, principally in Western Europe. For there the framework of collective security arrangements rests on the soon-to-be-invalid assumption of American nuclear superiority. Slowly, over a period of years, perhaps decades, the combined weight of Soviet conventional and nuclear superiority threatens to collapse the framework of Western European defense, *not* through direct aggression but through negotiated adjustment to geopolitical and power realities. The Soviet-sponsored European Security Conference is the first step in what predictably will be a long, confusing process, which will appear to represent the arrival of "peace" but which may actually represent the neutralization of Western Europe under Soviet auspices.

After the death of the despotic Stalin, the image of world Communism was humanized by the jovial peasant Khrushchev, but he himself was no humanist. He was an heir of Wilson's contemporary, Lenin, the great antagonist of Western civilization, and he made war against the enemy within the limits of Soviet power. When Khrushchev recklessly overstepped those limits and endangered the Soviet Union, he was replaced by men who, except for their unsmiling manner, are essentially like him. Reflecting their technical background, the style of the Brezhnev-Kosygin leadership is more cautious and methodical, but they too are Lenin's heirs. And so will be the men who succeed them. Important changes have occurred in the post-Stalin Soviet Union, but any evolutionary softening of the Soviet leaders' attitudes will require generations before it weakens the secret, ever-vigilant apparatus by which the ruling elite reproduces itself. To be sure, the Kremlin leaders must adjust to immense changes, such as the implications of the Sino-Soviet split and China's nuclear buildup, but they do so, like other men, within an established mental framework. As American political leaders believe in harmony and compromise among men, so Soviet leaders believe in conflict and mastery. The U.S. effort to achieve détente has been answered with a campaign of global indirect attack, aimed at forcing America into isolation.

Pride, strength, and confidence lie behind this strategy, inspired less by Marxism-Leninism than by Russian expansionism. The strategy is also fundamentally opportunistic. The prolonged U.S. entrapment in Vietnam provided the great opportunity. In the late 1960s an American defense analyst, comparing the U.S. involvement in Vietnam with Soviet moves in the Mediterranean and the Middle East, declared: "The Russians are loose in the world, and we're tied down. They mean to keep us tied down."

The prize they seek is Western Europe, where everything appears to be changing except the generation-old Soviet ambition to pry or woo the rest of Germany away from the West. As Washington has sought "convergence" with Moscow, the result has been a widening divergence within the Western alliance. The "hot line" between the capitals of the superpowers is the symbolic strangling cord of NATO, and American-Soviet summitry pulls it tighter. If a superpower deal seems in the making over their heads, the Europeans are encouraged to move toward closer political and economic ties with Moscow. This threatens to destroy the essential purpose of NATO. The alliance was created not only to deter Soviet military expansion. It was also to be a *political* structure enabling the Western allies eventually to negotiate with the Soviet Union a joint, comprehensive settlement of the unresolved issues left from World War II. The disintegration of this structure, in part through U.S. desire for an overarching bilateral accord with the Soviets, has left the European states vulnerable and tempts them to make their own individual deals with the Soviet Union. Pivotal West Germany has tried to do so. "Reading the European press," a distinguished American diplomat and strategist remarks, "you hear the voices of 1939. And in the German press, there are voices of the 1920s that raise echoes of Rapallo and a Soviet-German alliance."

Brezhnev's proclaimed goal of "a Europe without military blocs" is a formula for the removal of the American military presence and the neutralization of Western Europe. He has demanded the "complete withdrawal" of the U.S. Sixth Fleet from the Mediterranean, and has backed up the threat with a "permanent" and expanding Soviet naval force in those strategic waters. All along the southern flank of Europe, the Soviets are using the flexible instrument of naval power to probe the soft underbelly, exploiting Western weaknesses and differences. If the Soviets can dominate the eastern Mediterranean, the military security of Western Europe will be precarious. In time, the European sense of insecurity may bring political submission.

During the Vietnam decade, the U.S. and Western Europe became estranged. "It is a fact," André Fontaine, foreign editor of *Le Monde,* wrote late in 1968, "that there is not one government in Europe allied to the United States that would have dreamed for a second of sending a single soldier to Vietnam to fight on the American side. Strange alliance!" To many Americans, such an alliance seemed strange indeed. Europeans did not merely stand aside while the U.S. fought in Southeast Asia; many of them opposed the U.S. effort in Vietnam as unjust and immoral. The more polite and optimistic Europeans treated the war as a tragic aberration on America's part; they assumed that, once it was over, the U.S. would return to sanity and a Europe-centered foreign policy.

But the gross mismanagement of the U.S. economy during the Vietnam years, compounded by Nixon's inflationary policies of expediency, undermined these hopes. The U.S. dollar is the foundation of the trading and financial community of the West, and Washington has permitted it to collapse. Still worse, as the dollar has undergone a series of official and de facto devaluations, Washington, seized by a new economic nationalism, has seemed satisfied at the trading advantages thus gained at the expense of allies. The Europeans, it must be said, take no small satisfaction at the toppling of the once-lofty dollar and the humbling of the overbearing Americans. The U.S. still occupies a singular position in the eyes of Europeans, but no longer as the leader of a common undertaking. Now they regard the U.S. as an unpredictable and probably unreliable outsider. America is observed rather than followed.

The self-absorbed Europeans are chronically worried that the Americans will emulate them and succumb to the same parochialism. Therefore they continually seek evidence of an unchanging U.S. commitment, even as political and military circumstances change. As long as the U.S. remained generous and self-sacrificing, moved by ideals and proud of it, all was well within the Western alliance. As long as U.S. power was unquestionably superior, American motives were of little concern to the protected. Now that U.S. superiority and resolve have become doubtful, the weak are uneasy. It has become something of a ritual for each postwar administration in

Washington to recite familiar pledges designed to bolster European confidence. Now, however, the situation is being reversed; the Americans demand from the Europeans performance as well as pledges as the basis for continuing to assume ultimate risks on their behalf.

The Americans are as unheroic and humanly frail as the Europeans, and they find lonely vigilance onerous. Americans ask why they should be expected to stand, decade after decade, perhaps generation after generation, as the defenders of allies who decline to do more (though they are able) because they fear the U.S. will do less.

V.

In the behavior of a confident adversary and uneasy allies, a judgment can be read: the balance of global power is shifting against the U.S. Even as Brezhnev engages in amiable summitry, the Soviet Union continues to probe for evidence of American weakness. The Soviet Navy, modernized and assigned a new strategic role, is the spearhead of this process as it challenges America's supremacy on the world's seas.

The Soviet nuclear buildup in recent years has been accompanied by a rapid growth of the Soviet Navy. Raymond V. B. Blackman, editor of *Jane's Fighting Ships,* has written: "It is a sobering thought that no other country in the world in this day and age of sophistication and inflation can possibly build as many submarines as the Soviet Navy has at the present time . . . In short, the Soviet Navy has given the victory signal to the world." The same observation applies to surface combat ships. In 1973, Admiral Elmo Zumwalt, the U.S. Chief of

Naval Operations, was forced to concede that the American Navy had become numerically inferior. He said: "This is the year in which the Soviet Navy, which has always had well over twice as many submarines as we had, forges ahead of the United States Navy in total numbers of major surface combatant ships: We dropped from 229 to 179 (surface ships) as part of our annual process of reduction . . . as inflation and budget cuts take their inevitable toll. The Soviets have surged to 212. This is the year in which the proud United States Navy falls behind in what has always been its number one position."

In this respect at least, the Soviets are behaving as Westerners — the Western expanionists of a bygone day. They are using sea power, the classical instrument of expansion, along with the familiar bribes, favors, and arms by which Western imperialists won foreign clients. In the modern era, such imperialism is a crude anachronism. Nevertheless, the Soviets are succeeding, in part because the dominant opinion in America after Vietnam is that we have failed in our global "mission" — and that we *deserve* to fail for our presumption.

We Americans are "down" on the military today as part of a general deflation of our self-image. For more than a generation, we defined America's position solely in terms of military effectiveness. Our military power, so enormous, impressive, and unchallenged, stood as a substitute for hard thought concerning the nature of the modern world and the forms of contemporary conflict. What is galling about Vietnam is the realization that the U.S. won the conventional military war, but lost the unconventional political war. Trapped in the habits of mind of another era, we outfought the enemy, but were in the end *outthought,* both by the North Vietnamese and their

Russian sponsors, who themselves often disagreed.

In their effort to tip the scales of power, the Soviets have borrowed not only Western techniques, but also Western ideas. A pair of strategists have been especially influential. The first was a bookish American sailor, Alfred Thayer Mahan, who preferred his quiet study to the rolling deck of a ship. In 1890, Captain Mahan wrote in the *Atlantic Monthly:* "Whether they will or no, Americans must now begin to look outward." As few contemporaries did, he saw that America had external interests, and he declared that command of the seas was the chief element of national power and prosperity. When his classic work *The Influence of Sea Power on History* was published, Mahan gained instant fame abroad, particularly among the empire-minded Germans and Japanese, for he pointed out what was afterward obvious: three fourths of the globe was covered by water; navies ranging the earth's seas and oceans held strategic pre-eminence; and naval supremacy was essential to the fulfillment of imperial desires. Just as obviously, the new U.S. imperialists saw a powerful navy as the mainstay of American influence and independence.

Mahan codified the instinctive behavior of expanding nations in turning toward the sea. A decade later, a brilliant and remarkably prescient English geographer, Halford J. Mackinder, looked at the globe in an entirely fresh way and related land and sea power. Writing as the European sea empires were approaching their climax, Mackinder boldly foresaw the possible emergence of a new empire, capable of dominating the world. Taking the largest view imaginable, he identified the vast Eurasian land mass as a unit, which he described as the "World Island." From within the Island, the regions of the world appeared as separate peninsulas, vulnerable to invasion by land and envelopment by sea. The key to mastery of the Island and of the world, Mackinder suggested, was the broad northern region of Eurasia in which the rivers run into ice-bound or landlocked seas inaccessible to Western fleets. For this region, he coined the famous name "Heartland." Throughout history, conquerors sweeping westward across the Eurasian plains had been hampered by the infertility of the steppes and insufficient manpower, but modern cultivation, railroads, and industry would create a much stronger base for conquest. As early as 1904 Mackinder warned that a great industrialized power in command of the Heartland — either Russia, or Germany or China in control of Russia — could press simultaneously and by internal lines of communication upon all the peninsulas of the World Island.

At the time, Mackinder made little impression on his fellow Westerners. Like Mahan, he was taken up by German, Japanese, and, soon, Russian military scholars. It was not until World War II, when German and Russian armies were locked in battle on the Heartland, that Westerners belatedly discovered the relationship of geography to politics and recognized "geopolitics." Before his death in 1947, Mackinder assessed the consequences of Russia's victory over Germany, and described the Soviet Union as the greatest land power on the globe. "Moreover, she will be the Power in the strategically strongest defensive position. The Heartland is the greatest natural fortress on earth. For the first time in history, it is manned by a garrison sufficient both in number and in quality."

In Mackinder's view, North America was a mere satellite of the World Island. "There is a remarkable parallelism between the short history of America and the longer history of England," Mackinder wrote after World War I. "America is today a unit, for the American people have fought out their internal differences, and it is insular, because events are compelling Americans to realize that their so-called continent lies on the same globe as *the* Continent." As England's successor on a global scale, America requires naval supremacy to compensate for its inferior strategic position vis-à-vis the Heartland. Reflecting on the Cuban missile crisis, President Kennedy said: "Events of October 1962 indicated, as they had all through history, that control of the seas can mean security, control of the seas can mean peace, control of the seas can mean victory. The United States must control the seas if it is to protect our security."

But control is always subject to challenge. Mackinder asked a prophetic question: "What if the Great Continent, the whole World Island or a large part of it, were at some future time to become a single and united base of sea-power? Would not the other insular bases be outbuilt as regards ships and outmanned as regards seamen?"

In an epoch when nuclear weapons systems have been regarded as predominant, Mackinder's apprehension about men and ships seems old-fashioned. Yet it applies forcefully to present realities. In the first generation of the atomic age, the emphasis was on acquiring *strategic* nuclear forces. In the present and succeeding generations, the emphasis will be on living within the condition of mutual deterrence these forces create, while at the same time using new *tactical* conventional forces to affect the terms of international life in such critically important areas as the oil-rich Persian Gulf (the energy-jugular of Europe and Japan) and the Indian Ocean and its narrow approaches. Geographically, the non-Communist centers of order in the world, with the exception of Western Europe, are insular. Western Europe is a coastland of the

World Island, politically divided from the Soviet-dominated Heartland. Faced with the necessity of maintaining long external lines of trade and supply, the insular centers of order, if they are to preserve their community, have no choice but to maintain maritime supremacy.

For the remainder of this decade, the U.S. Navy will remain master of the seas. But U.S. sea power will be drawn across new stretches of ocean, reducing the likelihood that forces will be available to meet every contingency when and where they are needed. Meanwhile, the Soviet Navy presumably will grow and extend its operations. China, almost unnoticed in the West, has built the world's third largest navy, which soon may assert itself in the Indian Ocean and other "blue waters." The U.S. must not only expand and modernize its naval forces, including nuclear-powered ships. The U.S. must also enlist allies, such as the Germans and the Japanese, to share the burden of sea defense. These nations have the maritime traditions and resources to be effective sea powers, along with the critical dependence on seaborne trade to overcome domestic political reluctance.

Sea power is pre-eminently the power of *presence*. Ships sail in peace as well as in war; they are instruments of diplomacy. The movement of specialized task forces carrying airmobile and amphibious units in international waters provides a substitute for a presence ashore with a minimum commitment of force. Such task forces, with their highly visible and responsive units, can exert a stabilizing and deterrent influence. These forces also are independent of land-based military installations — a major consideration. Since 1955, U.S. bases abroad have declined by more than three-fourths, and most of those that remain cannot be counted reliable in every crisis.

During the October 1973 war in the Middle East, the U.S. suddenly found itself without reliable bases in Europe with which to defend the vital interests of NATO, a fact from which the Soviets, as we shall see, drew alarming yet quite logical strategic conclusions.

VI

The overriding American desire is to avoid crisis and, even more fervently, the possibility of direct military involvement — "another Vietnam." The most promising way to avoid unnecessary trouble and yet maintain our vital lines of seaborne trade and influence is to be prepared to intervene *quickly* and *decisively* where necessary.

We cannot foretell the future. We can only weigh and prepare for probabilities. The late Philip E. Mosely, professor of international relations and director of the European Institute at Columbia University, who gave much thought to the political consequences of the shifting balance of nuclear power, sounded this warning: "In any future period in which [the Soviet Union] might attain either nuclear equality or nuclear superiority, however that may be measured in terms of the ratio between offensive and defensive systems, we would be prudent to assume that Soviet policy would be tempted to undertake a more extensive, more acute, and more dangerous range of risks in order to pursue its declared long-range ambition to reshape the world according to its dogma."

During the Cold War we took very seriously the threat to our security contained in declared Soviet ambitions, even though the Soviet Union, outside Europe, lacked the means to fulfill those ambitions. In recent years, the Soviet Union has gained both nuclear parity and a truly global military capability, which we fail to recognize at our mortal peril. Karl Marx once wrote: "There is only one way of dealing with a Power like Russia, and this is the way of courage."

We are living, according to the well-known Yugoslav writer Milovan Djilas, in "the most crucial moment in history since World War II." Djilas is one of the best-informed sources available to the West on the workings of the Communist mind. A Communist revolutionary before World War II and a frequent wartime emissary to Stalin, he became vice president of Yugoslavia under Marshal Tito. His intellectual disenchantment with Communism led to his imprisonment. In his cell he wrote *The New Class,* a study of the bureaucratic police-state from inside the system.

The Soviet invasion of Czechoslovakia in August of 1968, Djilas wrote the following year, was not the end of a policy, but the beginning of one — "a new policy of aggression, not only by economic and political subversion, but by raw, naked military force. And unless altered in time from without, this course will inevitably lead to a collision with vital interests of the West which will have to be defended — even by arms." Djilas, who personally knows many members of the Soviet ruling elite, offers this urgent advice: ". . . the West must rid itself of any lingering illusions that the present Soviet leaders are sophisticated men who eventually will come to their senses." Instead, he describes them as frightened, heavy-handed bureaucrats, who will resist change within the system and their empire at any cost. If peace is to be preserved, Djilas declares, "the West must ensure that it possesses overwhelming military superiority" — the margin must be so great that "even the Soviet bureaucracy can understand it."

More recently, at high personal risk, prominent Russian intellectuals, led by the physicist Andrei Sakharov and the Nobel

Prize novelist Aleksandr Solzhenitsyn, have warned the too-eager West against accepting détente on Soviet terms, which leave the U.S.S.R. undisturbed as a closed, isolated, and overarmed police state. Sakharov, who gained membership in the prestigious Academy of Sciences at the extraordinary age of thirty-two for his leading role in creating the first Soviet hydrogen bomb, declared that détente without a simultaneous opening up of Russia would be "very dangerous." For the Soviet regime "hides its real face." "No one should dream of having such a neighbor," he declared, "the more so if that neighbor is armed to the teeth."

In justifying their occupation of Czechoslovakia, the Soviets declared the doctrine of "limited sovereignty" of states within "the Socialist Commonwealth," the scope of which Moscow would define as events dictated. It might be extended to embrace not only the Eastern European satellites but *any* socialist state in the world. The Chinese interpreted the Soviet action in this way and launched massive preparations to repulse a punitive invasion from across the Russian border, where more than a million Soviet troops were reportedly stationed by 1974.

While the Soviet Union has acquired the means of global maneuver and intervention, thus fulfilling the potential of a decade ago, our perception of the Soviet threat has declined dramatically. We have put the Cold War of the 1950s behind us, and we are unwilling to admit that a quite different contest has succeeded it — the *Second* Cold War. In this contest, we face not a weak opponent whose chief weapon is propaganda, but a strong opponent who matches us missile for missile, ship for ship, and who may not "blink" in a confrontation.

The Soviet Union made a thorough assessment of the October 1973 Middle East crisis, and, according to U.S. intelligence sources, reached a menacing conclusion: the United States is no longer capable of asserting power and influence on a global scale. Indeed, the Soviets, according to these sources, believe there will be only one truly global superpower before the end of the 1970s — the U.S.S.R. — and they expect to enjoy unprecedented freedom of action and achieve major political successes in areas of the world formerly within the American sphere.

Obviously, these are dangerous thoughts, for they may lead the Soviets into high-risk adventures and miscalculations with the potential for nuclear confrontation. At the same time, however, it must be said that the Soviets are not being unrealistic. As they see it, the continuing Middle East crisis is a superpower confrontation-by-proxy, and the Americans have been forced to retreat from an untenable position of all-out support for Israel. The Americans, in the Soviet view, are not only compelled to respect the U.S.S.R.'s military might and political influence. The Americans are also compelled to recognize their isolation from their most important allies, the Western Europeans. Under the stress of the Arab oil boycott, an act of economic warfare inspired by the Soviets as long ago as 1971, the NATO alliance effectively ceased to exist, precisely as Secretary of State Kissinger subsequently complained. According to the Soviet assessment, this episode has demonstrated conclusively that Western Europe "has no interest in supporting U.S. endeavors in any part of the world that does not fall strictly within West European regionalism."

To be sure, the Soviets expect that the powerful forces of economic interdependence inevitably will bring a compromise between the Americans and the Europeans, and that the profound differences revealed in the fall of 1973 will be tempo-

307

rarily papered-over with official statements. And they are bound to respect the statecraft behind Kissinger's personal peace-making, which led to Egypt's reversal of alliances and the U.S.'s formal treaty ties to the greatest oil producing country, Saudi Arabia. But it remained to be demonstrated that the U.S. could satisfy Arab expectations without betraying Israel. Over the long pull, the Soviets have cause to believe that the differences between the U.S. and the NATO allies will persist, and that these will inevitably come to the surface in future crises.

American analysts might dismiss optimistic Soviet speculation as self-serving, except that the Kremlin leadership reportedly has given concrete expression to its rising confidence. According to intelligence sources, the Soviets, on the basis of the enormous and unexpected success of the Arab "oil weapon" in splitting the U.S. and its allies, have advanced their strategic timetable by at least five years. Acting on the assumption that the oil weapon will come under their influence and eventual control, the Soviets are said to estimate that by 1975 they will have created the position of world advantage formerly not anticipated until the early 1980s. The Soviets expect to be able to use the Arab oil weapon to disrupt and dominate the economy of Western Europe, to preserve the American-European schism within NATO, to apply added pressure on vulnerable Japan, and ultimately perhaps to compel the U.S. to seek a separate "energy peace" with the U.S.S.R., based on Soviet control of Arab oil and desperate U.S. need for the energy resources of Siberia.

These Soviet expectations are not wildly far-fetched. Whatever we may think, far more important is what the Soviets think. The ambitious desires outlined above are likely to shape Soviet policy along much tougher lines. The Soviet threat to intervene unilaterally in the October 1973 Middle East crisis should be seen as only the beginning of tactics intended to force the U.S. to choose at every turn between confrontation and cooperation on Soviet terms.

"To endure the pain of power," Stewart Alsop once wrote, "a nation needs a conviction of its own righteousness. Our agonized effort to prevent a Communist minority from taking over by force in South Vietnam is surely at least as righteous as imperial Britain's wars . . . And yet we have no Kipling to celebrate the war in Vietnam, and a sense of our righteousness is precisely what we wholly lack."

We are, in a word, drained of the sustaining idealism with which we entered the world and assumed leadership only a generation ago. It is quite different with the Soviets. They are a rising breed of convinced imperialists, full of a sense of their own righteousness and ruthlessly willing to use power.

The first crisis America must deal with is not military or strategic. It is our own crisis of national identity. Born free, kept isolated and irresponsible too long for our own or the world's good, America came to grief in a small corner of Asia and now must come to terms with itself and its role in the world. In the Vietnam conflict, the fourth peninsula war the U.S. has waged in a half-century, our insular nation sensed, for the first time, its true geopolitical situation and destiny. Isolation can be chosen, suffered, or struggled against, with radically different consequences. The decision to struggle means maintaining our power and exercising it, and no longer apologizing for the results. The U.S. is neither missionary nor policeman. It is no longer the omnicompetent keeper of order. It is the keeper of the balance of power that preserves mankind's hope of a peaceful, humane order — and that is mission enough.

309

The Kennedy Legacy

I

MORE THAN A DECADE after his assassination, John F. Kennedy has entered history and the common American tradition. Enshrined in granite, postage stamps, and schoolroom portraits, the martyred President "who died too young" is part of the past and belongs to every citizen.

Less certain, however, is the status — indeed, the definition — of the Kennedy political legacy. It is not even clear to whom it will belong in the future.

The presumptive beneficiaries, of course, are Senator Edward M. Kennedy and the Democratic party. But their claim, on inspection, proves surprisingly disputable. If the Kennedy legacy is little more than a memory of a distinctive personal manner and "style," Teddy is the heir and can prove it by merely opening his mouth. But if the legacy is more substantial, consisting of positions upheld, policy themes stated, values exemplified, and virtues celebrated, there ought to be a fairly clear resemblance between what Kennedy stood for and what the present-day Democratic party stands for.

Alas, there is not. And when the late President's younger

brother pronounces on public policy, the family tie is apparent but their political kinship is not. The Kennedy legacy, it seems to me, must go to probate.

The left-liberal Democrats, Edward Kennedy prominently included, have disowned their party's recent past, as personified by President Lyndon Johnson. But the insurgency against the Vietnam war and the Johnson presidency went much further and cut much deeper than the Kennedy loyalists anticipated. It cut all the way to the root-truth of the matter: Johnson's great "crime" was to adopt Kennedy's world view, retain Kennedy's advisers, pursue Kennedy's policies, and honor Kennedy's commitments to the bitter end. And so, when the insurgency finally triumphed with the 1972 nomination of Senator George McGovern, the moral condemnation of the McGovernites fell on LBJ and JFK alike. Significantly, as the Democratic party turned itself into a movement dedicated to purging its past, only one candidate, Senator Henry M. Jackson, dared propose continuity of U.S. policy, and he was cast into darkness as an unrepentant Cold Warrior and superhawk.

Within the literary and intellectual realm, where Kennedy's adroit flattery once prevailed, an anti-Kennedy revisionist campaign is far advanced toward the objective of leveling Camelot. A typical revisionist judgment is to be found in Richard J. Walton's *Cold War and Counter-Revolution: The Foreign Policy of John F. Kennedy:* "As congressman and senator, Kennedy was never a liberal, and as President he prosecuted the Cold War more vigorously, and thus more dangerously, than did Eisenhower and Dulles."

Thus, on both the political and the intellectual front, the left has not only demythologized Kennedy (which is a healthy enough ambition) but has also declared war on his view of the world and the assumptions and policies he acted on to secure America's place in it. This, it seems to me, is an unhealthy enterprise which must be resisted. For the perils against which Kennedy rallied the American people have since multiplied to an alarming degree.

Can Senator Jackson and like-minded moderates pull the Democratic party back toward the center and reconcile it with both the Kennedy legacy and the realities of a dangerous world? I doubt it. Experience teaches that when a party transforms itself into an ideological vehicle, and true believers take the wheel, even an election crash produces only a limited corrective reaction. The relevant experience, of course, is Republican, vintage 1964. In spite of their champion's crushing defeat, Senator Barry Goldwater's followers, true believers and therefore returning delegates, held the decisive power at the 1968 Republican Convention. The McGovernites are likely to possess a similar preconvention veto power over the 1976 Democratic nominee, using the credible threat of a bolt to a left-wing third party. By the time the eventual nominee has appeased the zealots, he may establish in the public mind the same "radical" image that helped sink McGovern. Will Senator Edward Kennedy's charisma bemuse Middle Americans if he is perceived to be offering McGovernism-without-McGovern?

In 1972, Democratic election successes at the state and local levels made the McGovern candidacy appear merely an episode, an ideological fling certain to be repented by a swing back to pragmatic liberalism of the Hubert Humprhey stripe. This delusion will pass as the regulars come to realize that McGovern faithfully represents a strain of moralistic liberalism that has been growing stronger within the Democratic party since the late 1950s. The intraparty agony of the Vietnam years probably has made this tendency dominant — it has become, in effect, the operative "tradition."

From this outsider's vantage point, it appears that the future of the Democratic party lies well to the left of Great Society welfarism, mainly for the reason that this is where the people likely to determine the party's destiny want to go, even though the country may lag behind. In the atmsophere created by the Watergate affair and the collapse of the Nixon presidency, the McGovernites are apt to be more self-righteous and intransigent than ever — and more determined to regard JFK as at least half a villain.

Unlike the Republicans, who are a homogeneous minority representing compatible middle-class interest groups, the Democrats lack a core of fraternalism. Their New and Fair Deal dominance rested on an unlikely coalition of heterogeneous, warring minorities, whose common will to power overcame their rending contradictions. But now their will to unite has weakened, if it has not disappeared entirely. Opposing factions want power for purposes beyond the traditional mechanism of compromise. The old Democratic presidential majority was kept intact by the bestowal of balancing rewards, so that each element of the coalition saw a greater self-interest in sticking with the party than in defecting. Now, however, key elements have broken away and embraced the Republicans at the presidential level in return for little more than verbal reassurance.

The 1972 election saw Nixon take over most of George Wallace's following — some 80 percent in the South, more than 60 percent elsewhere — and this was by far the most im-

portant outcome. The future of American presidential politics, as has been apparent since 1968, will turn on where the
Wallacites go. In the Nixon-McGovern contest, most of them
gave up their identity as insurgent Democrats and became
presidential-level Republicans for lack of a better choice. (In
the South, almost half the voters split their ballots.) It is prema-
ture to say that the Wallacites have ceased their wandering
and found a new home. But they are more likely to stick with
the Republicans on the presidential line, it seems to me, than
to retrace their steps back to the Democratic party. The reasons are as much social and cultural as they are political.

II

The electronic invasion of political reportage has created
the illusion that our society changes at the same pace as the
images on the TV screen. On the contrary, powerful under-
currents move slowly and break the surface in their own good
time, regardless of particular campaigns and elections. To
put it another way, our politics has been changing for more
than a generation as the result of many *non*political factors —
racial migrations and *counter*migrations, new forms of conflict
arising from a culturally oriented class structure radically different from older concepts, fundamental changes in regional
economies and patterns of employment — all affecting the
way people live, feel, think, and ultimately, vote. Voting is a
consequence, not a cause.

The resentment of white Democrats who deserted their
party in 1968 and 1972 is more complicated than liberals assume. It is obvious, for example, that "racial balance" busing

is not a simple white-versus-black "civil rights" issue, but a conflict between lower-middle-class whites and upper-middle-class whites. Many of the latter have insulated their own children from the practical consequences of their "moral" commitment to school integration. In 1972, the Republican appeal to defecting white Northern Democrats explicitly linked social and cultural issues. Late in the campaign, in a radio speech, Nixon attacked the moralists: "It is time that good, decent people stopped letting themselves be bulldozed by anybody who presumes to be the self-righteous moral judge of our society. There is no reason to feel guilty about wanting to enjoy what you get and what you earn; about wanting your children in good schools close to home; or wanting to be judged fairly on your ability. Those are not values to be ashamed of; those are values to be proud of; those are values that I shall always stand up for when they come under attack."

Thus spoke Wallace's stand-in from the White House; and the target audience responded. In 1960, Nixon received slightly more than one fifth of the Catholic vote, and in 1968 about one third. In 1972, he gained a resounding 55 percent. We need only recall John Kennedy's blunt appeal to the party bosses prior to the 1960 convention — nominate me and get the Catholics back — to remind ourselves that Democratic strength among Catholic voters has been steadily eroding since the early 1950s.

Upper-middle-class, left-liberal Democrats tell each other (and the kindred, amplifying news media) that the "moral issue" of Watergate will elect a Democrat President in 1976. Given the enormity of the Republican failure in Washington, a Democrat has an excellent chance of winning the next presidential election, but *not* because he projects a virtuous image.

315

The new class and cultural politics does not work that way. It is based on specific, concrete *interests* affecting the voter's way of life, his family, and his children's well-being. In the eyes of Democrats-turned-Independents, a presidential candidate's apparent honesty will be less important than his position on inflation and the economy, crime, drug control, racial busing, and "scatter-site" low-income housing. To the extent that "morality" is a factor with such voters, it may well turn them against Edward Kennedy, who still moves within the shadow of the Chappaquiddick affair. (In anticipation of an EMK candidacy, bumper stickers have appeared bearing this message: "Nobody Died in Watergate.")

The Democratic presidential candidate more likely to win in 1976 is an economic liberal and social-cultural moderate/conservative, who incidentally enjoys a reputation for political clean-living. But because the Democratic Convention probably will be in the hands of the upper-middle-class moralists whom Herman Kahn correctly indicts for consistently misunderstanding the temper of America, this is the kind of candidate they are *least* likely to nominate.

In spite of themselves, therefore, the battered Republicans are not without opportunity in 1976 and beyond. What the Nixon administration has done, among many other things, is to destroy the new Republican "past" even before it could be recorded in the history books. Future G.O.P. orators will not point with pride to these years. Where their immediate political heritage should be, Republicans will face a void. To be thus deprived is intolerable to conservatives, whose natural home is yesterday. But where can they turn? Certainly not all the way back to Eisenhower, for that was long ago and, besides, Ike had a running mate. Where then?

316

Their deprivation, Republicans may discover, signals their liberation. Republicans are rather shameless borrowers of Democratic ideas and programs after they have aged. Why not take over the social, cultural, and political appeal of a President seemingly unwelcome in his own party? It is entirely conceivable to me that Republicans in the future will avail themselves of what now seems a free-floating resource — the Kennedy legacy.

Not all of it, to be sure, and not under the old labels. Quite apart from those right-wingers who have forgotten little and forgiven nothing about the New Frontier, moderate conservatives too are also still put off by the memory of Kennedy's splendid fakery, the vain arrogance of his courtiers, and the transparent improvisation of bold initiatives that were swiftly forgotten. But we have endured much worse in the White House during the past few years. "Style" doesn't matter. What matters crucially is the core of the Kennedy legacy.

That core is patriotism. From the first to the last of his thousand days in the presidency, Kennedy told his fellow citizens that America was a good country which could become better. He expressed the faith they felt in themselves, their values, and their ideals. He called for individual and national sacrifice on behalf of those ideals, and this struck a deep chord among young people. They were also drawn by his urging that the society pursue and honor excellence.

In the early 1960s, we remained innocent of the supposed evils of "elitism." Ordinary citizens were unoffended by the idea that they might elect better and abler men to govern them. The reign of mediocrity in Washington since 1969 has done much to restore the vitality of the idea that some men are better equipped to govern than others. There is nothing

317

wrong with government by "the best and the brightest" —
provided they are not snobs and their qualities include character.

John Kennedy had character. Though as quick to exploit
an opportunity or hedge a promise as the next professional
politician, he showed in many ways that he understood where
politics ended and principled commitment began. The skep-
ticism that intellectuals found so attractive in him was accompanied by an anchored faith in lasting things — family,
church, friendship, duty, loyalty, and courage — which ordinary men and women recognized and approved. When he assumed responsibility for a blunder — the Bay of Pigs is the
classic instance — he did so unequivocally, because he knew it
was right and necessary.

Contrary to his left-wing revisionist critics, Kennedy did not
heat up the Cold War to prove his virility. He accepted the
reality of great power conflict, sure to continue far beyond his
term, and he therefore accepted the challenges, especially in
Central Europe and in this hemisphere, that were his responsibility. Although liberal admirers have made much of Kennedy's speech at American University in June 1963, the one in
which he called on the Soviet Union to sign the limited test-
ban treaty and help "make the world safe for diversity," he did
not foresee an early and dramatic "end" to the Cold War, but
rather a protracted test of wills which might gradually yield to
mutual accommodation. Just sixteen days after his disar-
mament speech, Kennedy stood at the Wall in Berlin and
proclaimed his solidarity with the Berliners and his dedication
to "the advance of freedom everywhere."

Such rhetoric carried weight in that era because we possessed the strength to match our obligations. In remarks prepared for delivery in Dallas on November 22, 1963, Kennedy

was in a position to say: ". . . America today is stronger than ever before. Our adversaries have not abandoned their ambitions, our dangers have not diminished, our vigilance cannot be relaxed. But now we have the military, the scientific, and the economic strength to do whatever must be done for the preservation and promotion of freedom."

This is no longer true.

III.

America today is weaker and more vulnerable than ever before. Our political system has been subverted, not by foreign enemies, but by men who came to power barren of unselfish purpose and creative intelligence. Our economic strength has been undermined by the combination of haphazard, mistaken policies and systematic corruption of the necessary partnership between government and the private sector.

Since 1960, America, it seems to me, has come full circle to confront again the kind of questions raised and left unanswered by John Kennedy — questions of our values as individuals, our identity as a people, our purpose as a nation, and our resolve as a civilization under mortal challenge at home and abroad.

Of course, we no longer are the people to whom Kennedy addressed his soaring queries. We are more experienced, cautious, perhaps wiser, and surely more cynical. Idealism has vanished from public life, and the people regard all politicians with distrust. Some of us are freer — blacks, women, and young people. We have changed, even those of us who remain squares. We are more open and flexible and tolerant. We have newfound respect for individual and group differences, and new practical understanding of equality. Politically, we have scaled down our expectations and brought them closer to reality. We no longer demand inflated promises of earthly salvation on a New Frontier or within a Great Society — we will settle for a less inflated dollar with which to pursue our own dreams. The Nixon scandals have stripped away the false pomp and majesty surrounding the presidency and have ended its imperial expansion at the sacrifice of other institutions and our liberty. We shall not have another democratically elected leader masquerade as a king.

In this new mood of maturity, many see a turning away from the myth of America's uniqueness. America, they say, has become just another country. But this may go too far. As even the Watergate affair demonstrates, America *is* different, a nation created and preserved by ideals. No other country would have faced such a drawn-out crisis so steadfastly. No other country, with its laws and highest institutions thus corrupted, would have entrusted them to resolve the crisis. Until the past dozen or so years, the proof of America's uniqueness lay in its success. Since then, the proof has come through our response to failure. The American people have *not* failed as citizens — they have *been* failed. They are prepared to make far greater sacrifices than timid leaders realize, provided they are told the truth.

What ails America? There is no mystery about it. Our sickness of the spirit arises from a prolonged absence of just pride in what we have attempted and what we have accomplished. Our cure will come with the restoration of honest, truthful, and effective leadership that demands the best in us — as we remember John Kennedy once did. His legacy awaits the leader who can claim it.

320